D1011593

SINAI
THE GREAT AND TERRIBLE WILDERNESS

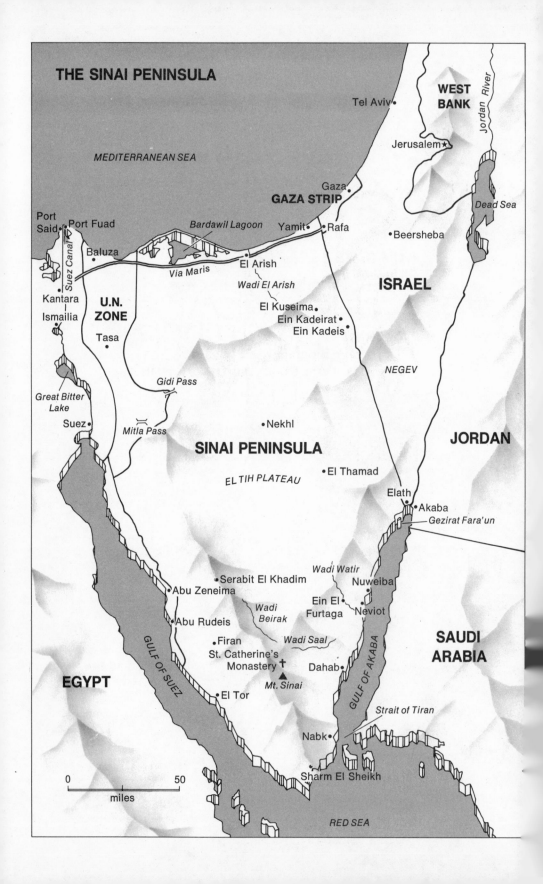

SINAI
THE GREAT AND TERRIBLE WILDERNESS

BURTON BERNSTEIN

THE VIKING PRESS / NEW YORK

11-21-05   G   13.95

LIBRARY OF CONGRESS CATALOGING IN PUBLICATION DATA
Bernstein, Burton.
Sinai: The great and terrible wilderness
Includes index.
1. Sinai Peninsula—Description and travel.
2. Bernstein, Burton. 3. Journalists—United States—
Biography. I. Title.
DS110.5.B46   953'.1   79-12794
ISBN 0-670-34837-6

Portions of this book originally appeared in *The New Yorker.*

Printed in the United States of America

Set in Video Garamond

Maps by Paul J. Pugliese, GCI

The photographs credited to Magnum were taken by
Micha Bar-Am; all others were taken by the author.

FOR MY FATHER,
SAMUEL JOSEPH BERNSTEIN (1892–1969),
BELATEDLY

And when we departed from
Horeb, we went through all
that great and terrible
wilderness, which ye saw by
the way of the mountain
of the Amorites, as the Lord
our God commanded us; and
we came to Kadesh-barnea.

—Deuteronomy 1 : 19

Foreword

IF ONE IS LUCKY, a solemn, self-indulgent promise of adventure may be fulfilled in the course of a lifetime. In my case, the promise I made to myself came rather late in life—in 1969, when I was covering the Arab-Israeli War of Attrition for *The New Yorker.* My travels during that dismal period of drop-by-drop bloodletting took me throughout Israel proper and the occupied territories, including the Sinai peninsula. For reasons that I hope this book will explain, it was the Sinai that captured my deepest fascination. I spent just a short time there, most of it under harrowing wartime conditions, but even so, I felt an immediate and mysterious connection with that strange, often misunderstood wilderness. I was determined to revisit the Sinai at a quieter moment in its anguished history, to travel throughout the peninsula at a pace leisurely enough to get some intimate sense of the land and the people.

What with one thing and another, the time was not right to carry out this personal pledge until the early spring of 1978. My luck held up. Despite all the complications of travel through the Sinai during the limbo of no-war no-peace after the 1973 hostilities, I was able to arrange for the necessary permissions, transportation, and guides. The result of that return to the Sinai was a series of articles in *The New Yorker,* which provided the foundation for this book. My intention was to present an overview of the peninsula's grand yet unlikely place in history—from the Stone Age to the present— and then zero in, like a zooming camera lens, on a particular area or group of people, exploring in detail.

Since my journeys through the Sinai in 1978, the region has

become more than ever the focus of attention. On the breathtaking roller-coaster ride to the March 26, 1979, signing of the peace treaty between Egypt and Israel, "Sinai" became as much a universal household term as "Carter" or "Sadat" or "Begin." In the world's imagination, the elusive word grew to be synonymous with the even more elusive word "peace"—after centuries of being its antonym. As of this writing, no one can say whether its synonymity will endure or whether the Sinai will revert to being an image for war. So far, the phased withdrawal of Israeli forces has been on schedule and without incident, and the treaty accords are holding up, despite the fury of ill-wishers. However, it is the Middle East, after all, and anything can happen. The Sinai has weathered war and peace since history began, and it is still there, timeless as ever. That is just one of the miracles of the place.

I want to thank all those who gave their time, energy, encouragement, and expertise to make this book possible, especially William Shawn, Editor of *The New Yorker;* Elisabeth Sifton, my editor at The Viking Press; Candida Donadio, my agent; Derek Morgan, an editor at *The New Yorker;* Richard Sacks, Peter Canby, and Thomas Teal, checkers at *The New Yorker;* Dr. Clinton Bailey, mentor and friend; Shmuel Moyal, Press Officer of the Consulate General of Israel in New York; Mahmoud Amr, Minister Plenipotentiary for Press and Information of the Permanent Mission of the Arab Republic of Egypt to the United Nations; Brian Urquhart, Under Secretary-General of the United Nations; Lieutenant General Ensio Siilasvuo, Chief Coordinator of U.N. Peace-Keeping Operations in the Middle East; C. William Kontos, Director of the United States Sinai Support Mission; Leamon Hunt, Director of the Sinai Field Mission; Owen Roberts, Deputy Director of the Sinai Field Mission; Michael Newlin, United States Consul-General in Jerusalem; Dolores Mann, Mr. Newlin's administrative assistant; Terry Kokas, Director of Public Affairs for the Greek Orthodox Archdiocese of North and South America; Zev Chafets, Director of the Government Press Office in Jerusalem; Mr. Chafets's assistants Linda Rembaum, Leora Nir, Pnina Randat, and Captain Nurith Rosen; Dr.

Morsi Saad El Din, Chairman of the State Information Service of Egypt; Moshe Pearlman; Mr. and Mrs. Yuval Elizur; Dr. Paul Marks; the late Meyer Weisgal; and, most importantly, the gracious and kind people of the Sinai.

Thanks are also due to the New York City Public Library, the library of the Mechanics Institute, the library of the Yale Club of New York City, the library of the Israel Museum, the Rockefeller Archeological Museum in Jerusalem, and the Hebrew University in Jerusalem.

Bridgewater, Connecticut   BURTON BERNSTEIN
June, 1979

Contents

Foreword   xi

List of Illustrations and Maps   xvii

CHAPTER ONE   1

CHAPTER TWO   30

CHAPTER THREE   58

CHAPTER FOUR   81

CHAPTER FIVE   110

CHAPTER SIX   153

CHAPTER SEVEN   173

CHAPTER EIGHT   193

CHAPTER NINE   216

CHAPTER TEN   234

Index   255

List of Illustrations

Gebel Halal	48
The oasis of Ein Kadeirat	48
Fishermen at El Arish	60
Bailey talking with Bedouin tribesmen at El Arish	65
The island fortress of Gezirat Fara'un	85
The 9th Brigade Road along the Gulf of Akaba	92
A wadi in the southern Sinai	92
Wadi Watir	95
The oasis at Ein El Furtaga	97
Sinai Bedouins at their evening campfire	98
The Plain of Raha	114
Sinai holy tomb	117
View from Mount Sinai	128
The courtyard at St. Catherine's	134
View from St. Catherine's Monastery	134
Interior of St. Catherine's Monastery	134
By the Well of Moses	135
The door of the church at St. Catherine's	135
Monks at St. Catherine's	135
The ossuary at St. Catherine's	150
The temple at Serabit	164
Sinai inscriptions	165
Steles at Serabit	165
Oil field near Abu Rudeis	177
Camel and ravens in the southern Sinai	180
El Tor	182

Gun emplacement at Ras Nasrani   187
Bedouin at midday prayers   188
Dunes in the southern Sinai   194
Sabkhet El Bardawil   199
The Mitla Pass   223
The Gidi Pass   223
Mountains of the Sinai   250–251

MAPS

The Sinai Peninsula   iv
Biblical-historical map of the Sinai   2
Four journeys through the Sinai, Israel, and Egypt   33
Israel's phased withdrawal from the Sinai after the
    peace treaty of March 26, 1979   236

SINAI
THE GREAT
AND TERRIBLE
WILDERNESS

ONE

ON ANY MAP OF THE Middle East, the Sinai peninsula sits dead center, an almost perfect inverted isosceles triangle, a sharp wedge that seems to cleave Africa from Arab Asia. Depending on one's political persuasion, it can be seen in several other contexts: as an eastern arm of Egypt, holy Egyptian soil, severed from its motherland only a little more than a century ago by the Suez Canal; as a natural and logical southern extension of Israel, a massive broadening of the Negev desert; as a northern adjunct of Saudi Arabia, separated from that immensity by the narrow Gulf of Akaba; or, simply, as an ancient land bridge connecting East and West, a handy route for caravans and invading armies. From any point of view, Sinai is a familiar, if not always clearly perceived, place-name. It has been a common word on the front pages of newspapers for decades. Every Sunday School student knows it as the "great and terrible wilderness" of the Exodus and, in Judeo-Christian tradition, as the earthly home of Jehovah, a birthplace of monotheism and Western law. Scholars know it as a setting for the development of our alphabet and as a land trampled by history. Yet, geographically, the Sinai evokes an image of vague, uninhabited desert, a lunar wasteland of sand and rock that, by accident of location, has come to hold great significance for many cultures.

The Sinai is more a wilderness than a desert. Its aridity and area are dwarfed by the intensely desertic vastness of the neighboring Arabian peninsula; the Sinai triangle covers 23,500 square miles, about the size of West Virginia, but within that space is a surprising variety of terrain. A fifteenth-century monk named Felix Fabri, one

1

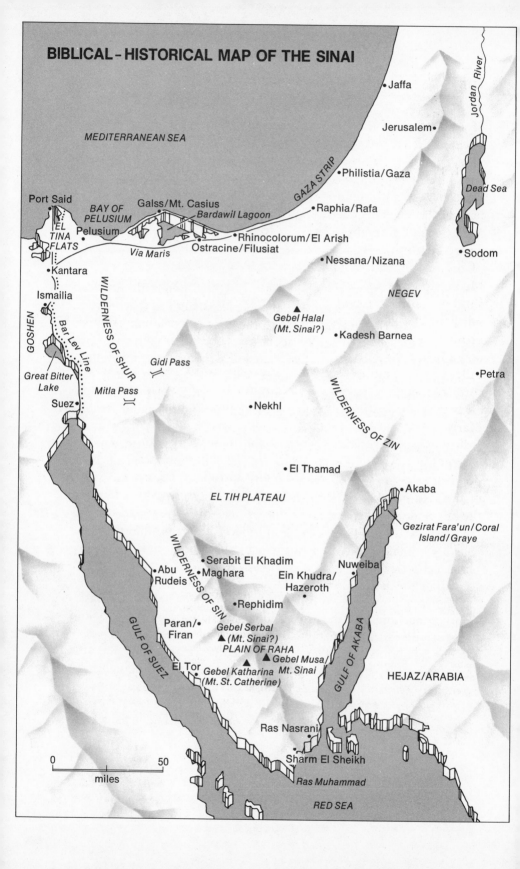

BIBLICAL - HISTORICAL MAP OF THE SINAI

MEDITERRANEAN SEA

• Jaffa

Jerusalem •

• Philistia/Gaza

Jordan River

Port Said •

BAY OF PELUSIUM

Galss/Mt. Casius

Bardawil Lagoon

EL TINA FLATS

• Pelusium

• Raphia/Rafa

Dead Sea

• Rhinocolorum/El Arish

Ostracine/Filusiat

Via Maris

• Nessana/Nizana

• Kantara

NEGEV

Ismailia •

GOSHEN

Bar Lev Line

WILDERNESS OF SHUR

▲ Gebel Halal (Mt. Sinai?)

• Kadesh Barnea

Great Bitter Lake

Gidi Pass

• Petra

Mitla Pass

• Sodom

Suez •

• Nekhl

WILDERNESS OF ZIN

• El Thamad

EL TIH PLATEAU

• Akaba

Gezirat Fara'un/Coral Island/Graye

WILDERNESS OF SIN

• Serabit El Khadim

• Abu Rudeis

• Maghara

• Ein Khudra/Hazeroth

Nuweiba •

GULF OF SUEZ

• Rephidim

Paran/Firan •

Gebel Serbal ▲ (Mt. Sinai?)

PLAIN OF RAHA

▲ Gebel Musa/Mt. Sinai

GULF OF AKABA

HEJAZ/ARABIA

El Tor •

Gebel Katharina (Mt. St. Catherine)

Ras Nasrani •

Sharm El Sheikh •

Ras Muhammad

RED SEA

0   50

miles

of a long line of pilgrims exploring the holy ground, wrote that "every day, indeed every hour, you come into new country, of a different nature, with different conditions of atmosphere and soil, with hills of a different build and color, so that you are amazed at what you see and long for what you will see next." The northern base of the inverted triangle runs along the Mediterranean Sea in a gentle arc for about 150 miles, from the Gaza Strip (technically, a part of Palestine) to Port Said–Port Fuad, the northernmost point of the Suez Canal. For approximately fifteen miles south of the Mediterranean coast, there is classic desert, replete with silken, shifting dunes, cartoonlike oases of waving date palms, and marshy salt flats. Like all deserts, this one advances by a process of sandy erosion, in some sections creeping southward by as much as a mile and a half every ten years. This northern desert region, paradoxically, supports most of the Sinai's seventy-five thousand residents, forty thousand of whom are Bedouins. It also contains the main caravan route between the Levant and the Nile Valley—the Via Maris.

From the Mediterranean coast south, the peninsula gradually narrows for 240 miles until both isosceles legs meet at the upside-down apex at Sharm El Sheikh,* which intrudes itself into the head of the Red Sea. The left, or western, leg of the triangle abuts on the Suez Canal and the Gulf of Suez, while the right, or eastern, leg

---

*The difficulty of transliterating Arabic words, particularly place-names, into other languages is as old as the words themselves. For instance, "Sharm El Sheikh" can be transliterated into English, with excellent justification for each spelling, as "Sharm e Sheikh," "Sharm ash Shaykh," "Sharm E-Sheikh," "Sharm Esh-Sheikh," "Sharm a-Sheikh," or any combination of these spellings with an *e* substituted for the *a* in "Sharm" and the final *h* dropped in "Sheikh." The basic reason for this confusion is that there are just three vowel sounds in Arabic, and their English equivalents are strictly a matter of how the individual English ear hears them and how various local Arabs choose to pronounce them. (The word "Bedouin," which will appear with some frequency herein, is actually a French transliteration of the Arabic *Badawi,* meaning desert dweller; the Sinai Bedouin refers to himself as something closer to "Buhdwi.") Some Arabists have invented signs for transliterating consonant, vowel, and glottal sounds, but this system (which includes the disturbing *q* not followed by a *u*) serves only to complicate matters further. The best system, I believe, is to approximate the Arabic sound with the simplest, most conventional, and least eye-disturbing English spelling; thus, "Bedouin" rather than "Badawi," and "Akaba" not "Aqaba."

follows the Gulf of Akaba up to the Elath-Akaba area. For 150 miles south of the northern desert strip, the terrain is mostly a gravel-and-limestone escarpment, ending abruptly at the forbidding El Tih ("The Wandering") plateau. Several roads and camel tracks cut through this middle wilderness with varying degrees of navigability, two of the most notable and navigable being the Gidi and Mitla passes, which played so large and crucial a part in the recent Sinai wars. In this central region the fewest and poorest Bedouins live, with little to sustain them beyond the knowledge that this is their accepted territory.

The southernmost third of the Sinai, from the El Tih plateau to Sharm El Sheikh, is the most dramatic and beautiful part of the peninsula. The irregular tableland, slowly tilting upward as the peninsula narrows, at last erupts in startling craggy brown, gray, and red granite mountains, the tallest, Mount St. Catherine, being 8,651 feet high. Mount Sinai (or Gebel Musa, the Mountain of Moses) is 7,497 feet. Just about everything that makes the Sinai a household name happened in this third of the peninsula—the revelation of the Burning Bush, the wandering in the wilderness, the law-giving, the theophany of Jehovah before Moses and the doubting Israelites, the flight of Elijah from Ahab and Jezebel. Here, too, are luxuriant oases, glittering sand and coral beaches, history oozing from the stones of the Egyptian Temple of Hathor at Serabit El Khadim and the fourth-century St. Catherine's Monastery, spectacular dry wadis that can become, during the brief winter rainstorms, thrashing Monongahelas, and, as often happens in the Middle East, oil.

Historically, the Sinai is a paradox. This seemingly worthless, underpopulated, undercultivated, static piece of gritty real estate has been the most besieged territory in the world—at last count, the battleground for at least fifty invading armies since recorded history began, surpassing even war-weary Belgium for the dubious title. It has been touched, in one way or another, by most of Western and Near Eastern history, both actual and mythic, and its sand and rock have been sacred to disparate cultures. The reason for its historical stature is its strategic position between East and West; it is the land an army must invade, conquer, and occupy in order to seize a grander prize somewhere else. As a result of this unhappy situation, it has been occupied by some alien force ever since the Early Bronze Age, about five thousand years ago.

Probably the only time its indigenous population lived in total peace and isolation was in prehistory. So far, only preliminary archeological investigations of the Sinai's prehistoric past have been made, mostly by Israeli archeologists who have had the run of the peninsula since the Six Day War of 1967. Their findings, still tentative, show the possible presence of troglodyte hunters in the part of the Sinai nearest the Negev. The hunters were most likely the *Paleanthropus Palestinensis*, a race of cavemen with both Neanderthal and modern characteristics, who existed 200,000 years ago in the Palestine area. Other archeological digs in northern Sinai have unearthed flint tools, arrowheads, needles, and a kind of hearth surrounded by ten holes, which may have been used for smoking hides or baking food. Also, in both northern and southern Sinai interesting prehistoric structures that archeologists call "desert kites" have been found—odd configurations of stone walls with occasional openings, whose function is a source of controversy. One theory holds that the kites were for penning herds of domestic animals and protecting them from raiders; another view is that they were for corralling game, probably gazelles, and entrapping them for mass slaughter. Variations of the desert kites were built until the Bedouins acquired firearms in the seventeenth century and the practical advantages of the kites became obsolete. Other mysterious prehistoric structures, so well preserved that they are still used by Bedouins, are the *nawamis,* circular, roofed stone huts with openings invariably facing west. The consensus is that the *nawamis* were once burial sites.

Studies by the archeologists Ofer Bar-Yosef and James L. Phillips of the Hebrew University of Jerusalem demonstrate that even as far back as the Late Pleistocene, about a million years ago, the Sinai experienced roughly the same discouraging climate as it does today, a short annual wet season and a long hot dry season, so there was no likelihood of any primitive agriculture. The prehistoric indigenes were nomads who traveled great distances from the shores of the Red Sea to the Mediterranean, following the game for food. This inveterate migratory trait of the native Sinai population has been proven by the discovery near El Tor on the Gulf of Suez of distinctive ornamental seashells that could have come only from the Mediterranean.

Traces of Early Bronze Age domestic ruins and pottery shards at Wadi El Sheikh, in the south-central Sinai, indicate a self-sufficient settlement life there, with the raising of sheep and goats, the dexterous use of tools, and, possibly, copper mining and smelting. But by then, the Sinai had already experienced its first invasion and occupation, by Mesopotamian Semites who had infiltrated from the northeast. Among other things, these Semites gave the Sinai its name. From out of the Chaldean city of Ur, the legendary home of the patriarch Abraham, came a cult that worshipped the moon god Sin, a deity of the Sin, Shamash, and Ishtar trinity (the Moon, the Sun, and Venus). Some scholars speculate that Yahweh (Jehovah) was once regarded as a moon god and that the early Hebrews were moon worshippers. Naram-Sin, a king of Akkad (*c.* 2200 B.C.), was so named because his conquest of Elam, a flourishing civilization north of the Persian Gulf, was considered the result of favorable lunar influences. He later conquered lands to the west called, according to a deciphered Assyrian fragment, Maganna ("Country of Copper") and Milukhkha ("Country of Blue Stone"). Perhaps these territories, rich in copper and turquoise, were collectively named Sin—and ultimately Sinai—after the deity that made the triumph possible. It is undoubtedly a coincidence, but a fascinating one, that the peninsula named for a moon god looks like nothing so much as the surface of the moon.

The primitive people of the Sinai during the Semitic conquest were known by various names in early history and legend. Generally, they were called the Mentu, but as lore was piled upon lore, they were known, by turns, as Horites (from *hor,* the Hebrew word for mountain), Rephaim (a race of giants), Amalekites (a wandering barbaric people, "the first of the nations," according to the Bible), Edomites (the cursed descendants of Esau), Thamudites

(perhaps the progenitors of the brilliant Nabateans), and the Midianites (nomads from the Arabian peninsula who foraged in the
Sinai). The peninsula was ethnologically Semitic, but soon it became geographically Egyptian. The Egyptians had a threefold purpose in colonizing the Sinai: to keep the northern desert (the *Shur,*
or wall, as they called it) a fortified buffer against invaders; to use
the north and central routes through the Sinai as military and trade
highways; and, most important, to work the copper and turquoise
mines at Serabit El Khadim, in the mountains across the Gulf of
Suez, conscripting the vanquished Semitic population as slaves
(Serabit El Khadim means "Heights of the Slave"). Throughout
the early dynasties, the Egyptians expanded the lucrative mining
operations. At first they were influenced by their slaves and adopted
a version of the moon cult, performing sacrificial rites to the Egyptian moon god Thoth, who was represented on mine walls as a
baboon- or ibis-headed figure. Later mine inscriptions depicted the
early Pharaohs as "smiters of the barbarians" (which is to say, the
enslaved Semites) and masters of all Egypt. Seneferu and Cheops
plundered the turquoise mines and vowed to protect the divinity
of the Sinai.

When the Hyksos, a Semitic people (one theory holds that they
were Hebrews) invaded Egypt through the Sinai and ruled the Nile
Valley from *c.* 1700 to 1580 B.C., the Sinai mines fell into disuse.
The Hyksos concentrated on keeping the peace in Egypt proper.
However, during the Eighteenth Dynasty, the foreign rulers were
overthrown and Egyptian expeditions to the Sinai were resumed.
A magnificent temple was built at Serabit to honor Hathor, the
Goddess of Turquoise (as well as Love, Mirth, and Joy), who was
represented by the features of a cow. Precious gifts were sent from
the Pharaohs to "Mother Hathor, Mistress of Turquoise," and the
Sinai turquoise, in turn, was transported to Nilotic temples. A huge
complex grew around the sacred house of Hathor, including a
courtyard, pylon, sanctuaries, purification baths, porticoes, steles, a
High Place of Burning, and a barracks area for Egyptian soldiers
who policed the slaves and protected the mines from marauders. At
some point during this period, an extraordinary intellectual event

occurred at Serabit. The Semitic slaves inscribed on the mine walls some markings, related to Proto-Canaanitic symbols, that were a major departure from the hieroglyphics the Egyptians had carved. Instead of merely being pictures representing words, these were symbols representing basic consonantal sounds, from which an infinite variety of new words could be constructed. It evolved into the Proto-Sinaitic alphabet, the key link, many epigraphists believe, between Egyptian hieroglyphics and the Phoenician alphabet, from which our own alphabet was derived.

For the next thousand years or so, till the Ptolemaic Dynasty of a few hundred years before the birth of Christ, a grand succession of invasions and retreats took place, all of them through the ravaged Sinai. Egypt colonized the East and was colonized in turn. Assyrians, Hittites, Babylonians, Persians, and Greeks all had their day against the Egyptians, slowly breaking the majestic power of the Pharaohs and controlling the trade routes between East and West. Even the Egyptians' own Hebrew slaves revolted and, fleeing east out of Egypt to freedom, they gave the Sinai its most celebrated and holy moment. The moment was, according to Scriptural tradition, really forty years of Exodus and wandering through the "great and terrible wilderness."

At this point, the history of the Sinai becomes totally mythic, the Scriptures and their multifarious interpretations being the sole sources. Personages, place-names, routes, and chronologies have for millennia been open to dispute and theory, but one salient fact remains: The Hebrews, having fled from Egyptian bondage (probably during the reign of the Pharaoh Ramses II, *c.* 1300 B.C.), slowly and painfully made their way across the Sinai, finally arriving in the Promised Land well to the north as a triumphant, unified, jurisprudent, monotheistic, and chastened people. They started out as Hebrews, became Israelites, and ended up as Jews. What they left behind in the Sinai was a crumbling Egyptian province, which reverted to its primitive Mentu life, the natives witnessing a long parade of new invasions.

From the fourth century B.C., the Ptolemies showed revived interest in the peninsula, mounting expeditions and building a few ports along the Mediterranean coast. While there, they encountered the Nabateans, an enterprising Semitic people from east of the Jordan River who had seized Akaba from their base in Petra and were using the Sinai to establish and control trade, even opening a land route from Akaba to Gaza. Along the trade routes, they left souvenirs of their presence by what have become known as Sinaitic Inscriptions, mostly Aramaic graffiti of salutation, warning, and advice. The Nabateans held their own against the Ptolemies, but they were eventually conquered by the Romans in A.D. 106.

During the era when Egypt was a Roman and Byzantine dependency—from 30 B.C. to A.D. 640—the Sinai grew in military, commercial, and social stature. The Romans maintained military posts along the Mediterranean coast at intervals of fourteen miles (the length of one day's march of a Roman legion), and traces still remain of some of these fortified positions. In those days, the Pelusiac, or eastern, arm of the Nile flowed through Kantara and entered the Mediterranean at a busy port called Pelusium. Farther east were Galss (also known as Mount Casius), where Pompey the Great, fleeing Julius Caesar, was assassinated by order of Ptolemy XIII; Ostracine, later called Filusiat (meaning "money") by the Arabs because of the profusion of Roman coins found there; Rhinocolorum, now known as El Arish, the current population center of the Sinai; and Raphia, present-day Rafa, the last outpost before Gaza and Palestine proper. With these Sinai fortifications, the Romans were able to hold their Middle East possessions in a suppressive grip, though, apparently, they could not prevent Jesus, Mary, and Joseph from escaping Herod's wrath across the Sinai to Egypt, and journeying back after Herod's death.

During the decline of the western Roman Empire and the ascendancy of the eastern Byzantine Empire, the Sinai reached yet a new zenith of vitality, and the reason was, in a word, Christianity. In the fourth century, Emperor Constantine and his mother, Empress Helena, embraced Christianity and decided for both tactical and religious reasons to develop the Holy Land and Sinai. A wind of Byzantine influence and culture swept the peninsula, with Rhinocolorum, for instance, boasting a cathedral, a monastery, and a convent, and the city itself covering an area of eight square miles. Other cathedral cities sprouted at Ostracine, at Pelusium, and near the site of the biblical Kadesh Barnea, where the Hebrews had spent most of their forty years during their Sinai wandering. It was a time of general prosperity for the Middle East, and the surplus population, particularly the more eccentric element, took to the desert as a means of acquiring sanctity and freedom from non-believers or oppressors. As early as the second century, many of these desert escapists headed from the Holy Land through the Sinai to Wadi Firan, a verdant, water-blessed valley in the southwest of the peninsula. Mostly anchorites searching for a retreat, they accepted the place as the life-giving Elim mentioned in Exodus, where there "were twelve wells of water and three-score and ten palm trees," and they revered nearby Gebel Serbal as Mount Sinai. They were at constant odds with the local nomads—the "Ishmaelites" or "Saracens" as they called them—but they not only survived, they thrived. Firan blossomed into a cathedral city and the seat of a bishopric, which included other hermit settlements as far off as Gebel Musa, the site, according to the instant tradition that was enchanting the Christian world, of God's addressing Moses from the Burning Bush. In 327, the elderly Empress Helena undertook a pilgrimage to the Holy Land. She visited the Gebel Musa settlement and, impressed that an actual bramble bush grew there, she ordered a small chapel to be built around it, dedicated to the Holy Virgin. Soon, in the active imaginations of the early Christians, Gebel Musa supplanted Gebel Serbal as the new true Mount Sinai. About 530, the small chapel had been enlarged by Emperor Justinian into a formidable church, fortress, and monastery, and centuries later it was rededicated to St. Catherine, the virgin martyr of fourth-century Alexandria. It has been inhabited by monks and pilgrims for more than 1600 years, which makes it one of the oldest continuously occupied buildings in the world.

By shrewdness, good fortune, and a lot of prayer, the Sinai Christians outlasted the boiling forth from Arabia of the Moslem hordes in the seventh century. As the Arabs rode pell-mell through the Sinai on their frenetic quest to subject the world to the new religion of Islam, they devastated almost every semblance of previous culture in their path. The cathedral cities, with the nigh-miraculous exception of the monastery fortress at Mount Sinai, fell with usually light resistance. Pelusium was valiantly defended by Roman mercenaries (the regular troops were in Rome defending that hapless city) but succumbed to the relentless Arabs after a long siege. The natives of the Sinai abandoned most of their pagan superstitions and welcomed their Bedouin cousins from across the Gulf of Akaba, embracing the attractive religion. It was and is a religion tailored for desert dwellers, and the Bedouins found in it a glorious new way of life for survival in the Sinai wilderness. The fact that they, direct descendants of the original Arabs of the desert, were among the earliest promulgators of Islam has sustained them and given them a sense of superiority over all other Moslems to this day. From the onset of Islam, the Sinai Bedouins were charged with the responsibility for protecting the hajj (holy pilgrimage) routes through the peninsula to Mecca.

The Moslem conquests inevitably clashed with burgeoning Christianity and the ensuing convulsion was the Crusades, which cursed the Sinai, increasingly denied to Christian pilgrims, with another hundred years of invasion, occupation, and mayhem. The prime Crusader objective was to capture Jerusalem from the infidel Moslems and transform the Holy Land into the Kingdom of Jerusalem, a goal bloodily attained in 1100. A slice of the Sinai, from Rafa to Akaba, was included in the Frankish Kingdom, and the old Roman fort at Ostracine was captured and held for many years. After Almaric I, as King of Jerusalem, invaded Egypt four times through the Sinai in the 1160s, the Egyptian and Syrian Moslem powers merged to strengthen their stand against the Christians. Almaric was defeated at Cairo by the forces of the charismatic Saladin, who pursued the retreating Crusaders as far as Gaza.

Just as the Moslems had infuriated the Christians by denying them access to holy places, so the Christians prevented Moslems from going overland on their hajj. Two key Crusader outposts were built at the head of the Gulf of Akaba, the larger one on Gezirat Fara'un ("Island of the Pharaoh," also known as Coral Island and, by the Crusaders, as Graye), which prevented for a while even the seaborne hajj. The Moslems, for their part, constructed a small fort on the peak of Mount Sinai, in order to defend the southern route to Egypt from the Crusaders. But by 1170, Saladin had retaken the Akaba area, and by 1182, he had led his howling forces across the central Sinai in the last great campaign against the Christians, which concluded with the fall of Jerusalem and a shaky peace at the end of the twelfth century.

For almost three hundred years following the final collapse of the Crusades at Acre, the Sinai rested unsteadily in the hands of the Mamelukes, the military clique, made up originally of converted slaves, that ruled Egypt. It was a period of relative peace—the East-West trade routes were reopened and thriving—with only occasional forays by foreign and Bedouin raiding parties to exact tribute. But by the beginning of the sixteenth century, the ambitious Ottoman Empire decided to take the Sinai and Egypt, the ultimate prize for so many conquerors. In 1517, the forces of Sultan Selim I invaded Egypt by the Via Maris and brought the area under Turkish rule. In the Sinai, the Ottomans built new forts at El Arish, in the desolate interior at Nekhl, and at Akaba, using them as stepping-stones for the further conquest of the Hejaz and the holy Moslem cities. With all the occupied territories divided up into tightly run eyalets and sanjaks (the Sinai alone was then part of two Ottoman administrative divisions), Turkish rule in the area lasted for four hundred years.

All was not serene, however. First, there was conflict with Portugal over the sea routes for trade with the Far East. The Portuguese defeated the Turks in an Indian Ocean battle, and as a result the Sinai ports withered from a lack of shipping. Then, more importantly, in 1798, Napoleon invaded Egypt and, six months later, the Sinai, to lay open the Levant and the rest of Asia. With ten thousand soldiers, including camel cavalry, he tore across north Sinai, routing the Turks from El Arish and ending up at Acre, then part of the Eyalet of Beirut. At Acre, he was stopped by the Turks and the British fleet. He fell back to El Arish, where plague, exhaustion, and thirst decimated his troops, and then to Cairo. Finally, in 1801, the

French Army left Egypt altogether. In its own way, the broiling Sinai was as formidable a foe for Napoleon as the frigid Russian countryside.

Another setback to Ottoman rule was the revolt against the Turks by the Albanian Viceroy of Egypt, Mohammed Ali, who, in 1831, sent his adopted son, Ibrahim Pasha, into the Sinai to engage the Turks. Ibrahim Pasha drove the Turks back to Syria, but he and his father were deprived of their spoils by the European powers, who interceded in favor of Turkey. A succession of viceroys (later called khedives) ruled Egypt and the Sinai, under the auspices of the Turkish Court, with influential British administrative control over the incipient Suez Canal area from 1862 on.

The opening of the Suez Canal in 1869 and the slow disintegration of the Ottoman Empire through palace intrigues, nationalistic rebellions, and internal corruption brought a subtle British hegemony to the western Sinai, along with a not-so-subtle sense of British imperial importance. The canal itself, the Red Sea, and the Gulf of Akaba became the main arteries for the newly introduced steamships, which were the instruments of communication and trade throughout the British Empire, especially with India. As far as the British were concerned, the Sinai was strategically vital to the maintenance of those arteries. Under an 1841 Ottoman firman, the Sinai was divided up in the following manner: Egypt, theoretically part of the Ottoman Empire but realistically under British control, was given the peninsula territory to the west of a boundary line running from Suez to El Arish; the territory to the east, with a southern borderline from Suez to Akaba, was deemed part of the Sanjak of Jerusalem, while the area south of the Suez-Akaba line was considered part of the Eyalet of the Hejaz. The firman was renewed in 1892, but Lord Cromer, the British consul-general who was really running things in Egypt, tried to insinuate Anglo-Egyptian sovereignty farther east into the Sinai, in order to increase the buffer zone protecting the canal. Anglo-Egyptian police stations were established in such dusty interior outposts as Nekhl and El Thamad, and by 1906, Britain made it clear to the militarily weaker Turks that it wanted the boundary line separating Egypt from Ottoman territory to run north to south from Rafa to Akaba, thus effectively severing the entire Sinai from Ottoman rule. Turkey offered a compromise proposal—a boundary line from El Arish to Sharm El Sheikh—but eventually it accepted the British ultimatum and recognized the new line, merely as an administrative division, not as an international border between the Ottoman Empire and Egypt.

To complicate matters further, Zionism, the brainchild of the Austro-Hungarian Jewish journalist Theodor Herzl, appeared at the end of the nineteenth century as a passionate alternative for European Jews fleeing the pogroms. Since the Zionists were having little success convincing the Turks that Palestine (or the Sanjaks of Jerusalem, Nablus, and Acre, according to the Ottoman designations then) was the natural homeland for the Jewish people, they suggested that north Sinai might make a surrogate homeland, with garden cities sprouting under Jewish hands along the Mediterranean coast from El Arish west to Egypt. For a while, the British were attracted to the notion and even sent an expedition of three Englishmen and four Jews to the region in 1903. But when they realized the difficulty of obtaining enough water for garden cities there, the British soured on the idea. (The concept of the Sinai as a Zionist substitute for Palestine died hard, however. As late as 1934, Ittamar Ben-Avi, a visionary Zionist and the founder of the Jerusalem Hebrew newspaper *Doar Hayom,* imagined a day when the government of Egypt might invite the Jews to settle and develop the Sinai. "Why should not Egypt issue a special 'Balfour Declaration' to attract to this barren land thousands and thousands of Hebrew people, young and enterprising?" he wrote. "Why would not Egypt create, near the El-Arish of the Beduin, a rich southern Tel Aviv, extending long green branches towards the desert and the looming hills—from which Amram's son once brought down God's message to the entire civilized world?")

The British fascination with the Sinai was not confined to diplomats and military figures. The holy ground that had seen the Exodus and so many other historic and religious migrations drew a procession of slightly balmy English explorers, who—often with little more than a pith helmet, a light cotton suit, a water bottle, a few camels, a bemused Bedouin guide, and scant knowledge of Arabic—wandered into the wilderness, sometimes, amazingly, meeting each other on some deserted camel track in the middle of nowhere. (The tradition of such haphazard exploration was started, actually, by a celebrated Frenchman, Alexandre Dumas *père,* who in 1839 visited the alleged locations of the Exodus and wrote a book about it called *Impressions of Travel in Egypt and Arabia Petraea.*) All the English explorers were impelled to write books on the subject of Sinai, and so the English-speaking world was treated to shelves of tomes such as M. J. Rendall's *Sinai in Spring; or, The Best Desert in the World,* Arthur W. Sutton's *My Camel Ride from Suez to Mt. Sinai,* and Alexander W. Kinglake's *Eothen.* Even an American, the Reverend D. A. Randall—a Thurberian clergyman from Columbus, Ohio—got into the Sinai exploration act. He intrepidly entered the desert, emerging some months later with notes for a book, which, in time, bore the spectacular title *The Handwriting of God in Egypt, Sinai and the Holy Land—The Records of a Journey from the Great Valley of the West to the Sacred Places of the East.* Of course, some English explorers were serious archeologists, Egyptologists, and Arabists of such standing as Sir William Flinders Petrie, Sir Charles L. Woolley, Edward H. Palmer, and the young T. E. Lawrence. Several of them had an ulterior motive in trekking into the Sinai—namely, to spy on the Turks, using exploration, archeology, and surveying as their covers. For instance, the Woolley and Lawrence expedition in early 1914 to the Turkish fringes of the Sinai was ostensibly undertaken for scientific research but was actually launched at the instigation of Lord Kitchener, the British Secretary of State for War, who was concerned about the German-inspired Turkish buildup in the area. The Turks easily saw through their little ruse and Kitchener finally called the "survey" off, but not before (if one is to believe anything that T. E. Lawrence ever wrote) Lawrence had walked to Akaba and then floated on a raft of empty ten-gallon drums to Gezirat Fara'un through shark-infested waters to reconnoiter the Turkish positions.

Lord Kitchener was well advised to be concerned about the

German-Turkish buildup, because when the First World War broke
out in July of 1914, the Suez Canal was a principal objective of the
Central Powers, which sought to stop the flow of Colonial troops
and supplies from reaching Europe. The Sinai was administered at
that time by a British governor, Lieutenant Colonel Alfred Parker,
who commanded only some Bedouin Camel Corps policemen
headquartered at Nekhl. It was obvious that Turkey would soon
enter the war on Germany's side, and the British reasoned that if
the Turks invaded the Sinai, the peninsula would have to be evacuated, since it could not be adequately defended; the Sinai itself, by
virtue of its rough terrain and inhospitable expanse, would function
as a natural barrier to the canal, it was thought. (Kitchener, however, once asked archly if the British troops were defending the
canal area or if the canal area was defending the British troops.) Just
before it formally entered the war in October, 1914, Turkey sent
patrols into the Sinai interior, organizing Bedouins as spies along
the way, and then, as a full-fledged belligerent, advanced in force
on El Arish and Nekhl. The Camel Corps was routed and the police
posts were destroyed. It was the start of a long, gory, and mercurial
battle for the peninsula, the worst the Sinai had experienced in its
long, gory, and mercurial history.

The Turks launched major attacks on the canal through the central Sinai, relying on gravel highways, railroads, and water pipelines, slowly constructed by German engineers, to facilitate their
plodding advance. When they finally attempted to storm the canal
itself in early 1915, it was abundantly clear to the British that the
Sinai was no longer the great natural barrier it once had been.
Although these Turkish assaults were ultimately beaten back, the
British realized that they could not hold the canal indefinitely without holding all of the Sinai, too. An Egyptian Expeditionary Force,
made up mainly of Colonial troops under Sir Archibald Murray,
painfully took back territory in the north from the Turks. Murray's
men pulled behind them a narrow-gauge railroad and a pipeline of
sweet water from the Nile (via Kantara, the biggest military city in
the world at that time), but they were turned back with heavy
casualties at Gaza, when some British troops were withdrawn to

fight in France and fresh Turkish reinforcements arrived. (The Gaza battles marked the first, but by no means the last, appearance of tanks in desert warfare.) Then, in June of 1917, Murray was replaced by General Edmund Allenby, who was ordered to capture all of the Sinai, Palestine, and as much of the rest of the Levant as he possibly could.

The panache of Allenby—riding through the desert in his open command car, bird-watching along the way, hiring a French chef to prepare meals for him in the field—had an invigorating and legend-encouraging effect on his troops and the Sinai Bedouins. A Bedouin prophecy held that the Turks would be driven from Jerusalem only when "the prophet of the Lord brought the waters of the Nile to Palestine," and as Allenby finished the tasks of laying the sweet-water pipeline from the Nile and the tracks and ties of what would later be called the Allenby Railroad, the prophecy seemed to be fulfilled. (It didn't harm his deiform image with the Bedouins, either, that his last name could be transliterated into Arabic as "Allah En Nebi," or "the Prophet of the Lord.") In any event, by brilliant stratagems, dogged fighting by British regulars and Colonials, and heroic tenacity, Allenby found himself being handed the keys to the city of Jerusalem by the mayor in December of 1917, just four months after the pipeline carrying Nile water arrived at Rafa, on the Palestine border. The victorious Allenby was accompanied into Jerusalem by T. E. Lawrence, who was freshly returned from his much-publicized guerrilla actions behind the Turkish lines and his momentous capture of Akaba from the drowsy Turks manning the fort there, and was soon to be known worldwide as "Lawrence of Arabia." The Sinai and a goodly part of the rest of the Middle East were safely in British hands.

Just a month before Allenby strode triumphantly through the Jaffa Gate, Arthur Balfour, the British Foreign Secretary and former Prime Minister, issued his controversial declaration that favored the establishment in Palestine (as the British were now officially calling the three Turkish sanjaks and the land across the Jordan) of a national home for the Jewish people, without prejudice to the civil and religious rights of existing non-Jewish communities there. The Balfour Declaration had the immediate local effect of a rabid skunk at a garden party—so much so that Allenby refused to allow its text to be published in Palestine for weeks—and it almost immediately set off the Arab-Jewish nationalistic turmoil that exists with screaming intensity to this day.

As the British and French arbitrarily carved up the Middle East to pay off old debts to various factions and chose sides on the question of Zionism, the Sinai was inexorably snared in the events. Some English officials, perhaps out of gratitude to Chaim Weizmann for developing a much-needed explosive during the First World War, took a decidedly pro-Jewish position, as witness the following letter written in early 1919 to Prime Minister Lloyd George by Colonel Richard Meinertzhagen, a member of the British Paris Peace Delegation and the Chief Political Officer in Palestine and Syria:

Paris   25.3.1919

My dear Prime Minister,

You asked me yesterday to send you an unofficial letter on the subject of the sovereignty of Sinai. I regard this question as supremely important—not at the moment but in years to come. May I enter more fully into the question than I was able to do yesterday.

We are very wise in allowing the Jews to establish their National Home in Palestine; we have also freed the Arabs from the Turkish yoke and we cannot forever remain in Egypt. This Peace Conference has laid two eggs—Jewish Nationalism and Arab Nationalism; these are going to grow up into two troublesome chickens: the Jew virile, brave, determined and intelligent; the Arab decadent, stupid, dishonest and producing little beyond eccentrics influenced by the romance and silence of the desert. The Jews, despite dispersal, have distinguished themselves in the arts, music, science and gave Britain one of its distinguished Prime Ministers.

In fifty years time both Jew and Arab will be obsessed by nationalism, the natural outcome of the President's self-determination. Nationalism prefers self-government, however dishonest and inefficient, to government by foreigners, however efficient and beneficial. Nationalism moreover involves the freedom of the State but ignores the freedom of the individual; it is a sop to professional politicians and agitators, and may involve gross injustice to the people.

A National Home for the Jew must develop sooner or later into sovereignty; I understand that this natural evolution is envisaged by some members of H.M.G. Arab nationalism will also develop into sovereignty from Mesopotamia to Morocco.

Jewish and Arab sovereignty must clash. The Jew, if his immigration programme succeeds, must expand, and that can only be accomplished at the expense of the Arab, who will do his utmost to check the growth and power of a Jewish Palestine. That means bloodshed.

The British position in the Middle East today is paramount; the force of nationalism will challenge our position. We cannot befriend both Jew and Arab. My proposal is based on befriending the people who are more likely to be loyal friends—the Jews; they owe us a great deal and gratitude is a marked characteristic of that race. Though we have done much for the Arabs, they do not know the meaning of gratitude; moreover, they would be a liability; the Jews would be an asset.

Palestine is the corner stone of the Middle East, bounded on two sides by desert and on one side by the sea; it possesses the best natural harbour in the Eastern Mediterranean; the Jews have moreover proved their fighting qualities since the Roman occupation of Jerusalem. The Arab is a poor fighter though adept at looting, sabotage and murder.

I now come to Palestine's position vis-à-vis Egypt. The Egyptians, even with superior numbers, are no match for an inferior Jewish Army. But as modern weapons—tanks and aircraft—develop, offensive power rests more and more on human bravery and endurance. That is why I regard Egypt as Palestine's potential enemy.

With Jewish and Arab nationalism developing into sovereignty, and with the loss of the Canal in 1966 (only 47 years hence), we stand a good chance of losing our position in the Middle East. My suggestion to you yesterday is a proposal to make our position in the Middle East more secure.

Previous to 1905 the Turkish-Egyptian frontier ran from Rafa in the North to the neighbourhood of Suez. The whole of the Eastern and Southern Sinai was part of the Hejaz province of the Ottoman Empire. In October 1906 Egypt was granted *administrative rights* in Sinai up to a line drawn from Rafa to the head of the Gulf of Aqaba, Turkey expressly *retaining the right of sovereignty*. General Allenby with British forces, unaided by the Egyptian Army, conquered and occupied Turkish Sinai which, by right of conquest, is at Britain's disposal. This bare statement can be verified by the Foreign Office.

If Britain annexes Turkish Sinai, the following advantages accrue:

1. It establishes a buffer between Egypt and Palestine.
2. It gives Britain a strong foothold in the Middle East with access to both the Mediterranean and the Red Sea.
3. It gives us room for a strategic base and, with Jewish consent, the best harbour in the Eastern Mediterranean.
4. It not only places us in a position whence we can frustrate any Egyptian move to close the Canal to British shipping, but it enables us to build a dual canal connecting the Mediterranean with the Red Sea.
5. No question of nationalism can arise in Sinai, as its nomad inhabitants are but a few thousand.

R. Meinertzhagen

While the debate concerning the future of the Sinai and Palestine crackled, the British judiciously decided to hold on to the peninsula as a separate province, in truth, a part neither of Egypt nor of the Palestine Mandate (the territory granted to England by the League of Nations). It was administered under an organization called the Occupied Enemies' Territory Administration, with Lieutenant Colonel Alfred Parker as the governor until 1923 and his deputy, Major Claude Jarvis, taking over the command from 1923 to 1936. The governor of Sinai was responsible for law enforcement, taxes, public works, public health, agriculture, and education of the native population, at that time about thirty thousand Bedouins and ten thousand assorted "town Arabs" in El Arish. These functions of government were administered by a body of about three hundred officials, including a Sudanese Camel Corps, which watched over four administrative districts (Northern, Central, Southern, and Kantara), each under a *mamour,* or district inspector. A prison and hospital were established at El Arish, with clinics in six other locations.

The British plan in the Sinai was to maintain the status quo until some permanent solution could be found for the troublesome peninsula. It wasn't easy. The Bedouins, in particular, were restive because during the anarchy of war they had become entranced with what to them was the ideal human condition of *mafish hakuma*, "no government," and they could pretty much run things their own way, for a change. With discarded weapons littering the area, ammunition galore, and heady rumors of Arab nationalism abounding, they dreamed of new glory and plunder, without having to toil in menial service, which is beneath Bedouin dignity. Intertribal raids for livestock, mostly, were commonplace, and hashish smuggling, from Turkey and Syria to Egypt via the Sinai, was the main commerce of the area, a kind of cottage industry. The British and their native policemen had their hands full.

Meanwhile, Egypt exerted more and more control over its own destiny. Nationalistic unrest compelled the British to relinquish most of their hegemony over the roiling protectorate, leaving them finally with little more than a military presence in the Suez Canal area. Sultan Ahmed Fuad Pasha proclaimed himself king, being succeeded by his son, Farouk I, and Egyptian influence spilled over into the Sinai. But then the Second World War turned things around and made the area militarily significant once again. The British Army occupation swelled for the second time in twenty-five years. Most of the hot action was, of course, in the western desert of Egypt, holding back the Germans at El Alamein, so the Sinai was spared another round of war's ravages, reverting to its role as strategic buffer and logistics base. With the end of the war, however, the complexion of the entire Levant changed radically: The pitiful survivors of European Jewry struggled against the power of the British Army and the enraged Arabs to settle in Palestine; Arab nationalism simmered as the old, tired colonial powers gave up one by one their Middle Eastern possessions; and Egypt, the most populous, most modern, most dynamic of all the Arab states, took undisputed control of the Sinai, with the blessing of the British, right up to the Palestine border. Clearly, confrontation between Arab and Jew was not far off.

On May 14, 1948—after the United Nations General Assembly had endorsed a partition plan for Jewish and Arab states in Palestine (with Jerusalem designated as a separate entity), after the Arabs had rejected the partition plan and were massing their armies to "drive the Jews into the sea," and after Britain had decided to throw up its hands over the whole ugly mess and end its Palestine Mandate —the State of Israel was declared, a harsh fact of life in the fantasy-ridden Middle East. Israel was immediately attacked from all sides, with Egypt sending her army through the Sinai to occupy the Gaza Strip and put pressure on the Israeli settlements in the Negev. Palestinian Arabs fled to neighboring states, both to escape the warfare and to await the promised Arab victory that would present them with a *Judenrein* nation. The Israelis managed to hold their own; in fact, after a short U.N.-arranged truce, the Israelis actually took the offensive, and by January, 1949, they had driven the British-equipped and -advised Egyptian Army out of the Bir Asluj–Auja El Hafir area on the Negev-Sinai frontier and were poised to take from the stunned Egyptians Rafa, El Arish, and the Gaza Strip. The great powers, alarmed at this totally unexpected turn of events, put heavy pressure on Israel to withdraw its forces from the Sinai. Israel complied, stating for the record that it didn't covet any Egyptian territory. For its part, Egypt was in no condition to continue the fighting, and, in February, 1949, it signed an armistice agreement with Israel, as did Jordan, Lebanon, and Syria, ultimately. Egypt retained the Gaza Strip and all of the Sinai.

The 1949 armistice agreements solved nothing. Arab hostility to Israel increased, with border skirmishes and terrorist attacks (in large measure from the Gaza Strip) heightening the tension to a sometimes unbearable level. As the great powers lined up on one side or another, it was obvious that there would be more war, with the Sinai as the convenient, empty, strategic battleground, as always, an immense playing field for deadly games. Between the 1948–49 Israel War of Independence and the present, no less than four more savage collisions have taken place in the Sinai between Israel and Egypt: the 1956 Sinai Campaign, the 1967 Six Day War, the 1969–70 War of Attrition, and the 1973 Yom Kippur War. Each had its own peculiar *casus belli;* each exacted its own peculiar brand of destruction on the peninsula, its people, and the combatants; each elevated the dreadful art of desert warfare; and each, in the greater scheme of things, only changed lines on the map.

The October 29–November 5 Sinai Campaign of 1956 was a joint Israeli-French-British effort created by the consolidation of several Arab forces under Egyptian command, Egypt's closing of the Gulf of Akaba to Israeli shipping, the increase in Egyptian troops in the Sinai and terrorist infiltration from the Gaza Strip, and, of most concern to the French and British, Egyptian President Gamal Abdel Nasser's nationalizing the Suez Canal and abolishing the British military presence in Egypt after a tenure of almost a hundred years. In just a hundred hours, the rampaging Israeli armored, infantry, and air forces ripped through the Sinai, approached the eastern banks of the Suez Canal, occupied the Gaza Strip, relieved the blockade of the Gulf of Akaba at Sharm El Sheikh, and generally devastated the Egyptian forces throughout the peninsula. Meanwhile, the British and French had mounted an invasion of Port Said, at the northern tip of the canal, hoping to regain control of the entire canal area and reverse Nasser's nationalization. The expedition failed because of angry popular reaction in France and England—and, more importantly, angry governmental reaction in America and Russia. Under such enormous pressures, all three countries soon withdrew their soldiers from the Sinai, Gaza, and the canal area, but not before a U.N. Emergency Force was established to guarantee free passage for Israeli shipping in the Gulf of Akaba and to provide a buffer zone between Egyptian and Israeli troops in the Gaza Strip. (Israel alleged that other promises were made concerning its use of the Suez Canal and the exclusion of Egyptian troops from the Gaza Strip; if these promises were indeed made, they were never kept.)

For a decade, the Sinai was relatively quiet. Maritime traffic to Elath was allowed to navigate the Gulf of Akaba, and El Fatah Palestinian guerrillas operated not out of the Sinai but out of Jordan and Syria, for the most part. However, in the mid-1960s, large quantities of Soviet weaponry, accompanied by Soviet advisers, poured into Egypt and Arab leaders vied with one another in making bellicose anti-Israel pronouncements. Israel, too, amassed a vast arsenal (much of it captured war booty from 1956), and by early 1967, it appeared that the Sinai would be the setting for more trouble. In June, when Nasser moved several divisions to forward positions there—after having peremptorily ordered the U.N. Emergency Force to withdraw, thus effectively closing the Gulf of Akaba to Israel once again—the clamor for a *jihad* (or holy war) against the Jewish state reached an intolerable pitch. Israel took it upon itself to strike first and hardest on June 6. Again, it was all over in less than a week. Mounting a military action that can only be called brilliant—and one that captured the imagination of the entire world—Israel swept the Sinai of all Egyptian troops, first reducing the Arab air forces to aluminum scrap. The cataclysmic defeat for the Arab armies was their most humiliating moment since the early Crusades.

Now it was Israel's turn to possess the Sinai as the great barrier, the fortified buffer, but the sense of security it provided turned out to be more costly than the jubilant Israelis first thought. The new, improved Israel, suddenly extended in area to more than three times its original size and embracing an additional million basically hostile people, found itself still confronted with Arab intransigence to a permanent peace. In the face of this, Israel refused to budge from its captured territories, and the result was a stalemate that inevitably erupted into more combat. The War of Attrition was, in actuality, a 1969–70 continuation of the Six Day War, most of the action again taking place in the Sinai peninsula. Over the Suez Canal area thousands of tons of artillery shells flew in both directions—the most massive artillery barrages since the Second World War—and both Egypt and Israel attempted commando raids deep into each other's territory. The Bar Lev Line, a series of sand-covered bunkers (reinforced with the tracks and ties of the old Allenby Railroad) constructed on the Israeli side of the canal, was under almost constant bombardment and sniper fire, but the Egyptian bank had more to lose, for that was where the canal cities of Suez, Ismailia, Kantara West, and Port Said were located. These cities and adjacent towns were being slowly attrited, their surviving populations decamping for already swollen Cairo. Israel's occupation forces, too, were suffering disturbing casualties, and its air force, used as "flying artillery" against targets inside Egypt, ran into clouds of antiaircraft SAM missiles. Soviet-manned missile bases, and later Soviet-piloted combat aircraft, added a dangerous new element to the already perilous situation, which probably contributed to the success of a cease-fire agreement sponsored by the United States in August, 1970. However, the Suez Canal remained unnavigable, blocked since 1967 with sunken and trapped ships, and, again, little was resolved. Israelis took advantage of the cease-fire to explore the wonders of their new Sinai real estate and, as permanent peace seemed less and less likely, to build new settlements in the peninsula, including a resort at Sharm El Sheikh (renamed Ophira, after Ophir, the biblical land in Africa with which King Solomon's fleet traded via the Gulf of Akaba) and an oil boom town near the offshore wells at Abu Rudeis along the Gulf of Suez. Israel was beginning to extract more from the Sinai than any occupier ever had taken before, and the local Arab populace was surprisingly calm about it all.

Anwar El Sadat, who succeeded to the Egyptian presidency after Nasser's death in 1970, threatened in pronouncement after pronouncement to recapture the Sinai from the Israelis. As the world listened with amused disdain, Sadat astonishingly made good his threat. No people were more astonished than the Israelis. On October 6, 1973—Yom Kippur, the sacred Jewish Day of Atonement —Egyptian infantry and armor crossed the canal and broke through the Bar Lev Line, moving several miles into the Sinai, while to the north Syria stormed the Israeli-held Golan Heights. Taken off guard and unmobilized, the Israel Defense Forces fell back with heavy losses in men, tanks, and planes; however, on the third day of fighting, a fully mobilized Israel went on the offensive along both fronts. On the tenth day, an Israeli raiding party crossed the central sector of the canal and troops poured into Egypt proper (or into "Africa," as the exultant Israelis put it), ultimately cutting off an entire Egyptian army stranded in the Sinai without adequate water or supplies. Both Egypt and Israel were hastily restocked with war materiel from Russia and America, respectively, and an Arab oil embargo on certain nations was put into effect in order to pressure them into an anti-Israel stance. Soviet and American forces were placed on alert. Attention was again focused squarely on the Sinai, and there was a collective gasp at the possible hideous international consequences of continued fighting in that stark, alien wilderness. At last, America and Russia, for differing reasons, agreed to a U.N. cease-fire proposal, and the collective sigh of relief was clearly audible. Another U.N. Emergency Force was sent into the Sinai, and Secretary of State Henry Kissinger proved useful to both sides with his dedicated diplomatic shuttling, which brought about a separation-of-forces agreement known as Sinai I, in January of 1974.

The separation-of-forces agreement gave Egypt an approximately five-mile-wide strip of the western Sinai along the canal, with only a thinned-out military presence allowed in the strip. Farther east into the peninsula another five-mile strip, serving as a U.N. buffer zone, abutted on yet another five-mile strip containing thinned-out Israeli forces. East of that strip, the Sinai was occupied Israeli territory, as it had been before the 1973 war. After a good deal more shuttling and haranguing, Kissinger worked out an interim agreement known as Sinai II in September of 1975, that slightly enlarged the Egyptian thinned-out-forces strip, granted an Egyptian civilian-administered region south to Abu Rudeis and within the widened U.N. buffer zone, provided for an electronic early-warning system manned by American civilians at the Gidi and Mitla passes in the U.N. zone, permitted one Egyptian and one Israeli surveillance station at the passes, and moved the Israeli thinned-out-forces strip farther east. For Israel's part, it had to give up more Sinai territory, including the precious Gidi and Mitla passes and the Abu Rudeis oil fields. For Egypt's part, it won back only a sliver of the western Sinai (though a valuable sliver) and it received massive American aid toward reopening the Suez Canal, which, under the terms of Sinai II, was made available to nonmilitary Israeli-bound cargo. Both parties were assured that neutral U.N. military and American civilian presences would separate them and that the agreement was to be regarded as a significant step toward a "just and lasting peace," remaining in force until superseded by a new agreement. All in all, Sinai II worked out well.

The problem of the Sinai, and perhaps much of the Arab-Israeli conflict, seemed to be on the road to a miraculous resolution with Sadat's courageous and startling initiative in November of 1977. By the time he flew from Cairo (carefully skirting the Sinai) to Jerusalem, where he addressed the Knesset, Israel's parliament, the euphoria was so high that all things appeared possible. However, between then and the Camp David talks of September, 1978, the issue of peace between Egypt and Israel—essentially rooted in the Sinai peninsula—had been thrown together with the other less soluble issues, foremost among them being the future of the Palestinians. As far as the Sinai itself was concerned, it emerged that neither side was all that willing to compromise—Israel insisting on holding on to strategic settlements in the Rafa area near its border, Egypt loath to give up even one grain of holy Sinai sand. The Sinai remained in substantially the same paradoxical predicament it had endured from its earliest moments of history: a fortified, occupied, blood-soaked triangle of wilderness, meaning many things to many people.

The revived optimism for a solid peace treaty after the September, 1978, Camp David talks quickly fizzled once Sadat and Begin returned to their respective countries and scrutinized the fine print and subtle shadings of the "framework" agreements. Not even the presentation of the 1978 Nobel Peace Prize to the two leaders brightened things. In fact, public opinion in both Egypt and Israel turned 180 degrees, from euphoria to pessimism, as distrust and doubt of the other's real intentions grew. When Egypt, under pressure from other Arab governments and dissatisfaction at home, hedged on such draft-treaty matters as exchanging ambassadors before self-governing Palestinian councils existed in the occupied territories and the supersession of the peace treaty over previous defense agreements with other Arab states, the Israeli attitude hardened. Other apparently minor questions thickened to ponderous issues. Many Israelis wondered not so silently, Why should we give up hard-won, tangible real estate—the Sinai—for airy promises of peace from a shaky dictator? And the Egyptians saw themselves being viciously ostracized by their allies and benefactors, just for an accommodation with their old, erratic enemy. The upheaval in Iran and the consequent halt of Iranian oil shipments, upon which Israel had been dependent, further complicated the touchy situation; the Sinai wells became all the more valuable to the Israelis. A new, confusing vocabulary of terms such as "linkage," "annexes," "side letters," and "American tilting" darkened the glow of Camp David. Like two petulant boys on a teeterboard, Sadat and Begin each attempted to give the other a hair-raising ride—with Carter occasionally lending his weight to Sadat's end of the seesaw—before they would ultimately alight, shake hands, and make up. Just when the teeterboard seemed about to collapse under the strain, Carter made his desperate, eleventh-hour trip to Cairo and Jerusalem in March, 1979, and miraculously exacted compromises from both of the still-petulant parties. The seesaw continued to quiver up to the last minute—2:00 P.M., March 26, 1979—when the final treaty drafts were signed in Washington by Sadat and Begin, with Carter adding his all-important signature as witness.

At that magic, curiously joyless moment, official peace came to the Sinai. It remains to be seen how durable will be the treaty—a finely detailed, heavily amended document that neatly sidesteps the crucial issues of the Palestinians and Jerusalem. Will the scrupulously phased three-year timetable for the total withdrawal of Israeli forces and settlers from the Sinai disintegrate at the first false move? Can Sadat survive the virulent attacks of his fellow Arabs? Would Sadat's successor respect the treaty? Will lip service paid to the future of the Palestinians and Jerusalem suffice? Or will the waging of peace be so enchanting that no power on earth can loosen the new bonds between two peoples eager for tranquillity? Is peace catchy? Millions on opposing sides of these questions wait with crossed fingers.

Somehow lost in all the centuries of wrangling over the Sinai is the more basic question of who really owns it. It is a question that could be applied to any border area in the world, perhaps, but in the case of the Sinai it is of paramount importance in the elusive search for Middle East peace. Authorities on international law, by the very nature of the loosely worded, unenforceable code, can make a good case for any position. Not even Israel denies that the

Sinai has been Egyptian since 1906, when the Anglo-Egyptian government pressured the Turks into moving back to the Palestine border. As for the Israeli settlements, the Fourth Geneva Convention of 1949 prohibits an occupying power from displacing a native population or transferring parts of its own civilian population into an occupied territory. The United States strongly adheres to this position; in February, 1978, Secretary of State Cyrus Vance infuriated the Israelis by announcing at a news conference that the Sinai settlements were "contrary to international law and that, therefore, they should not exist." However, other international-law experts feel that this Geneva Convention injunction was meant to prevent large-scale displacements of local civilians for slave labor and replacement of them with colonizers from the victorious side. The twenty Israeli settlements, constituting less than two percent of the peninsula area, were not seen as a serious violation of this tenet by those experts. Also, Israel could legally claim that, having occupied the Sinai in the course of a legitimate defensive action, it was entitled to retain parts of that land for reasonable defensive purposes, before or after a formal peace treaty. Such acquisition of conquered territory was considered lawful if it was agreed upon by both sides in the conflict, as in the case of Russia and Japan, Russia and Finland, and Poland and Germany after the Second World War. Israel is openly paranoid about "secure borders," just as Egypt and other Arab states are paranoid about "the return of *all* territories won through aggression." International law does not say much about hopeless stalemates.

In truth, the Bedouins and the citizens of the towns own the Sinai. The Bedouins relish the anarchic condition of *mafish hakuma,* and yet in all the centuries of their occupation by outsiders, they have experienced "no government" for just a few precious years. But, somehow, through it all, they survive, the Bedouins, for the most part, carrying on with their essentially Bronze Age way of life as though nothing has happened. They have been overlooked in all the squabbling, but they are as integral a part of the Sinai as the strategic passes, the drifting dunes, the flinty plains, and the mauve mountains. They are the living remnants of history.

TWO

THE FASCINATION THE Sinai has held over the past five millennia for such disparate groups as wandering Semites, ascetic Christians, and eccentric Englishmen rubbed off on me from the first moment I saw the place. Deserts, any deserts, fascinate—the harshness of life, the reliance on mere subsistence, the raw beauty of the terrain and its people—but for me there was more than strong attraction to the Sinai. I felt an eerie, instantaneous connection with the land and the Bedouins. It was the fall of 1969, and the War of Attrition was being waged with varying degrees of heat in the Golan Heights abutting Syria, the Jordan Valley, and along the Suez Canal. On an arduous trip into the Sinai to witness the action at the Bar Lev Line, I first experienced that strange connection, in spite of the devastation and chaos all around me. No atavistic vision or sense of *déjà vu* captured me; rather, it was the ordinary sights—a glimpse of a black-gowned Bedouin woman moving as if on tiny wheels across a distant dune, heading, seemingly, to nowhere from nowhere, the stark abruptness of the mountains, the omnipresent ruins of history preserved by the hot, dry environment. I promised myself that I would come back in more placid times, explore the entire peninsula, and get to know its people.

For various reasons, I could not revisit the Sinai until the early spring of 1978. As it turned out, there hadn't been such an opportune moment to travel in the Sinai for years. However, one can no longer, as the Victorian explorers did, simply hire a few camels and a Bedouin guide and prowl the wilderness. The exigencies of contemporary politics and travel in the Middle East are such that elaborate arrangements must be made. First, there was the matter of permissions and visas. My plans had to be spelled out in detailed letters to the Israeli government (the Israeli-held Sinai is, strictly speaking, a military zone and the Israelis want to know where you will be at any given moment), the Egyptian government (there was some hope of my being permitted to cross directly into Egyptian-held Sinai through the U.N. zone, and this scheme necessitated considerably more documents and discussions than the usual visa application), the United Nations Secretariat (journalists can visit the U.N. zone but they must be escorted by U.N. personnel at all times), the U.S. State Department's Sinai Support Mission (journalists are not particularly welcome to spend more than a few hours at the early-warning stations of the American-operated Sinai Field Mission, and I proposed to spend a couple of days there), and, lastly, the Greek Orthodox Church (which oversees the monks of St. Catherine's Monastery, who, because of rampant tourism in the monastery area, are extremely touchy about the number and quality of travelers staying on the hallowed grounds).

Then, most urgent for my journeys into the Sinai was the hiring of a guide, really a Sinai expert, who was fluent in English, Arabic, and Hebrew, who knew the unmarked tracks of the wilderness, and, above all, was available. The Israeli Consulate in New York put me in touch with a likely candidate, an American-born Israeli with the unexpected name of Dr. Clinton Bailey, a lecturer in Bedouin Studies at Tel Aviv University who had traveled extensively in the Sinai for the past ten years, living with and learning from the Bedouins. Also, he was the owner of a four-wheel-drive Land-Rover, which was indispensable for the kind of journeying I intended. He seemed perfect for my purposes; however, at the beginning of 1978, he was still recovering from a bad bout of hepatitis. But Bailey (and his physician) finally agreed that he could make the trip with me into the Sinai at the beginning of April.

So, armed with an accordion-envelope full of documents and letters of introduction, a sleeping bag, my trusty U.S. Army rucksack laden with miscellaneous camping equipment, and the, perhaps, naïve will and romanticism of a Victorian explorer, I arrived

in Jerusalem on Tuesday, March 28, ready for anything. My hotel
was the towering Jerusalem Plaza, whose Miami Beach opulence
would have quickly discouraged any nineteenth-century British ad-
venturer and sent him packing back to London. (For all its garish
irrelevance to the delicate beauty of Jerusalem, it affords a spectacular view from its upper floors of the Dead Sea and Moabite Mountains beyond.)

My first order of business was to meet with Dr. Bailey, whose
house was just a few minutes' walk from the hotel. Fortunately—
since we would be spending twenty-four hours a day together—we
hit it off right away. For one thing, it turned out that Bailey had
been a freshman at Dartmouth when I was a senior there, and
although I hadn't known him during my college days, we had many
Hanover and other acquaintances in common. The tall, curly-
haired son of well-to-do parents in Buffalo, New York, Bailey had
been something of a playboy in his youth. He left Dartmouth after
only one year, sporadically attended several other colleges, enlisted
in the U.S. Navy, experienced a sudden realization of his Jewish-
ness, and headed for Israel, where he became a serious student of
Arabic life and language at the Hebrew University, rounding off
his education with a Ph.D. from Columbia University's Middle East
Institute in 1966. More important, we both felt a strong sense of
connection with the Sinai and its people. Drinking dark coffee over
large maps spread out on the living-room floor of his pleasant,
Bedouin-artifact–filled house (which he shares with his three sons
and his lovely sabra wife, Maya, who calls him by his Hebrew given
name, Itzhak), we made detailed plans for our expeditions. I would
go on two Sinai journeys with Bailey in his Land-Rover. The first
and shorter one would begin on Monday, April 3, and cover the
northeast quadrant of the peninsula from the Bir Asluj–Auja El
Hafir area near the Negev-Sinai border to the barely accessible
Kadesh Barnea of biblical fame, via El Kuseima, and culminating
in a visit to the city of El Arish, where the monthly meeting between the north Sinai Bedouin sheikhs and the Israel military governor was scheduled for Tuesday, April 4. The second and longer
trip would begin on Friday, April 7, and would take in the entire

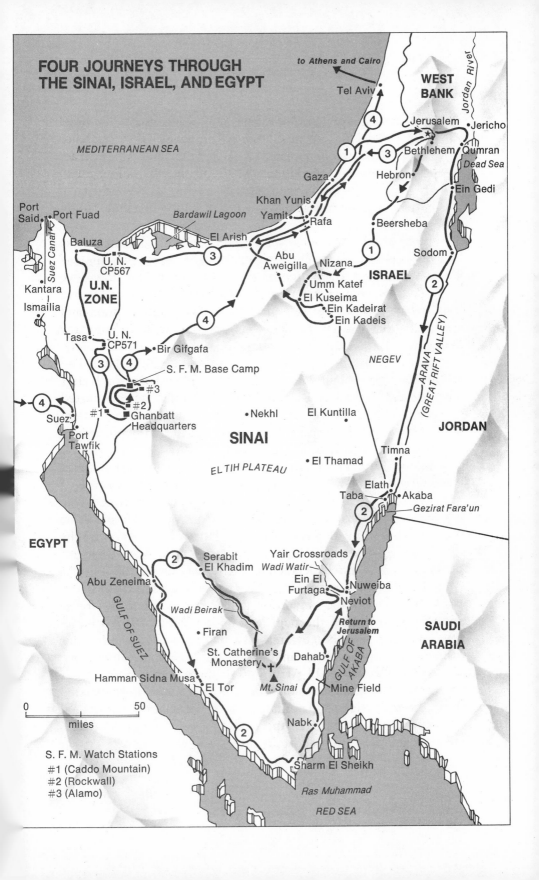

FOUR JOURNEYS THROUGH THE SINAI, ISRAEL, AND EGYPT

to Athens and Cairo

WEST BANK

MEDITERRANEAN SEA

Tel Aviv

Jerusalem • Jericho

④

① ③ Bethlehem • Qumran

Gaza Hebron • *Dead Sea*

Khan Yunis • Ein Gedi

Port Said • Port Fuad

Yamit • Rafa

Beersheba

Bardawil Lagoon

El Arish ③ Abu Aweigilla Nizana ①

Baluza Sodom

U. N. CP567 ISRAEL

U.N. ZONE Umm Katef El Kuseima Ein Kadeirat Ein Kadeis

Kantara

Ismailia *NEGEV*

Tasa U. N. CP571 Bir Gifgafa ④ *ARAVA (GREAT RIFT VALLEY)*

③ ④ S. F. M. Base Camp

#3 **JORDAN**

#1 #2

Suez Ghanbatt Headquarters • Nekhl • El Kuntilla

④ Port Tawfik **SINAI** Timna

EL TIH PLATEAU • El Thamad

Elath • Akaba

Taba ② *Gezirat Fara'un*

EGYPT ② Serabit El Khadim Yair Crossroads *Wadi Watir*

Abu Zeneima Ein El Furtaga Nuweiba

Wadi Beirak Neviot

• Firan *Return to Jerusalem* **SAUDI ARABIA**

St. Catherine's Monastery Dahab

Hamman Sidna Musa • El Tor *Mt. Sinai* Mine Field

0 — 50

miles Nabk

S. F. M. Watch Stations Sharm El Sheikh

#1 (Caddo Mountain)

#2 (Rockwall) *Ras Muhammad*

#3 (Alamo) *RED SEA*

GULF OF SUEZ

GULF OF AKABA

Jordan River

Suez Canal

central and southern regions of the peninsula. I had already arranged for two later journeys, one covering the U.N. and Sinai
Field Mission zones of the western Sinai and the other the Egyptian-
held area along the Suez Canal. All in all, there would be four
distinct Sinai journeys through virtually the entire peninsula.

As a pale-orange dawn broke over the color-mimicking Jerusalem limestone on Monday morning, I descended by elevator from
my eighteenth-floor room at the Plaza, hunched under the weight
of an Australian bush hat and a rucksack full of camping equipment.
The early-rising guests at the hotel, mostly committed joggers or
Orthodox Jews on their way to synagogues for morning prayers,
didn't quite know what to make of me. The "Israeli breakfast"
spread of fish, fruits, eggs, cheeses, yoghurts, breads, juices, and
coffee was just making its overwhelming appearance in the cavernous dining room, served by Arab waiters and busboys. Even with
all the eyes of my fellow breakfasters on me, I managed to cadge
a half dozen hard-boiled eggs and a few soft rolls for snacks along
the road. Having traveled through the desert before, I knew
enough to drink as much fruit juice and water as I could stomach
in preparation for the dehydration ahead.

Bailey and his Land-Rover—abrim with camping supplies, a
large plastic water bottle to refill the car's radiator, jerry cans of
gasoline, extra tires, and such miscellanea as Bailey's *kaffiyeh*, Web-
ley revolver, and canteens—arrived in front of the Plaza's main
entrance at 6:30. A knot of perplexed onlookers saw us off on the
road south to Beersheba, and I thought of how those Victorian
gentlemen must have felt as they left Jerusalem for the desert a
century ago, with strange, wondering eyes watching them disappear down a camel track. The ancestry of the sturdy but rattly
Land-Rover could be traced to the Six Day War of 1967, when it
was "liberated" from the Jordanian Army by the victorious Israelis;
it then passed through several owners until it arrived, battered but
game, in the hands of Dr. Clinton Bailey, who had run up tens of
thousands of hard kilometers in it. Sensing my doubts as we hurtled
down the road to the West Bank town of Bethlehem, Bailey said,
"Don't worry. It will get us there, and maybe even back again."

Bethlehem was quiet and touristy, as one would expect of that

Christian object of pilgrimage, which has survived the centuries as the birthplace of the Prince of Peace. But at Halhul, farther down the road, the tensions of the occupied West Bank became apparent. Even though few civilians or soldiers were to be seen, Bailey sped almost recklessly through the town's outskirts. Halhul had been the scene of recent rioting by Palestinian Arabs against the Israeli occupation troops, and Bailey said that he had just missed being caught up in that turmoil as he had passed through. He continued to drive fast through Hebron, also beset by recent rioting, and slowed down only when children emerged from the refugee-camp shanties, walking along the roadside on their way to school. The camps on either side of the road were, of course, deplorable, but no worse than any average Middle Eastern slum. Seeing them again put me in mind of what an Indian journalist had said during my visit here nine years before: "These camps would be a luxurious suburb in Calcutta."

As we dashed along a straighter, less hilly road toward the Negev and Beersheba, occasional patches of shin-high green wheat lent a perverse quality of agricultural richness to the sorry, parched landscape. The people who cultivated the wheat on small plots of irrigated ground were semi-Bedouins: that is, those Bedouins who have forsaken their mohair tents for concrete-block houses or deserted war-ruined buildings, in which they live with their livestock. (When they first took over these permanent abodes, they put their animals inside and continued to live in their tents, the mohair being better protection from the cold and rain than a stone roof. However, as they learned to improve their housing, the tents were dismantled.) Crossing into the Negev proper—Negev means "dry" in Hebrew and has come to mean "south"—I noticed that the patches of green wheat were less frequent. This was true desert, punished by its fourth year in a row of severe drought. Finding a spot of damp soil for planting wheat was hardly worth the trouble. Soon, we were in downtown Beersheba, a former desert crossroads which has blossomed into a city of 100,000 Israelis (both Jews and Bedouins), with fast-food outlets, traffic lights, rows of gas stations, and one of the largest prostitute populations in Israel—a frontier town gone mad.

From Beersheba south toward the old Sinai frontier at Nizana,

there was little on the desert floor but the detritus of war, some of
it dating back to Byzantine fortifications. This had been the main
armor and infantry training ground for the Israel Defense Forces
before they captured the Sinai in 1967. Since 1967, parts of the
Sinai have been used for training maneuvers—"another reason why
we should hold on to the Sinai," Bailey said. A few soldiers lounged
outside their tents and barracks, some of them Bedouins who had
enlisted in the I.D.F. as desert trackers, a basic Bedouin talent. (It
has been said that the sand is to the Bedouin what the morning
newspaper is to the Englishman—news and gossip, but with fewer
misprints.) Several of the trackers were black, the descendants of
slaves from Africa who had been put on the auction block in Arabia
and had traveled with Bedouin tribes performing the menial work.
The five hundred or so black Bedouins in the Sinai are freemen
now, but they are still considered outcasts—"below the salt," as the
British put it—and are not allowed to intermarry with lighter-
skinned tribal cousins. Every black is referred to, within his tribe,
as an *abd,* or "slave," even though he no longer technically fits that
classification. The Bedouins are, perhaps, the only people in the
world who still refer to blacks as "slaves."

The Negev has been the scene of a sometimes bitter conflict
between the native Bedouins, who are full-fledged Israeli citizens
(unlike the Sinai Bedouins), and the Israel Ministry of Agriculture,
headed by Ariel Sharon, a hawkish, blustery hero of the 1973 war,
who wants to expropriate some traditional Bedouin lands for Israeli
farms, industrial parks, settlements, and, since the peace treaty, new
military bases to replace those evacuated in the Sinai. Usually, the
Bedouins can claim only a historical tenure on the land in question,
offering some dubious legal deeds to back up the claim. As a result,
the Green Patrol, a controversial police arm of the Agriculture
Ministry, has moved in on Negev encampments and rudely shoved
the people and their livestock off the desired acreage to controlled
townships. This has stirred up a tempest in Israel (where any controversy becomes a tempest overnight), especially since the Negev
Bedouins are seen by liberal Israelis as being denied their demo-
cratic rights as citizens.

There is a larger question attached to the Negev ruckus: Should the Bedouin be discouraged from nomadism and livestock herding and, instead, be encouraged through vocational training to enter industry and other modern pursuits? Some Israeli ecologists feel the answer should be affirmative, because, they say, the Bedouins' insatiable, proliferating black goats, in particular, destroy desert plants and settlement crops. (Other ecologists say that black goats simply nibble and prune back the greenery, not unlike white goats.) Dr. Moshe Sharon, the Prime Minister's former adviser on Arab affairs, stated in 1978, "They [the Bedouins] used to have 30,000 head; today the number has grown to 250,000. Where can you find enough pasture in Israel to feed such flocks?" Bailey is a leader of the opposition to this view; indeed, he has presented his own plan to the government for keeping the Negev Bedouin on the land, herding livestock in the usual manner but within certain controlled areas under the aegis of the Nature Reserves Authority. "It is not our business to redesign the life of the Bedouin," he told me. "Help them, yes, but bully them, no."

The good paved road we rode to Nizana was originally constructed by the British after the First World War as part of the Ismailia-Beersheba Highway. Alongside the highway were the remains of the Ottoman railroad to the Sinai, which the Turks painstakingly built under the direction of German engineers, so painstakingly, in fact, that they gave the British time to mobilize and counterattack. The well-preserved arched-stone railroad trestles over the wadis demonstrated how fine the German engineering technique was, notwithstanding the poor German military timing. Then, suddenly, there was Nizana—the border post between Palestine and Sinai, the Turkish-British frontier of 1906, with a depot, water tower, and crumbling police station still standing—and just beyond a coil of barbed wire marking the old border, the Sinai. For some mysterious reason, it looked strikingly different from the Negev—more pristine, more majestic, more polychromatic, more timeless. The contrast reminded me of the geographic puzzle that presents itself whenever I cross the line from my home state of Connecticut to Massachusetts on Interstate-86; as if by divine command, the red earth and puny scrub of Connecticut immediately change into the dark, verdant soil and majestic pines of Massachusetts.

We stopped to explore the frontier post and stare at the ruins of a Byzantine city on an adjacent hilltop. To the banshee accompaniment of two Israeli Phantom jets turning south just over our heads, I read a bullet-riddled metal sign in English, erected by the Israeli government:

> THIS VILLAGE NOT [bullet hole] FROM
> BIBLICAL KADESH BARNEA IS THE
> ORIGINAL SITE OF THE BYZANTINE
> CITY OF [bullet hole]
> THE TURKS USED THE STONES
> FROM ITS RUINS TO BUILD
> THEIR ARMY ENCAMPMENT ON
>   [bullet hole] HILL
> WHEN THE BRITISH MANDATE
> TERMINATED IN PALESTINE ON
> THE 15TH OF MAY 1948 [bullet hole]
> WAS SEIZED BY THE [bullet hole] PTI [bullet hole]
>   ARMY.
> IT WAS CAPTURED [three bullet holes in a neat row]
> DEFENCE FORCES IN DECEMBER
> 1948, AND [bullet hole] THE EGYPTIAN-
> ISRAEL ARMISTICE AGREEMENT,
> [bullet hole] AS DECLARED A DEMILITARIZED
>   ZONE.
> AN EGYPTIAN BATTALION SEIZED
> CERTAIN STRATEGIC HEIGHTS IN
> THE ZONE IN OCTOBER 1955.
> THEY WERE DRIVEN OFF BY ISRAEL
> FORCES IN A DARING NIGHT
> ACTION AT THE BEGINNING OF
>   NOVEMBER.
> ARCHAEOLOGICAL EXCAVATIONS
> IN THE [bullet hole] BROUGHT TO LIGHT
> SOME [bullet hole] APYRI FROM THE
>   7TH CENTURY B.C.E.

The name of the Byzantine city erased by an anonymous bullet was Nessana, according to artifacts found years ago in its ruins. It was part of a complex of fourth-to-sixth-century Negev and Sinai Byzantine outposts, most of which were built on top of Nabatean settlements. Shivta, for instance, a city with three churches south of the Beersheba-Nizana road, made good use of the clever Nabatean system for gathering and storing every drop of runoff water. A site much farther south, at the Sinai hamlet of El Kuntilla, was discovered in the nineteenth century by Professor Edward Palmer, a British Arabist and historian, who erroneously believed it to be the Roman fortress city of Gypsaria. Recent findings there, by Professor Zeev Meshel of Tel Aviv University's Department of Archeology, indicated that it was an 800 B.C. Judean fortress and religious center, erected to guard the land route from Judea and Gaza to Elath. This may have been the route for Ophir gold and ivory brought, via Elath, to the Jerusalem Temple. Shells uncovered there from the Red Sea back up that speculation. Phoenician inscriptions on the walls at the Kuntilla site perhaps demonstrate the theory that Phoenicians could have hauled disassembled ships made of Lebanon cedar down the Sinai from Gaza to Elath for King Solomon's fabled Red Sea fleet. (The First Book of Kings hints that Solomon made an agreement with Hiram, King of Tyre, to outfit him with such cedar ships.) In any case, the Kuntilla site is definitely Jewish in origin, not Roman or Byzantine, according to Professor Meshel. Archeology is not really an exact science, and, in the eyes of some cynics, it tends to follow nationalistic predilections.

As for the sign's holey description of Nizana as a modern battle area, the documentation is far more complete. The push into the Sinai by the ragtag Israel Army during the War of Independence in late 1948 took place through this sector. To preclude heavy casualties, the Israelis decided against mounting a motorized assault straight down the Beersheba-Nizana road and had to improvise a plan for bringing their half-tracks and armored cars through the desert to attack the Egyptian positions. Some of the Israeli commanders recalled from their archeological hikes (everyone in Israel is at the very least an amateur archeologist) an ancient Roman track in dreadful condition running circuitously to Nizana through Wadi

Abbiyad. With bulldozers clearing a passable road through the wadi's sand and boulders, the Israelis, on Christmas Day, 1948, surprised the dug-in Egyptians, who surrendered by the hundreds after a short firefight. Large quantities of war booty fell into delighted Israeli hands, along with a stunned colonel of the Egyptian General Staff. All of the Sinai and the Gaza Strip was open to the Israelis, but they pulled back under pressure from the Big Powers and settled for the Negev as an integral part of the new nation. When the Egyptians violated the demilitarization of the area in 1955, another surprise night attack, this time by just infantry on a grueling forced march through the desert, again caught the Egyptians looking the other way. Hand-to-hand combat in the dark drove the Egyptians off. The same bloody battle area was used again as a route of advance into the Sinai in the Six Day War of 1967.

"Well, let's go to the Sinai," said Bailey. We clambered back into the Land-Rover and, with the hot hum of the mid-morning desert all around us, we drove across the frontier. It not only looked different, it was different. The Sinai road, far less traveled, was rough in spots, with drifting sand treacherously covering parts of it. Large mountains, ocherous in the bright sun, rose out of the south; one of the highest in the area, Gebel Halal, is considered by some biblical historians (believers in the Northern Route of the Exodus theory) to be the true Mount Sinai. The Israelis had recently, and unsuccessfully, prospected for oil there. One lone date palm was off in the dunes near a swatch of arable land on which a Bedouin had attempted to grow watermelon. Genista, a form of pale-green broom, sprouted in clumps. Its spiny branches are used by the Bedouins to cover their *arishas,* or arbor booths, which provide temporary shade or more permanent summer shelter. At a dot on the map called Umm Katef, near a dirt track leading south to El Kuseima, we saw the *katef,* a saltwort bush whose leaves are chewed by the Bedouins as a ready source of salt. Sometimes, when the larder is especially bare, they boil the *katef* leaves for soup, into which they dip pieces of *pita,* or flat bread. I chewed a few leaves and found the taste salty and rather uplifting. Not so Job, who said that he was so filled with woe that even such as the pluckers of the saltwort, the lowest of the low, were reviling him. (*Katef* means in English "pluck." *Umm Katef* means "Mother of Katef." *Umm* (Mother) or *Abu* (Father) before a place-name should not be taken literally; the looser meaning is "possessor of " or "characterized by.") More and more, the sand plains took on a greenish-black hue, as if they had been sprayed with some petroleum product. The dark covering was actually a layer of flintstone, which, in parts of the central Sinai, is so thick it makes the land look like a black sea—ideal terrain, Egyptian and Israeli military planners point out, for tank maneuvering.

When grinding through the Sinai in his Land-Rover, Bailey compulsively stopped and talked to every Bedouin he spotted. (If the Bedouin was too far off to approach the car, Bailey would at the very least honk his horn in passing salute.) This was how he gathered a great deal of his data on Bedouin life and lore, and while this habit could become slightly irritating for his traveling companions, it gave Bailey a rare lofty status for an Israeli in Bedouin circles. He was known throughout the peninsula as "Docto*rr* Bay*lee*," which moved me to dub him "Itzhak of Sinai." The Bedouins would exchange *salamats* (greetings) with him all day long, if he allowed it. They admired him and trusted him; some Bedouins counted him among their brothers, which was high esteem indeed.

On the dirt track leading south from Umm Katef to El Kuseima, Bailey saw a family of Bedouins huddled in the stingy shade of their roadside *arisha.* He pulled over in front of them and, leaning out the driver's window, shouted, *"Salamat! Salamat!"* A veiled woman wearing her everyday black gown, decorated belt, and turquoise-and-brass jewelry, a man in a red-checked *kaffiyeh* and a soiled caftan under a suit jacket, and four dark-skinned children slowly rose as one to greet him. "Docto*rr* Bay*lee*, *salamat!*" said the man. The woman and children hung back as the man and Bailey went through the lengthy Bedouin protocol of desert politeness. This involves, among other ceremonial procedures, never permitting an empty moment to sully the conversation; such moments, if they do unhappily occur, must immediately be filled by a new, totally redundant round of *salamats,* demonstrating peaceful intent in a hostile environment. At last, the man explained that he had just this morning built the genista-covered *arisha* for himself and his family, in order to await in relative shade the arrival of a traveling Israeli physician, who would examine them all in their booth. They knew the physician was due this day at this point on the road in his normal medical rounds. Some of the children, he said, were having stomach trouble. He seemed apologetic about not inviting us into his house, as it were, which is another pillar of Bedouin protocol, but the physician was due any minute now. Sure enough, as we drove off, under a barrage of *shukrans* (thanks) and *salaams* (peace), we passed the physician coming the other way in a four-wheel-drive truck.

I asked Bailey to tell me more about the family. "They are Bedouins of the Tarabin tribe," he said, wrestling with the steering wheel as we lurched over the rutted track toward El Kuseima. "The kids are darker than the parents, which might mean that they are the result of another wife, although I don't think the man could have afforded more than that one wife back there. As a Moslem, he's allowed four wives, but few Bedouins can support four and all the kids, too. Anyway, the Tarabin are a large tribal confederation in the Sinai—we'll be looking up their head sheikh, Suleiman Ibn Jazi, when we get to El Arish tonight—and they have spread out considerably over the years from the south Sinai to the north-central region and even over to the Suez area. The tribe has a lot of energy and a lot of people to feed, and that is why they have infiltrated other tribal areas. They were very tough guys once, about as tough as the notorious Howeitat tribe of T. E. Lawrence fame, but all Bedouins can be tough when they have to scratch out a living in poor conditions. The Tarabin became tamer when they expanded into Palestine and got the territory they wanted in the Negev. Before 1948, they were the biggest tribe in the Negev, but now they're mostly back in the Sinai. They still have many enemies among the other Bedouins."

For all their aggressiveness, Bailey continued, whenever a hot war broke out in their region, the Bedouins stayed well clear of the shooting. For them, discretion was the better part of valor. They didn't like to take sides; rather, they preferred to be simply left alone while the rest of the world committed collective suicide. They had never been disciplined troops, but they had always been good hit-and-run raiders ("ten-minute fighters," the Australian soldiers called them), with the emphasis on plundering livestock and other valuables, not taking human lives. "There is an old Bedouin proverb," Bailey said, "that translates roughly as 'When the shooting starts, get on the backs of camels to the tops of mountains.' In other words, bug out!"

About a hundred yards off the road, we saw a Bedouin man sitting beside a boulder with a loose Saluki dog, a scrawny, piebald version of the breed used by the Bedouins for guarding sheep and hunting. The Bedouin was staring straight ahead at nothing, apparently just waiting. What was he waiting for? I wondered, half aloud. "Who knows," Bailey answered. He tooted his horn and waved. The Bedouin waved back.

El Kuseima, such as it is, came into view at the end of the dirt track. A dusty *Beau Geste* oasis, it has been used as a police station by just about every power that has ever occupied the Sinai. One half of the outpost consisted of military buildings, housing a platoon of Israeli soldiers and their equipment. A tall radio antenna and hooded machine guns were on the headquarters-building roof; nearby was a helicopter landing pad with a bright orange windsock hanging limp in the dead air. Trucks and jeeps were parked in an orderly line, baking under the sun. A small white hootch bearing the legend "SALOON" lent a Wild West flavor, which Israelis seemed to cultivate in the sticks. The other half of the outpost was the Bedouin side of town: a small mosque, a half dozen low, decrepit, often roofless hootches, a water tower, and scattered shoes, sandals, plastic containers, and bits of odd metal littering the ground. Camels, donkeys, and goats wandered loose among the few date palm, casuarina, tamarisk, and acacia trees.

Bailey explained our presence in this unlikely place to some sleepy Israeli soldiers who came out of the headquarters building to greet us, somewhat suspiciously. As a reserve officer in the

I.D.F., he had little trouble convincing them of our innocent purpose. Then, we walked over to the Bedouin side of town, where Bailey, much more at ease than he was with his fellow Israelis, was joyfully welcomed in the usual "Docto*rr* Bayl*ee*" manner by several men emerging from the hootches. During the *salamats* and handshakes, he introduced me as "Burt," which came out as "Boo*rr*t" from the smiling, almost toothless mouths. We accepted —had to accept—their invitation to take hot, heavily sweetened tea with them in one of the huts that served as a small general store, offering such goods as hunks of laundry soap, plastic water bottles and sandals, ball-point pens, camel lead ropes, sacks of beans, flour, and tobacco (the sacks marked "UNRWA European Gift to Palestine"), and tins of bully beef, olive oil, tomatoes, tuna, and mackerel. After fifteen minutes or so of pleasantries, Bailey got to the point. He told them that we wanted to visit the two oases said to be Kadesh Barnea, the biblical resting place of the Israelites' wandering, and that while he knew the way to one of them, Ein Kadeirat, he wasn't exactly sure how to get to the less accessible one, Ein Kadeis. A Bedouin guide who knew the region well was required, he said. A short, swarthy, moustached, chain-smoking man with an abundance of woolly black hair stepped forward. I noticed that he was wearing long underwear, a shirt, a sweater, and a *galabiya* under a grimy suit jacket, in typical Bedouin contempt for the midday heat. He was Hassan Ibn Amir, a leading citizen and property owner of El Kuseima, whose grandfather, Salim El Awamra, was a close friend of Major Jarvis, the British governor of Sinai after the First World War. Hassan's father, Bailey further told me in a quick aside, was that rare creature, a flaming Bedouin nationalist and pro-Saudi. (Sinai Bedouins generally look askance at their wealthy Saudi cousins, whose traditional desert life has been recently fouled by oil and its attendant air-conditioning, Cadillacs, and high living in expensive foreign resorts. The Saudis have lost the knack of mere subsistence in the wilderness, and with it the title of "true Arab." Only their outward trappings are Bedouin, and those are often designed by Bond Street tailors.)

The seemingly endless cups of hot tea had a diuretic effect on me, and before the three of us left for Ein Kadeirat, I inquired, through Bailey, where I might discreetly void my bladder. The Bedouins chuckled and said that if I was diffident about such matters, I could go next door to another hootch, where there would be some privacy. I took their advice and found myself in a roofless square house, really just four battered walls, up to the tops of my boots in human and animal waste coated with regiments of hungry Sinai flies. This impromptu latrine was obviously part of the municipal establishment, an informal compost bin for general use, a natural extension of Bedouin town life. I recalled what Bailey had told me earlier: that the secret of getting along with Bedouins was not to be a missionary, not to criticize or patronize them for any behavior alien to Western life; rather, one must accept them for the timeless, proud, earthy people they are. To do otherwise is to loathe them and, in the end, to be their enemy.

It has been said that the Exodus is the most contentious event in the Old Testament, and one of the larger points of contention among biblical historians concerns what and where Kadesh Barnea is. According to the Bible, Moses and the Israelites wandered through the western and central Sinai wilderness for at least two years; after the theophany and law-giving at Mount Sinai, they made their way northeastward toward Canaan, stopping to rest for, some say, thirty-eight years at an oasis of abundance called Kadesh Barnea, so close and yet so far from their promised goal. For centuries, tradition had it that Ein Kadeis was the primary site of Kadesh Barnea, if for no more reason than the similarity in names. The Book of Numbers states unequivocally that in Moses's census taken during the second year of the wandering there were 603,550 men of fighting age (less the Levites); with women, children, and livestock thrown in, it would have been unlikely for Ein Kadeis, a bubbling spring and stream surrounded by some thistle and palms, to support this unwieldy host. (Sir William Flinders Petrie cleared up some of the contradictory arithmetic by pointing out that the Hebrew word *elef,* used in the Bible to number the Israelites in thousands, can also mean "family." By Petrie's calculation, the

Israelite host would have been roughly six hundred families, a more reasonable body to be trooping about the desert, with only one judge, Moses, to settle all their disputes and just two midwives to help with childbirth.) Ein Kadeirat, on the other hand, is a large and lush oasis several miles north of Ein Kadeis, with remains of ancient dams, reservoirs, and irrigation systems. It could comfortably support six hundred families for thirty-eight years, if they spread out a bit and rationed the natural resources.

The Israelites' extended stay at Kadesh Barnea, in the Wilderness of Zin, included several momentous biblical events. It was there that the Twelve Tribes were instructed to pitch their tents in formal order about the holy Tabernacle, the model for the latter-day Jerusalem Temple. It was there, too, that Moses sent out a reconnaissance party, one key man from each tribe, "to spy out the land of Canaan." The dozen reconnoiterers returned to Kadesh Barnea after forty days with a huge cluster of grapes, pomegranates, and figs as proof that the Promised Land "floweth with milk and honey," so to speak. However, they added, there were well-armed giants, the sons of Anak, blocking the way, next to whom the Israelites were "as grasshoppers." Of the twelve spies, only Caleb and Joshua suggested that they take on the giants and head forthwith into the Promised Land; the other spies—indeed, all the other Israelites—fearfully murmured and rebelled against Moses, Caleb, and Joshua for misleading them, a common reaction during the forty years of wandering by the volatile, "stiff-necked people." Since in God's eyes this lack of resolve showed treachery toward Him, He commanded that all those over the age of twenty, save Caleb and Joshua, would continue to roam the wilderness "until your carcasses be wasted." Only the young and pure would enter the Promised Land—thus the explanation for the thirty-eight-year stay at Kadesh Barnea, where the Israelites lived the life of Bedouins, strengthening their moral and physical fiber for the big move ahead. Laws, worship, and discipline were tightened (as an example, a man caught gathering sticks on the sabbath was executed by stoning), and open rebellion was dealt with sternly by the Lord, who caused the earth to open and swallow the leaders and fire to consume their followers.

Even Moses himself, human being that he was, was not immune to God's wrath. When he was instructed by the Lord to *tell* a rock to yield water during a drought, Moses, perhaps absentmindedly, *struck* the rock twice with his rod, as he had successfully done earlier near Rephidim. Water gushed,* but the Lord saw the act of striking as a breach of faith in the divine power to bring forth water by words alone. As punishment for this transgression, He condemned Moses and his brother Aaron to never entering the Promised Land (Moses's sister Miriam had already expired at Kadesh Barnea). Through these severe object lessons, the Twelve Tribes were welded into a disciplined, faithful army, capable after long, hard decades of conquering Canaan, albeit from the eastern side of the Jordan River.

I wanted to visit Kadesh Barnea not only to see the rarely visited place with my own eyes but to check out the various theories connected with its history, and to gain some experience traveling in harsh desert country in preparation for the harsher desert country ahead. So Bailey, Hassan, and I, crowded together in the front seat of the Land-Rover, bumped down the rough track toward El Kuntilla, passing a clinic, a school, an abandoned U.N. outpost, and, very gingerly, a poorly marked, uncleared mine field. Near the side of the track was a freshly bulldozed area that was supposed to be the site of a new Israeli settlement, called Moshav Kadesh Barnea, a pet project of Agriculture Minister Sharon; however, Defense Minister Ezer Weizman, the official technically in charge of the Sinai, had just recently forbidden any more work to be done on the settlement, to calm Sadat's fears after the peace initiative. The repercussions of this intra-Cabinet struggle were still resounding in the Israeli press.

After a few kilometers, we turned east to Ein Kadeirat, following

---

*Pools of fossil water are numerous in various spots throughout the Sinai. Sometimes, they can be accidentally found in aboveground limestone rocks; a Bedouin soldier under the British once energetically swung his shovel at a rock and almost fainted dead away when a Mosaic stream spewed forth.

an open aqueduct built by the British, which carried the cool Kadeirat spring water to El Kuseima. We stopped for a moment to give
some sugar wafers to two beautiful Bedouin children playing beside the aqueduct. Wide-eyed at our largesse, they overcame their
shyness and asked for more, which Hassan firmly vetoed, shooing
them off. As a respected leader of the five hundred or so Bedouins
of the territory around El Kuseima, he does not like to see begging,
particularly by children. At Bailey's prodding, Hassan told us more
about himself and the local Bedouins. He had inherited some farm-
land from his father and owned a share of the general store in El
Kuseima where we had tea. Originally, the local Bedouins were
members of the Kadeirat tribe, named after an ancestor called
Kadeir, and they belonged to the Tiyaha tribal confederation,
which occupied most of the extremely desolate El Tih plateau of the
central Sinai. But the Kadeirat had been conquered by the Tarabin
in a brutal invasion of the Negev and eastern Sinai two hundred
years ago, and they had been more or less under Tarabin influence
ever since. Much of their tribal land was now owned by the Sherafa,
people of the Sherifs, a holy family of Mecca and descendants of the
Prophet Mohammed. One hundred and fifty years ago, they had
fled Mecca during a blood feud and come to the northern Sinai as
merchants. They lent money to the Kadeirat, and when the Bedouins couldn't repay the debts, much of their land was usurped by
the Sherafa, who still lived a life of ease as absentee landlords and
merchants in El Arish. (The Sherafa also spread out over other parts
of the Middle East, becoming a powerful force in Jordan and heading the right-wing, fundamentalist Moslem Brotherhood there.)

Hassan treated us to a Bedouin story about the discovery—really,
the rediscovery, if one takes biblical legend to heart—of the plentiful water in the Kadesh Barnea region. Many centuries ago, the tale
goes, a Bedouin hunting with his two Salukis was walking along the

---

Gebel Halal, in the northern Sinai.

The oasis and archeological digs of Ein Kadeirat.

Wadi Kadeirat (which we were negotiating) and he stopped near
a big rock to sleep in its shade. His dogs heard a rumbling sound
underground and began to dig furiously with their paws. The
hunter awoke and saw that the dogs' paws were wet, that, indeed,
they had uncovered a spring. He then rushed about the countryside
spreading the good news to the other Bedouins, who proclaimed
it a rebirth of the blessed oasis that had succored Nebi Musa and
the Israelites. When I asked Bailey whether he believed this story
to be the truth, he hedged a bit and said, "What he is telling me
is what he believes is the truth. More than that I can't ask him for."
Bailey added that the "Kadeis" in Ein Kadeis probably has nothing
to do with the Hebrew word "Kadesh" in Kadesh Barnea; most
likely, it comes from the Bedouin word *kadus,* meaning "stone
trough."

Ein Kadeirat, looking for all the world like an idealized mirage
of a desert oasis, came suddenly into view just ahead. A wide
variety of brush and shade trees, including pine, casuarina, tamarisk, date palm, and acacia, grew thick along the lively rivulet that
led from the spring's source to the aqueduct. Some camels and
goats, both white and black, were nibbling happily at grass and wild
flowers, and grayish-brown birds, the small desert larks, were buzzing us overhead. There was even evidence of crops growing in
bustans, modest Bedouin gardens. It was lush, all right, and it must
have seemed like yet another divine miracle to Moses when he first
came upon it with however many murmuring Israelites in his
charge. Like those very Israelites, we raced for the spring's source,
now enclosed in a three-sided stone trough, and since it was up-
stream of the dung litter from the animals, we didn't hesitate to
wash our hot faces and fill our canteens in the silvery water. "Good
water, best in Sinai," Hassan said, flashing a great toothless smile.
Deferentially, he extinguished his latest Time cigarette in the
stream and then buried the butt in the sand.

Refreshed, we explored some of the sights of Ein Kadeirat: an
old stone-mound grave of an important sheikh, decorated with
threadbare white flags, thistle, and palm fronds; nearby caves used
as storehouses for produce; long-deserted archeological digs, which

now offered up only a soda bottle; and a dry reservoir and dam, about the size of a country-club swimming pool. It has been said that the reservoir was originally the work of Moses or, more realistically, the Nabateans, who collected duty from caravans coming through this area in 500 B.C. Its construction was not considered good enough to be the work of Romans or Arab Moslems. The reservoir was improved with concrete sides and bottom by the British, but a broken pipe leading from the spring had left it to bake dry in the sun. In its virginal state, it could have supplied water for six hundred families and their beasts, even for thirty-eight years.

After our sightseeing, Bailey, looking tired, complained of a twinge of pain in his liver, a legacy of his hepatitis. We decided to proceed directly to Ein Kadeis, several kilometers to the south, so that we would have some time to rest back in El Kuseima before going on to El Arish for the night. Sharing the Jerusalem Plaza's hard-boiled eggs, we consulted our maps and found that there was no clear route to Ein Kadeis. We would have to go around a large sandstone mesa and over a lunarlike plain strewn with gigantic rocks, called the Boulders of Kadeis, and then hope for the best. It would be a difficult ride in the Land-Rover, but Hassan promised us that he knew the way and that we would be back in El Kuseima drinking tea at three o'clock. Bailey shrugged a what-the-hell gesture and off we went around the mesa to the Boulders of Kadeis.

It soon became apparent that Hassan, while a delightful and informative companion, a noble Bedouin, and a generous man, was not exactly the most knowledgeable guide. In fact, when he directed us into some shallow quicksand, both Bailey and I felt it was a case of the blind leading the blind. He was basically a farmer and merchant, not an intuitive tracker like most Bedouins; also, it turned out that he hadn't been to Ein Kadeis in years and wasn't at all sure of the vague route. By shifting the four-wheel drive into first gear and placing flat stones under the tires, we managed to free the Land-Rover from the quicksand. The car shuddered and squealed but at last broke out of its trap, and keeping the momentum going, Bailey veered sharply into a stony field of new daisies, which gave us some better traction.

We looked around for signs of life, preferably a Bedouin who might know the shortest way to Ein Kadeis. Across the daisy field was something that appeared to be an *arisha* but on closer inspection was just a pile of scrap metal and rags. The terrain, fortunately, stayed hard and stony, and we made some good progress in the general direction of our destination. Finally, a Bedouin man, accompanied by two women, three children, and a flock of goats, came into view. As soon as he saw us approaching, he went into his mohair tent and brought out a carpet for us to sit on, not inviting his wife, or wives, to join us in the ceremonial greetings and tea. Hassan and the goatherd got into what sounded to me like a shouting match when Hassan inquired about the route to Ein Kadeis. Bailey explained that they weren't having an argument at all but were exchanging information normally; the shouting was the result of the goatherd's not having spoken to another man for a long time, and he was simply showing his enjoyment of this unexpected conversation by strenuously exercising his vocal cords. He was a handsome man, similar in appearance to Hassan except for more teeth and a dingy turban. Out of respect for his visitors, he often kissed his own right hand, as a sign of humility. The stentorian directions he gave Hassan were in terms of landmarks all but invisible to non-Bedouin eyes—a distant shrub, another tent, a dim white spot of limestone on a far-off hill. "Kadeis is three fingers to the right of the white spot," he told Hassan, sighting by his own three fingers and then checking his calculations with Hassan's three fingers.

With *shukrans* and blessings of peace, we roared off across the boulder plain, trying to keep the white spot in view as a reference point as it kept disappearing in the glare. Some hares, precisely the color of the sand, scampered ahead of us, and we found that we could almost stay even with them in ordinary rear-wheel drive. However, the Boulders of Kadeis became bigger and more concentrated. We bashed into a few, gnashing our teeth and hoping that we hadn't knocked a hole in the oil pan, and before long the going was so rough that Hassan had to leave the Land-Rover and walk in front of us, pointing out the way of least resistance and occasionally pushing a huge rock out of our path. Bailey, who was in more or less constant pain now, cheered himself up by recalling a Bedouin poem about a debased warrior who was reduced to wandering over the Boulders of Kadeis. It ended, according to Bailey's translation, as follows:

> And after I was a wolf who would prey inside camps
> And sat high in the saddle like the hero Jiddaya
> I am now but a walker with shattered bones
> Stumbling and rising on paths strewn with stones.

Struggling with the steering wheel, he recited those last lines again in Arabic and English, chuckling quietly when he had finished.

Our progress decreased to the discouraging rate of about ten yards a minute and then, after another floundering half hour, to zero yards. Hassan sheepishly turned toward us and held his palms outward in that universal gesture of despair. It was our first critical moment: Do we give up and turn back or press on by shanks' mare? Hassan and I were for continuing, if Bailey felt up to it. Bailey admitted that he had probably taken on too much for his first Sinai outing since his sickness, but, he said, we had already come so far and he had never seen Ein Kadeis before—we might as well go on by foot. It seemed, even allowing for the mirage effect of the midday sun on the desert plain and on our brains, to be at least ten kilometers to the white spot, over very harrowing terrain. We would need plenty of water, a few snacks for quick energy, and some protection against God-knows-what. So toting a cargo of full canteens, Jaffa oranges and sugar wafers in a musette bag, and Bailey's pistol, we struck out for Ein Kadeis, lurking somewhere on the shimmering horizon. It was hot, sweaty hiking, worse even than some hot, sweaty forced marches I had barely survived in the U.S. Army. I think we all regretted our decision after the first few kilometers.

Not surprisingly, the conversation, between gasps, turned to desert travel. I mentioned that T. E. Lawrence wrote, in *Seven Pillars of Wisdom,* that it was best to move at a steady, slow pace for as long as possible, without sleep; holding to such a regimen, Lawrence claimed he had crossed the Sinai from Akaba to Suez, with the help of camels, in fifty hours. Other Sinai explorers had written of being ruled by the sun ("The earth is so samely that your eyes turn towards heaven . . . you look to the sun, for he is your taskmaster," said Alexander Kinglake) and of experiencing the visual and aural phantasms one would expect of proper English gentlemen—a village church, a fresh lake, the ringing of vesper bells. Professor Palmer saw green oases and grazing camels in his mirages, which dissolved into a "tremulous vapor" as he approached them. Bailey said that it was extremely important to keep a flowing "Bedouin gait," not unlike that which Hassan was maintaining as he seemed to float over the desert a few yards in front of us. Also, you must eat little and sip water at regular intervals, never dehydrating yourself more than what you hope is eight percent, since it is very difficult to make up that eight percent before illness sets in. The way to tell if you are overdehydrating is to notice the color of your urine; if it is dark yellow or light brown, you are in trouble. (My urine was a darker yellow than usual at last observation, and so I took several quick pulls from my canteen as we walked along.)

I wondered whether the famous white spot, which seemed to be farther away than ever, would dissolve into a "tremulous vapor" and I would be moved to run screaming and frothing into the hills, never to be seen again. Just when I figured this to be more than an outside possibility, Hassan excitedly pointed at some animal dung in the middle of a narrow, shallow wadi. He trotted ahead and found some more droppings, then even more, which seemed to mark a trail, he thought, to a watering hole. We followed him with fresh spirit, and, magically, the white spot became before our unbelieving eyes a veritable limestone vein in a rock face. We saw in rapid order some damp ground, a few blades of grass, a tiny stream, and then a rank mud puddle filled with dung. Slimy sedge grew in patches around and in the puddle and swarms of gnats hung over it. At the other end of the puddle was a more lively stream that led to a stone-covered trough, a *kadus*. "Kadeis," Hassan announced, flashing another of his glorious, triumphant smiles.

Hassan and Bailey drank slowly and steadily from the stream. I finished off my good stuff from Ein Kadeirat and then, playing it safe, I filled my canteen with five Halazone water-purification tablets and the doubtful stuff from Ein Kadeis. I reasoned that I hadn't yet acquired a Sinai intestinal-tract lining. We splashed water on our faces, rested a bit, and then looked around. It was patently obvious that Ein Kadeis could not have sustained more than a dozen Israelite families for any appreciable length of time. Bailey conjectured that this meager oasis was merely an adjunct of Ein Kadeirat, which together with lesser wells and verdure in the vicinity constituted the biblical Kadesh Barnea. Perhaps, Bailey said, the Israelites used Ein Kadeis as just a headquarters. Odd helter-skelter piles of sun-bleached stones near the stream marked the graves of local Bedouins, but there was no telling from the stone markers how old the graves were. Bedouins tend to bury their dead near water because the bodies must be washed by tribal members of the same sex as the deceased. It is easier, if less hygienic, to bury them next to the water. The graves themselves are, by tribal law, as deep as a man is tall.

As we hiked back to the Land-Rover—each of us, for his own reasons, buoyed at having made it to Ein Kadeis—we were accompanied by scurrying platoons of small green lizards, called the *jarari* ("little runner") by the Bedouins. They are cute, friendly creatures, even when they are constantly underfoot. Since we were able to spy the Land-Rover for most of the way, the return trek seemed shorter and less taxing. Nevertheless, we didn't arrive at the car till four o'clock, two hours behind schedule. Bailey was quite pale and I was thoroughly bushed. Even Hassan seemed tired, not being used to this sort of activity. The Land-Rover was like a mobile blast furnace, but still it was good to be off our feet.

There was one more obstacle delaying our return to El Kuseima. A Bedouin, the first we had seen since the man who had given Hassan directions to Ein Kadeis, appeared beside the car, shouting at us and gesturing madly. He was inviting us to join him for tea at his tent nearby. Bailey patiently went through a new ritual. He said several times in Arabic to the man, "May God cover your house with honor, but we are in a big hurry right now and we cannot stop." At last, the Bedouin nodded with satisfaction and let us pass. A curt "No, thanks," Bailey later explained, would not have sufficed; the Bedouin would feel dishonored because others might hear that we had passed him in the desert and were not invited to take tea at his tent. But Bailey had assured him that he and his house were blessed and he would be safe from any slander. The strange, time-consuming incident reminded me of a story in Major Jarvis's book, *Yesterday and To-day in Sinai,* about two Bedouins riding camels at full tilt by an old man's tent and being asked to stop. The camel riders hurriedly apologized but they were greatly pressed for time and couldn't accept the customary desert hospitality. The old man, cut to the quick, took up his long rifle, the *jezail,* and fired twice at the departing camel riders, killing one outright and wounding the other. The wounded rider fired back at the old man, killing him. The resulting tribal and legal entanglements kept the British Sinai administrators busy for weeks. Desert Bedouins take their hospitality very seriously.

Hospitality is no less sacred an institution for town Bedouins. Hassan's promised tea party at the general store began at five o'clock and grew to a dozen Bedouin men, as well as Bailey, Hassan, and I. We all solemnly shook hands and traded what seemed like hundreds of *salamats,* after which there was a reciprocally advantageous exchange of information between the Bedouins and Bailey—the former telling the latter tales of local lore and the latter telling the former gossip about various Sherafa he had met throughout the world. As we were saying our thanks and good-byes, I gave Bailey some Israeli money to pass on to Hassan, as a tip for his services. Hassan adamantly refused to accept the cash—I was "Boorrt," his friend, he said—but after much discussion, he agreed to let me purchase from the store a fine handwoven camel lead rope, called a *rasan.* (It was a compromise weighted in my favor; I don't own a camel but the *rasan* became an interesting and handsome decoration for my living-room wall.)

Some of the Bedouin hospitality had infected the Israeli soldiers at the nearby outpost. Bailey and I dropped by there to tell them we were leaving for El Arish, and the soldiers on K.P. filled our arms with Jaffa oranges, white bread, and several containers of a kind of half yoghurt–half sour milk, which is thin enough to sip through a straw. The Bedouin sweet tea and the Israeli yoghurt–sour milk combined alimentally and symbolically to refresh us after our long, hard day—which figured to be longer and harder still when we discovered that the left rear tire of the Land-Rover was totally flat.

Considering the beating the car had taken, we were lucky to have just a flat (the puncture in the side of the thick tire was from either a stilettolike acacia thorn or a piece of barbed wire). A Bedouin mechanic who worked for the I.D.F. outpost had just come off duty but he cheerfully volunteered to change the tire for us. The changing of the tire developed into a village event, with Hassan, his friends, Bedouin kids, Bedouin women (making their first appearance of the day, having returned from foraging the livestock outside of town), and male and female Israeli soldiers, all kibitzing and staring at one another. I passed out oranges and sugar wafers to the kids, who accepted them with stiff formality before their elders. At seven o'clock, the taskmaster sun extinguishing itself in a fast dim behind a western hill, the Land-Rover once again ready for travel, our handshakes and thanks repeated to Hassan and the others, we drove north through the darkening desert toward Abu Aweigilla and El Arish.

THREE

PERHAPS BECAUSE OF the cool dusk or the wholesome snack or the onset of yet another expedition, both Bailey and I found our second wind. This new burst of energy arrived not a moment too soon; the road north to El Arish was covered over in parts with fine, often deep sand, perilous at times since we had to build up speed and plow on through in four-wheel drive, skidding and weaving wildly. And it was doubly worrisome in that a terrorist could easily have planted land mines in the soft stuff, a favorite P.L.O. tactic. We needed all the alertness and concentration we could muster to make headway.

As we passed the rambling, deserted old Egyptian Army base at Abu Aweigilla, the moonless night sky abruptly sprouted stars, as only a desert sky can, the North Star in the inverted Little Dipper's handle directly in front of the windshield. To the west, slowly descending parachute flares dropped at intervals for I.D.F. night maneuvers added to the celestial show. At a crossroads, we were halted by some soldiers manning a checkpoint. The soldiers warily shone their flashlights onto our faces and asked Bailey where he was from. I was astounded to hear him reply, "Sde Boker," a Negev community made famous as David Ben-Gurion's home, where Bailey had actually spent eight years helping to found the Institute for Desert Research. After we were allowed to proceed, Bailey explained that he had told the soldiers he was from Sde Boker rather than Jerusalem, his real hometown, because it aroused less suspicion. Jerusalemites, being presumably more sophisticated and liberal, are automatically more suspect in outlying military zones, especially when they travel with foreign journalists. There would probably be no more checkpoints till El Arish, whose lights were blurring the sky straight ahead.

El Arish, the provincial capital of Sinai and the peninsula's major town, is an unorthodox place even for the unorthodox Sinai. It was founded about three thousand years ago by Actisanes, an Ethiopian ruler of Egypt, who shunted off all his deadliest enemies and confirmed criminals to the lonely spot, first cutting off their noses so that they could be identified if they escaped. Consequently, the town was called Rhinokoloura (city of cut noses) by the Greeks and, later, Rhinocolorum by the Romans. Sitting astride the Via Maris, it became a natural battleground and war route for every invader of the Sinai—Syrians, Hittites, Assyrians, Persians, Greeks, Romans, Crusaders, Turks, French, English, Egyptians, and Israelis. Each army left its mark—usually in the form of stragglers who intermarried with the locals (some Bosnian and Albanian colonial soldiers under the Turks were particularly eager to become Ari-shiya)—and the results were a gallimaufry of ethnic strains and the emergence of a singular Arabic dialect. Major Jarvis, who in his way was intrigued by the polygenetic quality of the place, wrote that El Arish was "populated by all those who had not the guts to go on" and that the citizens have an "extraordinarily crooked, suspicious outlook on life generally." The present population of El Arish is about thirty-five thousand people, almost half the population of Sinai: five thousand Palestinian Arabs, ten thousand descendants of the multifarious stragglers (the aristocracy of the town), ten thousand Egyptians, and ten thousand "desert rats" (a mixed bag of strays from all over the Middle East who came to make money as merchants)—plus, of course, visiting Bedouins and the Israeli occupation forces. The townspeople exist by fishing the Mediterranean, trading, smuggling, and date farming.

The Wadi El Arish, the largest riverbed in the Sinai, drains the highlands from as far away as the El Tih plateau. Its wide mouth spills into the Mediterranean just north of the town, and at times of severe flood, as in 1975, the winter torrent can wash out every-

Fishermen with their nets on the beach at El Arish.

thing in its path, depositing, as the water recedes, new silty real estate for those foolish enough to settle on it. Since biblical days, Wadi El Arish has been generally interpreted as the "River of Egypt," the word "Arish" considered a variant of an Arabic term for Egypt; more likely, "Arish" comes from the Bedouin word *arisha,* for arbor booth, a construction in abundance throughout the area. As the pre-treaty headquarters of the North Sinai Military Government, the city had taken on a greater political importance than it enjoyed in Ottoman days. The fact that the sleepy coastal town lived in comparative serenity under the Israeli raj, surrounded by Israeli settlements and military bases, stuck in the Egyptian craw —more so even than Gaza, which the Egyptians never really considered their national soil. During one of the periodic stalemates in treaty negotiations, Sadat hinted broadly that he would welcome some generous gesture on Israel's part—for instance, the return to Egyptian sovereignty of El Arish. Begin, who had contemplated making exactly that gesture just before Sadat appeared in Jerusalem, soon changed his mind. Sadat, he said, would get "nothing for nothing." However, it is interesting to note that the initial pullback of Israeli forces from the Sinai, under the treaty of March 26, 1979, directly involved El Arish. Phase One of the withdrawal called for an evacuation of personnel and equipment from a narrow forty-five-mile strip along the Mediterranean coast to a point slightly east of El Arish within two months. (The town came under Egyptian control two months after the treaty signing—all of it, that is, except for a military laundry building, which will be used by the Israelis for a while. Sadat and Begin met there on May 27, 1979, in order to announce the formal opening of the border, at the El Arish line, between their two nations. With typical flexibility, the local citizens welcomed the Egyptians as if they had never left. Both El Arish and Beersheba were designated as alternating sites for further peace-treaty discussions between Israeli and Egyptian delegations.) After nine months, the Israelis were obligated to return to Egypt two thirds of the peninsula—from the El Arish line south to Ras Muhammad, just west of Sharm El Sheikh. Within three years, the entire Sinai, up to the old Palestine Mandate frontier, would presumably be in Egyptian hands.

As we entered the town, one thing was gnawingly clear to Bailey and me: we were starved. Our plan was to look up Bailey's good friend, the Tarabin Sheikh of Sheikhs Suleiman Ibn Jazi, at his house (and accept the certain invitation to spend the night there), but before that, we thought it discreet to have our first real meal of the day. It was past nine o'clock and only a few places were open on the main street—a couple of cafés filled with backgammon players and coffee drinkers, some shops empty except for the owners, a well-lit mosque. Fortunately, what Bailey called "the best restaurant in El Arish" was still open for business along the rialto. It was a nameless sidewalk café, its edible offerings (mostly lamb and vegetables) hanging alfresco and fly-covered near a charcoal brazier. But the smell of sizzling lamb made it seem like the old Chambord. We ordered large bottles of Israeli Gold Star beer, shish kebab, salad with chick peas, and warm *pita*. While we greedily devoured the meal, various town Arabs—some with red hair and blue eyes, indicating, perhaps, a certain Crusader dalliance—wandered by, staring at us curiously. Bailey patted the pistol in his jacket pocket and asked me to keep my eye on a sour-looking youth casually loitering behind him. "He's a P.L.O. candidate if I ever saw one," he mumbled, while chewing the crisp meat. If he was a P.L.O. candidate, he must have decided that we were hardly worth his trouble; we had an uneventful and delicious repast. Only once during the meal did an I.D.F. jeep patrol show its flag in the center of town.

Driving through the dark, unpaved alleys off the main street with a knowing hand, Bailey pulled up in front of the beige one-story house of Sheikh Ibn Jazi. We locked the Land-Rover and stumbled through a small courtyard to the door, where we were welcomed by one of the sheikh's sons, a well-tailored young man in Bedouin garb. Naturally, he asked us to come in, take tea, and stay as long as we wanted. He apologized that his father was out for the evening at a local party, but his father's house was our house. Inside, a large, Spartan, rather shoddy living room held several male children, a veiled Bedouin woman (who scurried off to another part of the house when we appeared), a young girl in modern dress, and an outsized black-and-white television set tuned to a Cairo channel. A news documentary was on, showing an impressive military parade. While Bailey chatted with the son, the veiled woman, Ibn Jazi's El Arish wife, brought in some tea in the small clear glasses the Bedouins favor. By design or accident, her veil slipped to mouth level for a moment, and I saw that she was quite beautiful, with dark almond-shaped eyes and high cheekbones. A guest is not supposed to notice such things, and so I quickly averted my eyes. At last,

Bailey, stifling a yawn, asked if we could bring in our gear and spread our sleeping bags in the adjacent sitting room, where male Bedouin conclaves are held, feasts presented, and guests allowed to sleep. That request generously granted, we settled into our sleeping bags on top of stuffed mats and carpets spread about the room. I had the energy for one more question before I dropped off into the dead sleep of the totally exhausted: If the sheikh is so powerful and prosperous, as befits his station, why does he have such a, well, decrepit house? The answer, through unstifled yawns, was that most Arabs who haven't been Westernized are not ostentatious in their house décor; they prefer to put their money in gold, jewelry, livestock, cars, and land. (Jazi made his fortune by smuggling many years ago.) Bailey added, his voice weakening, "When you meet him tomorrow morning, you'll see he is a simple man who leads a simple Bedouin life, both here and at his tents in the desert. His wives in the desert are even racier than this one. By the way, that little girl wearing the dress, she's the daughter of one of Jazi's sons-in-law, who's in jail in Egypt for being an Israeli spy." I wanted to find out more about this, but it was too late, I was already asleep.

Then, what seemed like two minutes later but was actually three o'clock in the morning—*Crash! Bang!* Girlish laughter. Loud voices. Blaring Arab belly-dance music. And worst of all, a blinding, bare ceiling light bulb rudely switched on. "Bay*lee,* Bay-*lee!*" said a deep voice. Assuming I was in the middle of a frightful dream, I stayed turtlelike in the shell of my sleeping bag for a moment. When I dared to poke my head out, I saw a magnificent, gray-moustached Bedouin dressed all in white, sporting a silver Rolex watch on his left wrist and carrying a tape recorder the size of a bread box. He was shaking Bailey's hand and chattering in Arabic at the top of his lungs. Just behind this apparition was a handsome, slightly epicene teen-age boy, who was filling the room with smoke from his cigarette and tipsily gyrating his hips to the music. The Bedouin man in white was, of course, Sheikh of Sheikhs Suleiman Ibn Jazi, returning home from his evening out on the town. The male houri, Bailey told me after the introductions were made, was Majid, a fifteen-year-old non-Bedouin waif of the El

Arish streets, who had been hired to sing and dance for the guests
at the late party the sheikh had attended. Majid apparently had
taken a little too much to drink at the festivities. Since he had
pleased Jazi with his singing and dancing, he had been plied
with Kent cigarettes and protectively taken home by the sheikh
for the night. To demonstrate Majid's talents, Jazi turned up
the tape recorder full blast and commanded the boy to perform
to the music. Even over the screeching noise, I could hear the
rest of the household stirring in other rooms. After ten unbe-
lievable minutes of this, Jazi tired of Majid's performance and
turned off the tape recorder. For his part, Majid was cross-eyed
and ashen with fatigue, cigarettes, and drink. Extinguishing one
last Kent in an ashtray, he wrapped himself in a blanket and
fell asleep like a kitten.

Not entirely convinced that I wasn't in the middle of a dream,
I extricated myself from my sleeping bag and listened to Jazi describe the party to Bailey. With Bailey simultaneously translating,
I learned that the party had come about for a typically convoluted
Levantine reason. An El Arish merchant, who trucks sundry goods
to Bedouins in the south Sinai, has two wives, one of them from
the Hejaz. The beautiful eighteen-year-old daughter of the Hejaz
wife, sired by an earlier husband, was ripe for marriage and was
brought to El Arish to meet her stepfather's sixteen-year-old son by
another wife. (Although they were step-siblings, their marriage
would not be considered incest.) The purpose of the party, given
by the merchant, was to break the ice between the two youngsters.
Majid was hired to dance and sing, wine flowed (despite Koranic
strictures against the use of alcohol), and *tout* El Arish was invited,
including those two old smugglers Jazi and Breik Odeh Abu Abdullah, the hard-drinking, fun-loving sheikh of sheikhs of the Muzeina
tribe. (The Muzeina and Tarabin are traditionally enemies but not
when they are off their own turfs.) The ice-breaking scheme was a
failure, however. The girl had whispered to Jazi that her step-
brother was too young for her. She said she needed a real man to
please her, not a baby—someone, for instance, like Jazi's son Ayish,
a professional camel racer who worked in Elath. And so the matter

Bailey (right) talking with Bedouin sheikhs at the
El Arish conclave.

was left hanging. The next move was up to Ayish, although the girl
could not reject the suitor chosen by her parents, unless she was
willing to become an outcast. All in all, it was one hell of a bash,
apparently, and Jazi would have gone on for hours telling us more
about it if he had not suddenly grown sleepy. With apologies for
his fatigue, he retired to his bedroom, leaving us to resume some
fitful dozing to the accompaniment of Majid's erratic snoring. The
last words I heard Bailey say, in answer to my unasked questions,
were "Don't be a missionary."

In spite of everything, breakfast at the Jazis was at six-thirty. The morning sun poured in through the sitting-room windows and the household was running in high gear when I awoke. The house and facilities seemed even shabbier in the daylight. The bilious green walls of the sitting room, I noticed, were peeling and faded, the carpet and mats were soiled and dank. How odd that one must remove one's shoes when entering this room—not, obviously, for hygienic reasons, but as a sign of respect. But there I go being a missionary, I thought. The head of the house, smiling and chipper in the same white garb of a few hours before, joined Bailey, Majid, and me in the sitting room for breakfast. Behind him were his favored son Ayish, in jeans, red shirt, and red-checked *kaffiyeh,* and two younger sons. The sheikh and Majid were already puffing on Kents. As breakfast—hard-boiled eggs, fresh tomatoes, goat cheese, *pita,* and hot tea, all on a large round platter—was served by one of the younger sons, another guest dropped in. He was introduced not by name but by reputation: the best *simsimiya* (a crude triangular banjo) player in the south Sinai.

Bailey and I were beckoned to attack the platter first with our fingers, as honored guests, and then the others dug in. It was a tasty and satisfying breakfast. While we ate, Ayish talked about his work in Elath and his camel racing. He had won a recent Elath race and been rewarded with the publication of his photograph in a newspaper, a cup worth five Israeli pounds, and a purse of one thousand pounds. "The Jews are clever," Jazi said. "They give you a cheap cup, a picture, and a thousand pounds." Then Jazi produced a dog-eared letter written in English, which he asked Bailey to translate into Arabic for him. It was from a Dutch hippie who had lived in the desert with the Tarabin the year before and been adopted by one of the sheikh's brothers, Salim. The hippie, it turned out, was now in a Dutch jail (for unstated reasons), and he wrote, movingly, of how he yearned for the freedom of the Sinai and the good company of the Jazi family. The sheikh smiled and made a clicking noise as he listened to Bailey's translation. "The Dutch boy is a Bedouin now," he said, "and Bedouins hate jail. It is not for men." He dictated an answering letter, which Bailey wrote down in English. It was full of warmth and hope, and when Jazi carefully signed it, he looked very sad. After breakfast, I wandered into the living room, where Jazi's wife was cooking at a brazier in the center of the floor. She was unveiled, but when she saw me, she immediately turned her face away, not before flashing a charming smile, however. I noticed that she was wearing lovely bangles over her forehead. Bailey judiciously called me away from the living room and said it was time to drive across El Arish to our nine o'clock appointment with the military governor, Colonel Moshe Dahan, at the headquarters building on the seashore. Jazi invited us to have lunch with him between my interview with Colonel Dahan and the meeting of the north Sinai sheikhs at one o'clock. We accepted, offered thanks, and left with Majid, who wanted a ride across town. Outside the house in the alley, we saw the sheikh's Mercedes-Benz sedan, with oculiform symbols covering the fenders and hood, placed there to ward off the evil eye.

On the way toward the seashore, we left our punctured tire to be fixed at a garage. When Bailey asked Majid where specifically he wanted to go, the lad, suddenly petulant and cocky, said nowhere, really, just near a store along the beach. It was clear he had no permanent home. We drove him to the beach and he asked to get out of the car. He tossed us a practiced, insouciant wave and sauntered toward a small store, breaking into a squirmy little dance every so often. The Arabs outside the store laughed at him.

The long El Arish shoreline, with wide stretches of clean sand, groves of leafy date palms, and picture-postcard scenes of fishermen hauling nets into their dories, is unspoiled and impressive. Only the unsettled state of the area has kept, say, an El Arish Hilton from dominating the strand. A resort developer wouldn't even have to provide beach umbrellas for his guests, since the date palms supply generous shade from the Sinai sun. (The palms are owned communally by the citizens of El Arish, who all share in the summer-harvest profits.) Just off the shoreline sits the rectangular Military Government compound, a former Egyptian Army headquarters, with rooftop machine guns pointing toward the sea. Two thunderous sonic booms from Israeli jets rattled our teeth as we drove into the compound, reminding everyone within earshot that an official state of war still existed. A guard directed us to a wardroom on the second floor, where sexy Israeli girls in tight, short-skirted khaki uniforms milled about with the male soldiers, displaying the hectic informality that marks an I.D.F. post. Since we were a bit early for our appointment with Colonel Dahan, Bailey made use of the time to put in a good word for one of Jazi's relations, whose house had been raided by the police recently and a large amount of foreign currency confiscated. At precisely nine o'clock, we were ushered into Colonel Dahan's office.

The colonel, a gracious, forthright sabra of Moroccan-Jewish parentage, rose from an enormous desk (a relic of the Egyptian administration) and greeted us. Although he spoke some English, Arabic, and French (he had attended the Sorbonne), he said he preferred to answer my questions in Hebrew. I asked him what the general situation was in his jurisdiction, which runs south to the bottom of the El Tih plateau. With Bailey translating, he answered, "It's quiet. Sinai has always been the quietest of all the occupied territories, maybe because the people here are so used to being occupied. There is an atmosphere of dislike for the P.L.O. by both Bedouins and Arishiya, especially after the Sadat initiative. The north Sinai residents are convinced that peace is bogging down because of the P.L.O. Most want peace with Israel. The incursion into southern Lebanon by the I.D.F. last month was actually well received here. Since Sinai II was signed in 1975, there has been no real trouble. Before then, we had to deal with some Egyptian intelligence units and Bedouin spies."

I told the colonel about an encounter I had had with a Bedouin spy during my trip to the Suez Canal in 1969. Along the coastal road I noticed a crouching Bedouin who made a pencil mark in a small notebook every time a vehicle of some sort passed. I asked my I.D.F. escort officer about this, and he said, "Oh, he's just the local spy. The Egyptians pay him to record all the traffic on this road. It helps the economy and we don't mind. It's impossible to keep our military traffic a secret out here, anyway. He's a good chap and he does his job well."

The colonel grinned. "Well," he said, "they can go to jail if they're caught. We are still in a state of war, after all. Mostly, though, the Bedouins are anxious about security. One sheikh said to me recently that he felt much safer in the Sinai than in Tel Aviv."

I asked Colonel Dahan to describe what I could expect to see at his meeting that afternoon with the north Sinai Bedouin sheikhs. "We have a restaurant in the main building and we give them all lunch," he said. "Before the lunch, though, I listen to their private problems. Every week I make a trip through the area by helicopter, car, and camel to hear more of their problems. Then we go into the big conference room and I announce general information, speaking Hebrew with an Arabic translator. Each of them, if he wants, presents his complaints. They usually ask for different things, but if there are disputes to be settled, we try to let them settle the problem within the tribe or tribes. We are not a court, really; just in a few cases will they ask for Solomonic judgments. Crimes outside of Bedouin tribal adjudication go through the civilian courts in Israel, if they do not involve security matters. Offenses against security— like spying, stealing from the army, or smuggling—are tried by the Military Government, through the Legal Department of the I.D.F. A decision by the Military Government cannot be appealed to civilian courts, but the accused can ask for a lighter sentence or a new trial with new judges." The recent highly controversial decision by the Military Government to fine parents of young demonstrators in the occupied areas the equivalent of five hundred dollars was not a major issue in the Sinai, the colonel added, since there was so little demonstrating.

As for the smuggling (which Bedouins view as merely a profitable occupation), the colonel said there was far less now in the Sinai than there was during the Egyptian administration. While some smuggling involves goods such as tape recorders, bolts of cloth, and even burglar alarms, most of it is in hashish. The hashish used to travel northeast to southwest, from Syria and Turkey to Egypt; nowadays, however, it goes in the opposite direction, from Egypt to Israel, often accompanied by coffee, which is also glutting the

market in Egypt but is dear elsewhere. It is comparatively easy for
the Bedouins to transport contraband through the U.N. zone, but
the I.D.F. presence beyond that zone makes smuggling difficult.
The Bedouins have readopted an old trick they used with some
success during the British occupation of the Sinai: shipping water-
tight rubber bags of hashish by boats along the Mediterranean coast
and weighting them down with sacks of salt. If the boats are chal-
lenged, the smugglers ditch the bags in the water; the salt dissolves
in a few days, causing the bags to rise to the surface, where they
can be picked up at a more opportune time. The hashish is familiarly known as "Sinai Sheikh."

We left the colonel to his preconclave duties and drove back
through the town to the garage, where the repaired tire was waiting
for us. In the late hot morning, El Arish falls into Levantine torpor.
Citizens lie about in whatever shade is available—a rusting derelict
car, a doorway, the remains of a Turkish fort. But down the street
from the garage, one incident brought the populace to life for a few
wild moments. A chubby Israeli girl in tight shorts and a skimpy
halter sashayed down the dusty road in front of the El Arish Preparatory Boys School, and within seconds at least twenty Arab lads,
gawking and whistling, were following her, as if she had just descended into their town from Mars. Bailey asked a red-haired boy
why there was so much commotion. "It is shameful," said the boy.

Lunch at Sheikh Ibn Jazi's was no ordinary noontime snack. As
soon as we entered the courtyard, I knew something special was in
the offing when one of Jazi's grandsons ceremoniously handed
Bailey and me two small towels and some pink perfumed soap and
led us to an outdoor spigot. After our ablutions, he took the soap
and towels from us and showed us into the sitting room. There,
cross-legged around a carpet, were the sheikh and his sons. In the
middle of the carpet was a round salver, looking like a platter for
the world's biggest pizza, on top of which was a mountain of soft
white rice and chunks of boiled goat meat, the heady juices blotted
up by a thin layer of *pita* between the rice and the salver. The sheikh
was smiling broadly. He gestured to us to sit down in the circle and
be the honored guests, which we did, first removing our shoes. He

explained that just a few hours earlier he had slaughtered in the backyard his prized year-old goat, a tethered, fat, fodder-fed animal he was saving for a special occasion, and here it now was for our delectation. Usually, at such feasts, the goat's heart, lungs, and kidneys are roasted and presented to the guests as appetizers, but since the main course was all ready, there was no need for hors d'oeuvre. The tangy aroma was overpowering—it was certainly the freshest meat I would ever eat—and although I wasn't very hungry, I dug in, compressing the meat, rice, and a bit of *pita* into a ball with my right hand and popping the results into my mouth. Our hosts joined in after Bailey and I had swallowed our first portions. The meat was a trifle gamy, as expected, tasting not unlike a freshly stewed rabbit I had once eaten in the Adirondacks. But best of all was the soppy, pungent combination of *pita,* rice, and goat gravy, with which I stuffed myself, washing down the heavy golf-ball-sized nuggets with hot tea. I had the feeling that the luncheon feast had been laid on, somehow, to make up for the incident at three o'clock that morning. But maybe not; Bedouins, if they can possibly afford it, will find any excuse for a feast.

Suitably honored and bloated, I excused myself and attempted for several minutes to wash the goat grease off my hands with the perfumed soap. (Days later, it was still under my fingernails despite vigorous scrubbing.) I wanted to do nothing more than sleep for a few hours, but there was the Bedouin meeting to attend in just twenty minutes. (As a south Sinai sheikh, Jazi would attend the conclave in the southern jurisdiction the following week.) Bailey, meanwhile, was sprawled on a mat, transcribing on his tape recorder a cassette, played on the sheikh's machine, of a Bedouin reciting his own poetry from a jail cell in Egypt, where he was serving a term for spying. As in all recitations of rhymed-doggerel Bedouin poetry, there is a litaneutical quality, the listeners lovingly repeating the rhyming words in a trance of satisfaction. It was a relaxing, even soporific, entertainment, especially after a feast.

When Bailey had finished copying the tape, we shook hands all around and said our good-byes. I told the sheikh that my house in Connecticut was his house, whenever he chose to visit me. He replied that it was a dream of his to come to America sometime. He and his sons walked us to the parked Land-Rover and stood there in a clump waving as we drove off. I understood a little of what the Dutch hippie must have felt for the Jazis.

Back at the Military Government compound, in a grassy, tree-shaded yard next to the main building, there was a crowd scene out of *The Desert Song.* At least forty finely arrayed sheikhs, a veritable ocean of *kaffiyehs* and *galabiyas,* strolled about, chatting among themselves and with several I.D.F. officers and plainclothes intelligence agents, who were questioning the sheikhs for any snippets of useful information picked up in the desert. When the sheikhs spotted Bailey, many of them broke off their conversations and rushed to shake "Docto*rr* Bay*lee's*" hand. Each, it seemed, had a long story to tell him, and it wasn't until a Druse captain called them all into the conference room that Bailey could stop talking and pumping hands.

The conference room contained rows of wooden benches before a cloth-covered dais and a long table laden with fruit, cakes, and bottles of orange soda. Travel posters promoting Israeli tourism were hung here and there on the walls. The sheikhs settled themselves on the benches and waited patiently for Colonel Dahan to enter. At last, he strode in, accompanied by two other officers, and all the sheikhs rose. Dahan walked down the bench rows, shaking hands with everyone and briefly exchanging greetings, and then he took a seat at the dais. It was at once regal and cordial.

A lieutenant colonel called the meeting to order and told the assemblage (in Hebrew, translated into Arabic by the Druse captain) that some unauthorized building of houses had come to the government's attention and he wanted to remind them that this was illegal. He introduced Colonel Dahan, who, through the Druse captain, said that the new fiscal year began in April and the government was interested in furthering development projects in Bedouin settlements. (This news was met with general silence. The colonel asked if they had understood the translated Arabic, and the sheikhs shouted back that they had.) The government, he continued, hoped to construct new schools, mosques, shops, clinics, wells, and to broaden its immunization program for Bedouin children. (Murmuring of approval.) The child-mortality rate was decreasing, thanks to better medical services available to cooperating Bedouins. (Louder murmuring of approval.) And the government will offer to build houses for Bedouins, and when there are enough houses, electricity will be installed. (Silence. "There goes the neighborhood," Bailey whispered to me.)

Other announcements: The mayor of El Arish was ill and expressed his sorrow at not being able to attend the meeting; at the Negev border, three hundred head of livestock had crossed into Israel and could be legally confiscated, although the government would compensate for any losses; the wells at Auja would be available to all Sinai Bedouins, but they must not cross the border with their animals.

The colonel said he would now answer questions of common interest. There was a round of applause, and before it was over a sheikh from the Ein Kadeis region, the image of Anthony Quinn, walked up to the dais and confronted Dahan face-to-face. In a booming voice, he complained that a young Bedouin tracker in the Israeli Army had grabbed the prettiest local girl, who was bewitched by his uniform and status. The sheikh demanded an investigation, and Dahan said he would look into it immediately. In the same pattern of direct talk, other sheikhs approached the dais to complain about such matters as unfair water and welfare-rations distribution ("God didn't create us all equal," the colonel said. "We must help the neediest first"), maverick Bedouins crossing tribal lines without permission ("The chiefs get blamed," the sheikh said), infrequent medical services ("It will get better," the colonel promised), and afternoon monthly meetings ("If they began in the morning, we would get home earlier," the sheikh reasoned).

There were no more grievances and the meeting simply petered out, with no formal closing. The sheikhs lined up at the refreshments table and happily downed the food, talking with each other, the officers, and, of course, Dr. Bailey. It struck me how much this give-and-take conclave resembled the British system of dealing

with the Bedouins during their occupation of the Sinai between the
World Wars. I mentioned this to one of the I.D.F. officers and he
agreed. "But during the Egyptian occupation," he said, "there
were never conclaves. They built cisterns and schools for the Bedouins here, but they didn't allow for open complaints. I think the
Bedouins appreciate more our way." As the talk and eating wound
down, Colonel Dahan said he had a few last-minute announcements
to make. About the Bedouin tracker and the pretty Bedouin girl,
the military police in the area had been informed of the situation,
and if abduction was involved, the tracker would be properly punished by the authorities. As for livestock crossing the Negev line
without permission, an extension of time would be granted in order
to round them up and take them back to the Sinai. Also, the May
meeting would begin at ten o'clock in the morning. This was
greeted with applause and the sheikhs dispersed, some to their
parked Mercedes-Benz cars, some to taxis, some to pickup trucks,
some to buses, some just walking off down the road. Colonel Dahan
looked pleased.

The remainder of our itinerary called for a drive along the Via
Maris to the Rafa salient, where we would visit Yamit (meaning
"Seaside"), the hub of the new Israeli settlements in the northeast-
ern Sinai, at issue in the possible return of the peninsula to the
Egyptians; a stop at an I.D.F. base near Rafa, in order to pick up
Bailey's oldest son, Michael, who was finishing up a stint with
Gadna (Youth Corps), a paramilitary organization for boys and
girls fourteen to eighteen years old; then a dash through the Gaza
Strip and on to Jerusalem by nightfall. We gassed up and checked
the Land-Rover. A khamsin—a hot, nettlesome wind blowing in
from the Sahara that can drive saints to murder—was in the air, and
we didn't want to stop more than we had to.
    Crossing and recrossing the abandoned Allenby Railroad tracks,
we made our way through the Via Maris traffic past ruined villages,
ugly scrap heaps of war, huge hothouses for growing exported
flowers (one of Israel's biggest cash crops), and Bedouin women
and girls tending their flocks. When Bailey blew his horn and

waved at the women and girls, they all waved back in unison, a lovely sight. If we had pointed at them instead, Bailey said, they would have hidden their faces, fearing some lewd interest. Eucalyptus trees lined the highway. They were not native to the region but were brought here as seedlings by the British, who thought the trees would dry up the swamps and help prevent malaria. They proliferated and did help control malaria, so much so that the Bedouins assumed the eucalyptus bark was the reason malaria decreased. They named the strange tree *kina* ("quinine") and took to chewing the bark on the sly, which rather amused the British.

Approaching Yamit, off the road through the dunes toward the sea, we saw the infamous Dayan Fence, which had been erected in 1971, at great expense, to keep the Bedouins out of the Sinai settlement area. Now, Bedouins were placidly grazing their animals within the chain-link and barbed-wire barrier. "You can't keep Bedouins out of anything by fences," Bailey said. "If they want to use the land, they'll use it." The same was true at Yamit proper, a sprawling complex of prefabricated modules, shops, plazas, and community buildings on a dune at the edge of the sea. Bedouin tents and flocks were side by side with the concrete development, which looked like a half-finished beach colony in Orange County, California. Kids in bathing suits ran about, while mothers wheeled infants in strollers around the plaza. It was all super-neat, super-clean, super-new, and full of promise. Yet, nobody seemed to be smiling. Arie Kagan, who runs the adjacent Field School (one of many kibbutzlike retreats throughout Greater Israel) told me that he had moved to Yamit from Tel Aviv because of the excitement of working in a pioneering town. He viewed the future with mixed emotions, hopeful about Sadat's peace initiative but disconsolate that Yamit might be under the Egyptian flag one day. "If we are Egyptian," he said, "I will go back to Tel Aviv, but I do not want to move from here." He pointed at the sand between the houses. "It is sand now, maybe grass later," he said wearily. "I don't know."

Back in 1972, Moshe Dayan, then the Defense Minister in Golda Meir's Labor Party government, submitted an ambitious proposal for a "new city" in occupied Sinai to be named Yamit. The master plan (termed "creeping annexationism" by Dayan's critics) called for agriculture, industry, tourism services, a large seaport, and an international airport within twenty-five years, all cared for by an estimated population of 250,000 Israelis, making it potentially Israel's third largest city, after Tel Aviv and Jerusalem. Strategically, it would be a wall between a hostile Gaza Strip and a less hostile Sinai. The idea caught on, although on a reduced scale, and many sabras and immigrants (including several Americans) who could afford the eleven-hundred-dollar down payment for a plot of land rushed to settle in Yamit and its cluster of satellite moshavs. (Menachem Begin himself purchased a small retirement house in nearby Neot Sinai.) Dayan ordered a security fence built around the Yamit region, ostensibly to keep terrorist infiltrators out but really to prevent Bedouins, who were attracted by all the activity, from using the land.

By the time Sadat went to Jerusalem in November, 1977, there were seventeen hundred people living in Yamit and four thousand in the entire Rafa-salient settlement area. At their talks in Ismailia on Christmas Day, 1977, Prime Minister Begin offered Sadat complete Israeli withdrawal from the Sinai in return for a full peace treaty. However, once Begin was back in Jerusalem, he disclosed an enormous qualification: Israeli settlements in the northeastern Sinai would remain under Israeli protection even after the peninsula had been given back to Egypt. To this, Sadat replied, "I do not agree to the presence of a single Jewish settlement on my land. Let them destroy them. Neither do I allow a single Israeli civilian or soldier to remain." Those were strong words—especially alongside the U.S. State Department's announced opinion that the settlements were illegal and an obstacle to peace—and the resulting impasse went far toward contributing to the long-term breakdown in peace negotiations. As for the four thousand Israelis already ensconced in the disputed territory, they felt deserted by the very persons who had enticed them there in the first place. When Moshe Dayan, in his new capacity as Foreign Minister of the Begin government, paid a visit to the region in January, 1978, he was assailed by an angry, jeering crowd of Yamitniks. Changing his tune some-what since 1972, Dayan told the people that "we never once pro-posed extending Israeli sovereignty over the Rafa salient." He did say that if peace came, perhaps the settlers would be protected by Israeli armed forces, but, he added provocatively, they would not be under the Israeli flag. One heckler interrupted him, shouting, "We don't want to live in a ghetto. Our settlements must be an integral part of Israel."

While I was in Yamit, I hoped to talk with the person who had the most sensitive finger on the community's jumpy pulse—David Artom, the secretary of the nine-man Governing Council, which controls all the area within the Dayan Fence. He was unavailable at the time, but I managed to reach him by telephone on the following day. "I am optimistic, no matter what," Artom told me then. "Yamit will be a city of one hundred thousand people. I firmly believe this. Look, there are three facts of life here right now: One, nobody has left Yamit since the Sadat initiative; two, sixty-five families have moved here since then; three, fifty-eight apartments were sold as part of our moshav plan, in fact. So I am optimistic."

Who were these people of Yamit? I asked him. "They are not so much farmers," he said, "but many are agricultural specialists. Also, we have I.D.F. personnel from nearby bases and construction workers and other laborers for the private-enterprise industries. They can rent instead of buy, if they are essential individuals. Fifteen percent are immigrants—from the U.S.A., Russia, Latin America, mostly—and the rest are sabras or people in Israel for more than five years. We all get along well."

And how about the local Bedouins? "When Yamit was started," he said, "there were hardly any Bedouins here. Since then, more and more have come from the El Arish area. Some are employed as workers in the plants or as menial laborers. We trade with them and make economic improvement for them, a better life than in El Arish. We have no security problems. There is no anger at us. We have good cultural relations, even with the Palestinian Arabs who work in our plants."

What kind of relations do the people of Yamit have with their own government? "Ah, we are upset," Artom said, suddenly sounding less enthusiastic. "We are upset with our government, but not with Sadat. However, no Israeli government would permit Egyptian reign here. If somehow the Israelis did withdraw, then we would all have to move, but no government will dare do it. We will give up for real peace ninety-nine percent of Sinai but not the one percent here. Ninety-nine percent is a lot to give up, after all. We do not fear the Egyptians coming up to our fences. We look forward to it. The economic cooperation will be good for all concerned. One day, we will be a city of one hundred thousand. You will see."

(Artom's optimism was misplaced, apparently. An Israeli government will indeed permit Egyptian reign in the Yamit area, when the final phase of the peace-treaty agreement takes effect in 1982. Yamit may well be a city of one hundred thousand someday, but it will be a metropolis under the Egyptian flag. Whether any Israelis will be citizens of that metropolis depends on a stable, viable peace coming to the Sinai. Meanwhile, the people of Yamit have three years to protest sullenly and to dismantle their homes and lives.)

We left Yamit on a sandy bypass alongside the Allenby Railroad, a more direct route to the Rafa I.D.F. base, where Michael Bailey was waiting for a ride back to Jerusalem in his father's Land-Rover. The disagreeable khamsin wind was getting worse, but the sudden aroma of orange and almond blossoms from the groves along the road helped calm our nerves, and the sight of Bedouin women and girls leading their flocks to their tents for the night lent an air of pastoral peace to the short trip. At one point, we saw Bedouin boys joyfully racing their camels beside the unused tracks.

The Rafa army base, at the end of a dirt road off the Via Maris, was another strong reminder of the awesome military power of the diminutive State of Israel. Every mechanized vehicle imaginable was parked in hangarlike sheds: tanks, trucks, jeeps, half-tracks, wreckers, even motorized Bailey bridges. (Whenever Bailey has difficulty explaining his name to his countrymen, he says in Hebrew, "Like the Bailey bridge," and they immediately know the correct spelling and pronunciation.) As we drove through the acres of military might, Bailey said that the Rafa base was one of the most vital. "Without this base, the Arabs would eat up the settlers in no time."

The Gadna barracks were on the fringe of the base. Sunburned, serious, healthy teen-agers in T-shirts and shorts lounged about, looking like a scrupulously posed photograph in a Zionist magazine. Bailey chatted for a few moments with a standard scoutmaster-type, the leader of this Gadna unit, and then Michael, two other boys, a girl, and their rucksacks were squeezed into the Land-Rover.

It was dusk by the time we reached the Via Maris, and it was abruptly Palestine. Rafa is smack on the old Sinai-Palestine border. The timeless, pastoral Bedouins were replaced by dour, urban Palestinian Arabs, staring us down as we rolled along in front of their shanties. The Rafa refugee camp seemed slightly worse than it was when I had traveled on this very road in 1969. Yet, the Palestinians were making more money now than they did then, receiving good pay for work in Israeli industries. Why weren't their houses and their temperaments in a happier state? Again, it was partly a case of the Arab putting his money into jewelry, cars, camels, land, anything but his house. That and an undisguised loathing for everything Israeli, including our Land-Rover. I noticed that Bailey, like my driver in 1969, had increased his speed and rolled up his window.

We raced through Gaza, that dusty, miserable, crowded city with its wicker-furniture factories, orange-processing plants, garages humming with prosperity, and the familiar 7-Up bottling plant, an unlikely landmark I recalled from my 1969 trip. A totally unfamiliar sight at bus stops along the road stunned me—Israeli prostitutes peddling their wares for Arab laborers returning home from work. Bailey tsked. "Some Israeli girls put themselves through college that way," he said. "The Arabs may have lost the shooting wars against us, but they are winning the sexual ones. A Jewish woman is considered a great treat."

The burden of hate and khamsin seemed to abate once we had

crossed into Israel proper, south of Ashkelon. Things looked neater, greener, cleaner, cooler. At the turnoff to Jerusalem, we let out the two Gadna boys, who were going to hitch rides north to their homes; the girl, Jerusalem-bound, stayed on. She and Michael dozed off in spite of the noisy traffic. There was that quick and magical desert evaporation of the sun—as if a greater power had pulled a switch—and at eight-thirty, Bailey deposited me, bearded and bedraggled, at the main entrance of the Jerusalem Plaza. I had been away from that touch of Miami Beach for only thirty-eight hours, but I had been to another world.

FOUR

6 A.M. FRIDAY, APRIL 7. I am reliving my Jerusalem Plaza "Israeli breakfast" ceremony of the previous Monday morning, stuffing myself with fish and cheese, quaffing as much fruit juice and water as I can hold, and purloining hard-boiled eggs and soft rolls. Bailey is supposed to pick me up at seven. During the last two days, he has been to Tel Aviv to teach his classes at the university. He telephoned last night to say that he was still exhausted, hoarse from lecturing his students and me, and experiencing occasional twinges in his liver; however, he was game to go through with our big trip to the southern and central Sinai—at least five days in the most rugged wilderness, with small promise of comfort. I am still tired myself, having spent the last two days doing research in museums and libraries, interviewing various Sinai experts, and arranging my future trips with the Israeli, U.N., American, Greek Orthodox, and Egyptian bureaucracies.

At exactly seven o'clock, there was Bailey and his chock-full Land-Rover, incongruously pulling up at the Plaza's main entrance. He was cheerier than I had expected him to be. The doorman, shaking his head with Talmudic foreboding, helped me put my gear in the Land-Rover, and we drove off into the hazy orange sun through East Jerusalem and the suburb of Silwan, on the road to Jericho. We were waved through a few I.D.F. checkpoints and roadblocks—this, after all, was a route of Arabs traveling between Israel and Jordan, as part of the "Open Bridges" policy, and the I.D.F. was nothing if not security-obsessed. Just about the time we had returned to Jerusalem from the northeastern Sinai on Tuesday

81

night, a reserve soldier, hitchhiking back to his army camp in the
West Bank, was shot in the head right in front of the Rockefeller
Museum in East Jerusalem by three terrorists, who then fled to the
warrens of Silwan. (A few hours after that incident, a man from
Haga, a civil-defense patrol unit made up of older Israelis, went
berserk and fatally shot an Arab youth at the same spot. He was
taken into custody, and the youth was buried at an angry funeral
on Wednesday afternoon.) So there was tension as usual in the
West Bank, but I was relaxed as we plunged down the steep road
to the Dead Sea valley, recalling the familiar landmarks from my
1969 trip. Only one unfamiliar sore thumb stood out—a new settlement of the Gush Emunim, an ultranationalistic Orthodox sect that
is dedicated to establishing Jewish encampments in the biblical
lands of Judea and Samaria.

At the leaden, discouraging Dead Sea, we turned south, away
from Jericho, down the good, paved road toward the Arava, the
hottest, driest segment of the Great Rift Valley, a series of geological faults that run from the source of the Jordan River some four
thousand miles to Mozambique. With the Dead Sea and Jordan's
red-granite mountains of Moab and Edom on our left, and the
pocked escarpments of the Judean desert on our right, we sped past
King Hussein's luckless luxury hotel at the head of the Dead Sea
(which was scheduled to open in early June, 1967, just when the
Six Day War began, and has yet to welcome a paying guest), the
ruins of Qumran (where the Dead Sea Scrolls were discovered),
Ein Gedi (a thriving Israeli town and resort), Masada (the site of
the celebrated hilltop fortress where Jewish zealots held out for
three years against the Romans, until their mass suicide), and, at
last, Sodom (equally celebrated, biblically and etymologically).
From the inactive fleshpots and the active potash works of Sodom
at the southern tip of the Dead Sea—the nadir of the world, 1,302
feet below sea level—we broke onto the new road through the
Arava. It was miserably desolate and oppressive, with little to break
the scrubby monotony. For what amounted to a border road between two nations technically at war, there was hardly any military
presence, only hitchhiking Israeli soldiers toting their ever-present

weapons. We gave lifts to two of them, a blond sergeant on his way home to Arad, in the adjacent Negev, from a tour of duty in southern Lebanon (about which he was close-mouthed), and a pert girl heading to Elath. An occasional well-fortified kibbutz or moshav appeared along the road, showing off its brightly painted houses and shiny automobiles as evidence of new wealth from winter cultivation of melons and vegetables and from governmental tax breaks and subsidies. A sort of Howard Johnson's–style highway stop rose before us like a mirage; assuming it was real, we pulled in for cold drinks and gasoline. It was jammed with cars and buses full of Israeli tourists off on holiday, and it seemed like Jones Beach on July Fourth.

Farther on, near the site of King Solomon's copper mines, now called the Timna mines, we sensed something approaching a sea breeze from the direction of Elath, at the apex of the Gulf of Akaba. Since the Timna copper mines had shut down, the major industry in Elath was fast becoming tourism. It was no longer just a frontier town and port, but more a busy sea resort, about the size of Pompano Beach, Florida, with boulevards, cabanas, supermarkets, restaurants, hotels, souvenir booths, tennis courts, condominiums, fast-food stands (*felafel,* as well as hot dogs), excursion boats, backpackers, bikini-clad women, topless men, and Bedouin workers. We let off the girl soldier at a supermarket, where we bought some provisions for the days ahead, canned foods and biscuits, mostly, along with some Time cigarettes and candy for any Bedouins we would be staying with. Elath was an example of how Israelis managed to pluck prosperity from the flames of adversity. Even the roadside Bedouins, peddling camel rides, *kaffiyehs, galabiyas,* and photograph poses to the tourists, were doing business the envy of any Disneyland higgler. Several of them took time out from their hawking to wish "Docto*rr* Bay*lee*" Godspeed in the Sinai. A friend of one of the peddlers, a Tarabin named Suleiman, was going to Nuweiba, a third of the way down the peninsula along the Gulf of Akaba, and we offered him a lift.

The conventional guidebook description of the Gulf of Akaba is "a ribbon of cobalt blue," rimmed by mountains "of stark, sweeping majesty." The imagery is, at least, accurate. The Sinai, which begins just south of Elath, makes itself felt immediately as a very special part of the world. Even guidebook clichés seem timid. It is, quite simply, breathtaking. But before we plunged into the wilderness, Bailey suggested that we stop at something called Raphy Nelson's Saloon and Beach Club, at Wadi Taba a few kilometers beyond the frontier. It was a wild and woozy scene, a haphazard resort in the Polynesian manner thronged with hard-drinking, sybaritic Israelis, not a common sight in that country. Well-endowed women cavorted about under the thatched roof of an open-air bar, while two young beach bums amused themselves by painting garish nudes on an old piano. Sunbathers, like pop-art sculptures, were here and there along the sandy, trashy beach. When our Tarabin hitchhiker took a look at the scene, he fled back to the discreet safety of the Land-Rover; however, I saw some Bedouins working within the beach club.

Raphy Nelson, a bearded, bare-chested man who, I suspected, had designed himself to resemble Ernest Hemingway, came over and welcomed us. He said, between hugs and kisses with arriving customers (all of whom seemed to know him intimately), that he had come to this "end of the world" at Wadi Taba seven years ago, started his saloon with next to nothing, and has been enjoying its success ever since. Today, he told us, was more hectic than usual because—"can you believe it?"—Frank Sinatra, Gregory Peck, and Mrs. Johnny Carson were going to pay a call any minute now, in person! I recalled having read in the *Jerusalem Post* that Frank Sinatra and a jet plane full of his friends had arrived in Israel in order to dedicate a Sinatra-sponsored building at the Hebrew University. The last mirage I had expected, or wanted, to see in the Sinai was Frank Sinatra and his friends at play, so Bailey and I beat a quick retreat from the compulsive hilarity of Raphy Nelson's, with one very relieved Bedouin hitchhiker. (As it turned out, Sinatra and company never showed; they had apparently been driving their government hosts crazy with last-minute changes of schedule.)

As soon as we had started south again on the coast road, the graceful multiple trunks and branches of doum palm trees, the spiny

The island fortress of Gezirat Fara'un. *Magnum.*

caper bushes, the eroded granite walls on our right, and the deep-blue gulf on our left erased the Raphy Nelson chaos from our minds. A few kilometers farther on, we came opposite the Gezirat Fara'un, a tiny, irregular offshore island-fortress originally named for a Pharaoh, although no Pharaoh was ever known to have set foot on it. Some biblical authorities say that the Israelites set foot on it, after having departed from Kadesh Barnea. It may have been the site of Etzion Geber, at which the wanderers turned north toward the Promised Land. The island's history during the Crusades is on much firmer ground. From the early Crusades on, the Gulf of Akaba was of extreme importance to both the Moslems and the Christians as a strategic point of control over trade and pilgrimage. Renaud de Châtillon, a Christian commander, captured Gezirat Fara'un and built a sturdy European-style castle on it, which he called Graye. Stealing a page from King Solomon, he brought two ships in pieces from Jaffa down through the Sinai and assembled them at Graye, with the intention of sweeping the Red Sea of Arab vessels and taking Mecca. One of the ships foundered, however, and the other was captured by Saladin, who, stealing his own historical page, carried sections of ships across the Sinai on camels, also assembled them near Graye, and seized the entire region from the sea. It was said that Louis IX ("Saint Louis"), King of France and committed Crusader, was held prisoner at Graye by the Moslems until his ransom was delivered. The ruins of the fortress are well preserved, and archeological research has uncovered some biblical, Nabatean, and Byzantine artifacts under the Christian and Moslem constructions there.

Just a few kilometers south of the island is a compact deep-water bay, enclosed by granite cliffs, known locally as The Fiord, and indeed looking like a tropical version of Scandinavia. It is a lovely, lonely spot for sunbathing and skin diving among the coral reefs, when the excursion boats from Elath and the private yachts aren't anchored there. The underwater reefs seemed to be slabs of jade in the bright sunlight, and this coloring against the umber of the mountains, the gold-yellow of the sand, the mauve coastline of Saudi Arabia across the gulf, and the unrelenting azure of the sky was exhilarating. The spectacle moved Suleiman to recite a poem for Bailey, not specifically about nature but about a Tarabin coward called "The Remainer." During the mobilization of the Tarabin tribe for war against the Tiyaha, several generations ago, everyone took up arms except for one man, "The Remainer," who insisted on staying behind because he had no stomach for fighting. When the Tiyaha found him alone, "The Remainer" swore by the sea and all the mountains of Sinai that he would never fight them and he pleaded for their protection. The Tiyaha, impressed, let him go unharmed, and the Tarabin, also impressed but for different reasons, wrote him into their tribal lore. It was a rare case of Bedouin conscientious objection.

Farther along the coast road, I noticed a cluster of fishermen's huts and tents along the shore, and I asked Bailey if the Bedouins made a decent living by fishing the gulf. He said they did well enough, but the Tarabin and Muzeina Bedouins, who populated the gulf coast right down to its southernmost point at Sharm El Sheikh, were mainly herdsmen and menial laborers for the Israelis these days, in spite of their proximity to the sea. Suleiman, for instance, told Bailey that he worked for the Elath Department of Sanitation. When he felt the call of the wilderness, he hitchhiked to Nuweiba and took his camel up into the mountains to forage until his money ran out and he had to return to Elath. He made do in this fashion and maintained his ties to traditional Bedouin culture. Bailey asked him about smuggling, which had once brought prosperity to the Tarabin and Muzeina. "Ah," Suleiman said, his eyes lighting up, "if there was good smuggling still, there would be money to sell. Now, without so much smuggling, we have not great money, but enough. After eight hours of work, you rest. In good smuggling times under the Egyptians, there was more money but no rest. We were tired from little sleep and trouble from the police. The Egyptians were always accusing you of something and throwing you in jail. I do not miss smuggling, although I cannot afford to buy fodder for my camel. And with this drought, my camel has only broom plants to eat, and young camels must eat many different plants in different seasons or they will not eat at all. It can be hard, but I do not miss smuggling."

The fine highway we were barreling along would be the pride and joy of any American county. This permanent connection between Elath and Sharm El Sheikh was completed in 1971, its broad, paved surface following the track that the Israel Army's 9th Brigade, under the command of General Abraham Yoffe, raced down to capture Sharm El Sheikh from the Egyptians in 1956. In honor of that event, it is named the 9th Brigade Road. As the highway

wound around steep mountain sides and crossed wadi deltas and
dunes spilling into the gulf, it presented a new vista at every turn.
If your attention was elsewhere for as little as thirty seconds, you
missed an extraordinary sight. "My God, look how beautiful it is!"
Bailey suddenly shouted. "How can Israel give this back? We need
it more than the Egyptians do. The Mediterranean is nothing compared to this. Begin says he'll return the Sinai to the Egyptians over
three years. I think he should propose to rent it from them for at
least fifty years, see how things go, and then maybe give it back."
But were this beauty and space worth the constant threat of war?
I asked. "Who knows?" Bailey said. "For me, it's irreplaceable."
An I.D.F. roadblock just outside of Nuweiba punctuated the argument with contemporary reality; as usual, Bailey told the soldiers
on duty that he was from Sde Boker, and they waved us on.

Nuweiba (which means "bubbling springs") marked the tribal
boundary between the Tarabin and the Muzeina. It was actually
three distinct places: Nuweiba Tarabin in the north, consisting of
a thick grove of palms, a shallow bay, some driftwood fishermen's
shacks, and the ruins of a fort; Neviot, a moshav established in
1971, thriving on agriculture and tourism; and, just to the south,
Nuweiba Muzeina, a somnolent, sparsely inhabited oasis, which
came to life in the late summer when Muzeina flocked to the palm
groves to pick dates. Suleiman, being a Tarabin, wanted to be
dropped off at Nuweiba Tarabin, so we turned onto a sandy track
and stopped in front of an *arisha* with a sign reading "COFFEE."
Suleiman insisted on buying us some refreshment, and we were
invited to sit on a carpet under the booth, amid a dozen or so
Bedouins, El Arish merchants, and Salukis, all of them sleeping
away the midday heat in the shade. One fat Bedouin seemed quite
dead, his *kaffiyeh* covering his face like a shroud and his hands
folded on his chest; he finally stirred to disperse a cloud of black
flies from his body. (The Sinai flies are really no different in appearance from other flies, but being desert dwellers, they tend to be
more hungry, all the time.) In a room off the *arisha,* a transistor
radio crackled with Arab music and a man cooked a sour-smelling
stew for lunch. A few of the Bedouins awoke as we sat down,

shoeless, on the carpet; they all seemed to know Bailey, who talked quietly with them. Suleiman bought us orange sodas, surprisingly cold thanks to a Styrofoam ice chest. After downing my soda in two gulps, I went off to explore the nearby fort ruins.

The story of this nineteenth-century fort is a good example of how convoluted life in the Middle East can, and probably always will, be. When Egypt was under Turkish suzerainty, the khedives were charged with overseeing the hajj routes to Mecca, one of which passed Nuweiba. But toward the end of the nineteenth century, as British influence grew in Egypt, there was a question of which troops would be manning which forts at key spots. The English wanted their forces as close to Akaba as possible so that they could keep an eye on the Turks, and vice versa. A complicated compromise was struck, in which the Turks would continue to occupy their fort in Akaba but would build a new fort at Nuweiba for the British. Constructed of native rock and coral, with the latest designs in ramparts and shooting slits, it was never used in battle. Deteriorating beyond its years, it was now just a dung-filled corral for donkeys and goats. Hardly a tourist or archeologist ever stopped by.

I thought I had witnessed the last culture shock in the Sinai at Raphy Nelson's boisterous beach club, but I was wrong. Neviot, the Israeli moshav cooperative between the two Nuweibas, prospering from flowers and vegetables grown under silvery plastic strips that hold the moisture, seemed a conventional enough settlement at first. But witnessing the scene at the Neviot cafeteria on the beach, I was transported back to, say, Provincetown, in the mid-1960s. At the cafeteria, legions of hippies, in various modes of dress and undress, were munching listlessly on gray hamburgers or, more often, just staring straight ahead at nothing in particular. There was a definite North European look to them; Neviot had been discovered by rootless youths from Sweden, Denmark, and Germany, as well as Canada and America, several years before. The atmosphere was sullen and anachronistic. A German counterman sang early Beatles songs as he served up hamburgers and French fries, a few Bedouins, not at all upset at the near-nudity, walked among the loungers selling trinkets, an emaciated blond girl sketched a beach scene while a male counterpart played backgammon by himself.

Bailey and I ordered some lunch and carried our trays to a table occupied by a tanned young man in a bathing suit. He was from Toronto, he told us, and had gravitated to Neviot after a working stay at a kibbutz in the Galilee. I asked him how he spent his days at Neviot. "Well, just mostly hanging around," he said. "That's what all of us do, just hang around. I like it. It beats working. Nobody really talks. We just get stoned and look at each other. We crash on the beach back there, and a lot of us go to Elath once a week for cheap food, so we can live on about a dollar a day. The guys who are better off buy food here at the cafeteria or from the Bedouins. Some of those Bedouins are making a small fortune off of us. They come down the beach on their camels every morning, waking us up and selling dope, food, and all kinds of junk. They even offer to take us on camel rides into the mountains. The regular Bedouins hate those guys. The moshav is happy, though. They make good money from this place and they don't mind us camping out around here, just so long as we stay clear of them. But it's all going to end for me soon, I guess. My folks are coming over here to bring me back to Toronto. It was nice while it lasted."

Our schedule called for us to turn inland up the Wadi Watir, one of the peninsula's widest and grandest dry riverbeds, and arrive by nightfall at Ein El Furtaga, a verdant oasis where the Tarabin have their tribal seat. Before leaving the 9th Brigade Road and heading into rough country, we decided to stop first at the Yair Crossroads gas station and rest area, just outside of Neviot, to fill up with fuel and water.

On the way to the gas station, while I tried to shake off the depression from our visit to Neviot, Bailey said, "Are you ready for another culture shock? Well, whether you are or not, you're going to meet Zvi Swet." Zvi Swet, Bailey explained, was a "fighting Jew," a British Commando during the Second World War who had fought in just about every daring raid the Allies could dream up. Two weeks before the end of the war, he stepped on a land mine and lost both of his legs. He recovered and went to Palestine, where he married a Vienna-born woman named Ruth, and turned against his former comrades-in-arms with a vengeance. Confined to a wheelchair, he became a chief of operations of the Stern Gang, an uncompromising underground terrorist unit that wreaked havoc on the British troops in Palestine and, occasionally, on the Haganah, the Jewish defense militia. Even after Israel had won its independence, Swet refused to temper his nationalistic fury, and bad luck continued to dog him. His sons were either killed or badly wounded in later wars, and his daughter, a medical-corps officer, contracted and barely survived a rare disease. During the sunburst of optimism after the 1967 war, Swet came to the Sinai and opened a gas station at Nuweiba, before there was a Neviot. He and his remaining family built it all by themselves ("He can do more work from his wheelchair than ten men with good legs," Bailey said), and they were still adding on boutiques, snack bars, and living quarters. They started a new life in the Sinai because Swet was tired of his Tel Aviv neighbors' pitying him. He wanted independence. When Begin offered to return the Sinai to Sadat, Swet drove to Jerusalem to see the Prime Minister personally and gave him hell, as one old terrorist to another. He told Begin that what was fought for must be kept.

At the Yair Crossroads—churning with automotive activity, Bedouin encampments beside the gas pumps, and new construction—Bailey introduced me to Swet and his wife, while the Land-Rover was seen to. From the description, I had expected to meet an unreconstructed firebrand. Instead, Swet was a bald, soft-spoken, gray-bearded bear of a man with the most gentle eyes I had ever seen, his massive torso ridiculously imprisoned in a metal wheelchair. Over coffee and those thin Israeli yoghurts, we talked about his life in Nuweiba.

"I rent this land from the government," Swet said. "Now, it appears I won't have more than a three-year lease from Begin. In Neviot, my competition across the way, they get government concessions—and hippies and drugs and whatever. This place, I have built from nothing, with no concessions. I have only Bedouins

working for me. I think I get along better with them than anyone else does. I understand them and they understand me. They say to me that we Jews were here in Sinai first, so it's all right for us to be here now. They are wise. And they are changing, too, but slowly. Listen, I will tell you an anecdote. For years, the Bedouins working here at my gas station have always looked at a broken car or truck and said the problem was due to Allah. 'Inshallah,' you know? Like saying, 'What can you do?' and throwing up your hands. But just recently, a Bedouin said to me that a flat tire was flat because it needed air. It was the first time he didn't say, 'Allah did it.' And they are good mechanics, proud of their work. They have time on their side, too. When, for instance, a carburetor is broken, they form a committee and take it apart and let everybody offer suggestions on fixing it. And they fix it! Amazing."

A small argument was developing nearby between an Israeli tourist and a Bedouin on a camel over a photograph taken by the former of the latter without proper payment. Swet wheeled himself into the fray and settled the matter, in a mixture of Hebrew and Arabic, within thirty seconds. It was an inspiring performance, and we all applauded him when he returned. He smiled shyly and said, "I have learned to be a peacemaker here. Living on the border between the Tarabin and the Muzeina, I have to be sometimes the umpire. The gas station is the nerve center of the two tribes. Not long ago, a Tarabin approached a Muzeina woman not nicely. Soon, both tribes were lined up facing each other near here. All Sinai knew immediately about the insult through a kind of bush telegraph—the taxis and the El Arish merchants in their trucks. On both sides, their faces turned green and blue with anger. Stones began to fly and one Bedouin pulled his *shibriya* knife from its sheath. That's when I wheeled between them and broke it up.

The 9th Brigade Road, along the Gulf of Akaba coast, to the southern Sinai. *Magnum.*

A wadi in the southern Sinai. *Magnum.*

Then, I built a booth for both tribes and we had an *atwa."* (An *atwa* is a truce conclave between Bedouin combatants, in which possibilities for peace are explored. Later, some compensation from one side to the other—maybe through *diya,* or "blood money"— furthers the process. More ritual negotiations take place until peace —a *sulha*—is perhaps achieved. It has been said that Sadat made both an *atwa* and a *sulha* in his 1977 peace initiative and visit to Jerusalem.) "They are still in the *atwa* negotiating stage. But if you get a stone on your head, you don't forget about it so easily. Some trouble might break out again and I will have to be the umpire."

I asked Swet what I knew was a painful question: What will he do if the Egyptians are given back the Sinai? He swallowed hard and said, "I knew many Egyptians when I was in the British Army. In the 1940s, they rarely went past Kantara on the canal, they felt nothing for this place. Now, suddenly, all the Sinai is holy soil to them. When the time comes to give the Sinai back, I will decide. I have already been offered a lot of money by a Swedish company for this gas station, but I turned it down." He paused for a moment. "If the Egyptians would want me to stay, maybe I would stay." I told him that I planned to be in Egypt soon. "If you see Sadat," he said, "tell him I want to speak with him, to explain to him how it really is here. We will sit down and talk like *mensch,* and we will see who is right. That is how I talk in Jerusalem with my own government."

Ruth, a large earth-mother sort of woman, noticed the arrival of a truckload of the ubiquitous Arishiya merchants. "Here come the swindlers to cheat my Bedouins," she said. "I'll have to deal with them before they bargain the clothes off our backs. When they swindle, they are sometimes afraid to sleep near the Bedouins and they ask if they can sleep outside near us." She hurried off to greet the merchants.

Swet watched her go and said, "You know, we sleep outside

A solitary walker in Wadi Watir. *Magnum.*

almost every night, under the stars like the Bedouins. There is no
danger, no trouble in all the years I've been here. When you sleep
in a house, your thoughts are only as high as the ceiling, but
outside, they are as high as the stars. That is what I love about the
Sinai—the space, the freedom, the stars. . . . Bailey, when you're
in the hills, please try to make a tape recording for me of that
Bedouin wedding song I like so much, the beautiful, sad one. I can't
hear it enough." Bailey said he would try. We shook hands with
Swet, wished each other well, and drove off down the coast road
to Wadi Watir.

The distance from the junction of the coast road and Wadi Watir
to Ein El Furtaga was just eighteen kilometers, but it was eighteen
kilometers into the hard, isolated, mysterious world of the Bedouin
loose in nature. A sign in Hebrew, Arabic, and English at the
mouth of the wadi warned "FOUR-WHEEL-DRIVE VEHICLES
ONLY." The advice was well given. Wadi Watir is a meandering,
erosion-chiseled notch running from the gulf to the inland mountains, a strapping stepchild of the Grand Canyon, with granite walls
rising almost vertically on either side of a boulder-strewn floor,
sometimes as narrow as fifteen yards, sometimes as wide as two
hundred. Once we were inside the notch, the sun was blocked by
the sheer walls, and as Bailey struggled to avoid the boulders and
soft sand, it grew chilly enough so that we needed our jackets. No
sign of animate life was to be seen, just neatly cut intersecting
branch wadis, spiny caper bushes, and the rubble of ageless avalanches. The only man-made objects were occasional piles of stones,
marking tribal borders (if the stones are black, they have the added
significance of a black curse on any enemy who happens along), and
flood gauges attached to the wadi walls.

The late-fall and winter flash flood (the *sayl,* at once dreaded and
life-giving) is especially dangerous in the longer, deeper wadis.
Because there is so little vegetation to absorb the mountain rains,
a roaring, ruinous torrent can career through a previously bone-dry
river valley just a few hours after a rainstorm twenty miles away.
One famous Sinai *sayl* in 1867 washed away an entire Bedouin

camp, leaving forty persons dead. There has been an added hazard since the Arab-Israeli wars: land mines and unexploded artillery shells were often unearthed and carried downstream in the torrent, like live unguided missiles. No sane Bedouin would camp near a wadi during the rainy season. Bailey, in his investigations of star lore as the governing factor in Bedouin encounters with nature, was told this bit of ancient verse by a Muzeina: *"In tila Suhayl/La tamin is sayl/Law kan agab il layl"* ("If Canopus rises, don't trust the flood, even if it be the end of the night").

The oasis at Ein El Furtaga. *Magnum.*

"Don't trust the flood" is drummed into every Bedouin child's head.

In early April, the flash-flood danger was nonexistent, but in riverbeds such as Wadi Watir there were still watermarks ten feet high on the walls and brimming rock pools which had trapped the runoff water. The pools were introduced by, at first, a damp spot on the wadi floor, then a mud puddle, then a tiny rivulet boasting some grass. One cool, shaded pool we passed, looking like a bottomless Scottish tarn, was perfect for a dip, in spite of the chill in the air. We stopped and approached the rim of the pool, only to discover a solitary man in a bathing suit reading a book on an opposite ledge. He was an Israeli who must have hiked in to this choice idyllic spot, wanting to be left alone. It seemed best to leave him in his splendid isolation, and we drove on.

I could tell by a widening rivulet, disappearing underground and suddenly reappearing before us, that Furtaga was not far off. After another kilometer or two, there it was around a bend—a large oasis in a broad plain, studded with clumps of palms, small *bustans* fed by diverted water channels from the main stream, scattered booths and tents, and prowling camels and Salukis. We circled the plain, Bailey pointing out one of Sheikh Ibn Jazi's mohair tents ("Even though I have some money, I can make any place my home," Jazi once told Bailey), and then we parked the Land-Rover before a small rise, upon which were the booth and tent of the sheikh's brother Salim Ibn Jazi. "Docto*rr* Bay*lee*" was welcomed with the usual warm *salamats* and handshakes, and, of course, we were invited to have dinner and spend the night with Salim. A campfire of acacia sticks had already been started and tea was brewing in a blackened brass pot in the middle of the fire (a Bedouin adage holds that a good man has a charred teapot because it shows that he is hospitable). Some neighbors and Salim's sons came forward to greet us, as well as some more of the omnipresent El Arish mer-

---

Sinai Bedouins at their evening campfire. *Magnum.*

chants, their red truck parked behind the booth. The Arishiya, too, were invited to be Salim's guests for the night; he obviously trusted them more than most Bedouins did, or, perhaps, he owed them more money.

We sat with our shoes off on a rug in front of the booth, sipping tea in clear glasses and exchanging interminable *salamats*. The men chain-smoked the Time cigarettes and the younger boys chewed with delight on the candy we had bought in Elath. One of the boys, a frail lad with a runny nose, a nasty cough, and a feverish glaze to his eyes, sat next to me and stared at my tape recorder. I let him examine it closely, while Bailey translated, in muted asides, the talk around the fire. All the women and girls of Furtaga were far up the Wadi Watir with their flocks, looking for pasture. The men were making do without them, cooking, eating, trading, smoking, and minding the houses and camels ("Camels are man's work, too strong for a woman," Salim said). Since Salim was an employee of the Nature Reserves Authority, the warden of the Wadi Watir area, he had better reason than the others for remaining behind.

As the tea flowed and the dusk settled, the conversation took new turns. Salim complained that some Tarabin young men did not want to tend their camels and live the traditional Bedouin life, but preferred to work in Elath until they earned enough money to buy pickup trucks. In some families only one son stayed around long enough to be trained in the old ways. His complaint had a universal ring to it. When Bailey told him that he could no longer drink liquor because of his hepatitis, Salim laughed and said that was good news, since alcohol is forbidden by the Koran. Some Salukis set up a howling clamor, and Salim told the story of how he had become a Saluki breeder. He had owned a bitch named Rashrash in the 1940s, and one day he met some Saudi merchants coming up the wadi herding horses to sell in Egypt. They had a hunting falcon and a male Saluki with them, too. The Saluki hung around to mate with Rashrash, and that was the beginning of Salim's noisy kennel. Since the subject was dogs, I asked if they would like to hear a tape recording of Igra, my golden Labrador retriever, singing along to the "Marseillaise." (My dog prefers to sing to Berlioz's arrangement of the "Marseillaise" even more than to Mahler's Second Symphony; I had taped her performance while testing my recorder before leaving home.) Igra's wailing to the anthem elicited mixed reactions: the consumptive boy was absolutely enchanted; the others simply stared at the machine with bemused smiles, nodding their heads; the Salukis immediately stopped their howling, as if they sensed a greater talent among them. For me, the musical interlude lent a fine touch of Surrealism to the already haunting scene, another culture collision to round out the day.

Bailey produced his own tape recorder with the intention of taping some Bedouin poetry and oral history before dinner. I excused myself and took a walk up the wadi in the dying light. It was the quintessential moment. Never had my feeling of connection to the Sinai been so strong. The wadi and the plain were changing from minute to minute into ever-darker shades of purple, which created the illusion of the rock walls closing in on me. I picked my way around a booth covered with caper plants (probably a way station providing some small shade), a disdainful camel, some acacia trees (holding in their upper branches, booby-trapped with deadly thorns, family supplies and possessions wrapped in tent fabric), and an indistinct mound, which turned out to be a lone Bedouin prostrating himself for his sundown prayers, facing southeast toward Mecca. I stopped short, not wanting to intrude further into the supplicant's devotion—so quiet, so personal, so total—and, yet, by just standing there staring, I was intruding. I walked on in a wide circle behind him.

Long before the emergence of Islam, the Bedouins had followed religious patterns of their own design—superstitions, really, based on their star lore, animism, and practical desert laws and customs. They believed in unlucky astrological periods, when, for instance, the moon is in conjunction with Libra, Sagittarius, and Scorpio. To this day, many Bedouins (the older ones, especially) will not attempt a difficult task, a journey, a raid, or sexual intercourse during such periods. (It is believed that a child conceived during unfavorable times will be retarded.) There are poems spelling out each of the astrological prohibitions.

Professor Palmer, in his wanderings about the Sinai, made a detailed study of the Bedouins' extant pre-Islamic superstitions and rituals. He found, among other things, that the Bedouins have long believed a great spirit created man first, and then gave him camels, goats, sheep, and donkeys for his use, along with time and seasons. When man forgets this god, the serpent will sting him—although a *hawi*, a venom-proof medicine man, may be called upon to neutralize the sting. They believe, too, in the end of the world and a general resurrection, with the good able to repel attacking vultures and the bad helpless before the eye-pecking birds. Charms and philters prepared from animals can help ward off such cataclysmic hazards; for example, if a vulture is killed and buried for forty days, then boiled until its flesh is gone, the first white bone can be used to summon a genie who will reveal wonderful secrets of nature and survival, including aphrodisiacs. Burnt owl feathers and boiled hyena flesh also bring about miraculous cures. The revered rabbit and the leopard are considered to have been human in an earlier life and therefore cannot be eaten. A mythical, never-seen beast called the *hudhud* (because it is heard in the mountains crying "Hud hud") is also man's brother and must never be disturbed. Even after the Bedouins enthusiastically adopted Islam, some still performed non-Moslem prayers rooted in old superstition. When a man awakens in the morning, the spirit of god is on his right shoulder and the devil is on his left. He must pray and sprinkle himself with water, otherwise the devil will be with him all day long. The same ritual must be done at sunset, too, to protect him for the night.

I followed the intermittent stream up the wadi, the camel droppings and slimy vegetation in the water filling the air with a thick, fetid smell. The only sounds were the erratic bubbling of the stream, the chirping of crepuscular birds, and the Salukis calling to one another with echoing howls. I could almost hear a celestial light switch click, as the cloudless, moonless sky suddenly flashed with stars, the brightest firmament I had ever seen. I felt insignificant and alone in space—the way every Bedouin must feel much of the time —and I recalled what Bailey had told me about the Bedouin philosophy of existence in the wilderness. It can be summarized as "I against my brother, my brother and I against our cousin, my brother and I and our cousin against the world." The harshness of life, of course, demands this departmentalization of loyalties—individual, family, clan, tribe. Blood feuds continue until the fifth generation, unless they are settled by a *sulha.* Memories are long in the desert. The Bedouin has both dependency on and distrust of his neighbor, a kind of built-in suspicion usually absent in settled, policed communities. Since he rarely extends himself past the tribe, nationalism or regionalism hardly matters. He doesn't take political sides, as a rule, and because he acknowledges no earthly master outside the tribe, he can never be truly conquered. His fundamental quest in life is for food and shelter on the simplest subsistence level. Mere subsistence is an end in itself. More than that a Bedouin does not generally covet. Great ambition is alien to him. (The present-day Saudi Bedouins are a glaring exception.) The compulsive emphasis on hospitality is really a tit-for-tat posture. Without it, he would never be able to herd his livestock far from home or go to market or seek refuge in hard times. Because he usually has (or wants) so little, generous sharing is tantamount to an act of bravery, the mark of a man. The town Arab does not need this posture, this show, and that is why there is mutual loathing between him and the Bedouin. Ibn Khaldun, the fourteenth-century historian and promulgator of Arab civilization, was of two minds about the Bedouins: on the one hand, he respected them for their courage and simplicity; on the other hand, he derided them for being unmanageable, ignorant nomads. He wrote in *The Mukaddimah* that they were "the most savage human beings that exist. Compared with sedentary people, they are on a level with wild, untamable animals and dumb beasts of prey." Yet the noted contemporary American biblical scholar William Albright has said that the Bedouins "are the heirs of over thirty centuries of camel-nomadism and of some thirteen centuries of Islam. They reflect the most highly developed pride of race and family. The most ignorant and the wildest Bedawi may be capable of displaying courtly manners and unexpected eloquence. The Bedawi tradition of freedom and cul-

ture is so high that the humblest tribesman considers himself im-
measurably superior to the peasant and even to the semi-nomad—
who in his turn despises the peasant. On their part the peasants may
hate the Bedouin and call them 'wild beasts,' but they admire them
all the same, and Arab oral literature is full of their praise."

Homing in on the glow from Salim's campfire, I made my way
back down the wadi to the booth and dinner. The dim glow from
other campfires around the plain gave an eerie, extraterrestrial
quality to the night, that Sinai moonscape again. I stopped at the
Land-Rover and was surprised to discover that it was unlocked.
Bailey had made a point of always locking the car, even if we were
away from it for only a few minutes. He appeared beside me
through the shadows and I asked him why he had left the car open.
He said it would be an insult to our hosts to lock it, even though
he was leery of the El Arish merchants. "We'll be up at first light,
anyway, before the Arishiya have a chance to swipe anything," he
said. From our box of Elath supermarket provisions, he took out
cans of kosher chicken soup ("It's Friday night, isn't it?") and
something called turkey balls. They would be added to Salim's stew
(Salim's permission having already been granted), and together
with fresh *pita* being prepared and sugared tea, that would be our
dinner. There was no freshly slaughtered goat, just a plain potluck
meal. I fished out a bottle of Scotch from my rucksack and took two
long pulls from it. The undiluted whiskey had never tasted so good.
I was suffused with inner warmth and peace, and I offered some to
Bailey, who, of course, shook his head regretfully. "Hard cheese,
old man," I said.

We walked to the carpet spread out near the fire and I watched
one of Salim's older sons prepare the *pita*. He was kneading a large
blob of flour-and-water dough into a family-size pizza. When he was
satisfied with its diameter and texture, he simply threw it onto the
fire, brushing hot coals over it with a stick. Almost immediately, it
smelled delicious. Then, about ten minutes later, with his bare hand
he turned the *pita* over, repeating the ember-covering process. The
bread was charcoal-black in spots and looked like a flat, round dish
made of scorched plaster. Meanwhile, Salim stirred the stew over

the fire in a big brass pot, the heady traces of chicken soup, turkey balls, and, I guessed, lamb mixing strangely in the night air. The other Bedouin adults were settling their accounts with the merchants for a few purchased items of clothing and food, doling out with precision and ceremony their Israeli pound notes, one by one. The Arishiya just as carefully re-counted the bills after they were handed them. Words of thanks were exchanged and everyone at last took his place on the carpet.

The younger boys were not only allowed but encouraged to sit in on adult male activities, just as the younger girls tended the flocks with their mothers. There was no Bedouin generation gap. I noticed that when the consumptive boy displayed a certain boredom while waiting for dinner—he idly rapped a twig against an empty can—his punishment was just a "tsk-tsk" from Salim, and the child instantly stopped the rapping. This gentle discipline was in marked contrast to that of town Arabs, who, with more children in tighter quarters, tended to be irritable toward their young and often beat them. It was Bailey's theory that since the Bedouins led an outdoor, measured life, the children knew instinctively how far they could go, and the parents were more patient. The town Arabs, however, are confined and pressured by life, and their tempers are short.

As a rule, only one out of every ten Bedouin boys attended school regularly, and almost none of the girls. (The Israelis provided the schools but did not press for total attendance.) There was no tradition of formal education. In the Bedouin culture of subsistence and survival, education came from the elders, who taught the child by example and imitation. Consequently, few Bedouins learned to read and write, which accounts for the emphasis on oral history, law, literature, and entertainment. One of Bailey's missions in life was to set down on paper the oral history of the rich Bedouin culture. He felt that no time should be lost because as more and more sons left the fold to work in towns, the lore of their fathers might be forgotten. The time-honored Bedouin routine of herding animals, raiding to supplement income, and, perhaps, growing produce to eat and sell was in danger of fading away, too—all the more reason for the elders to fear formal education. One brilliant young

Bedouin man, with tribal backing, was sent off to England for medical training. He received his M.D. degree and emigrated to California, where he is currently attached to a hospital. He wrote home that he missed the Sinai but, even so, he could not see his way clear to returning. It will be a long time before another young man is sent off by the tribe for advanced education.

A thin white candle was lit near the campfire and dinner was proclaimed ready. The candle was an uncommon addition to the evening meal. It was in our honor, as was the ceremonial presentation of a separate tin pan of stew and a large hunk of *pita* to Bailey and me. The protocol of hospitality behind this was that, as guests, we could eat all we wanted, without having to worry about enough food for the others, who would eat out of the brass cooking pot. Following Bailey's example, I broke off a small piece of *pita* and, using it as a spoon, I covered a larger piece with stew. The *pita* was harder and denser than oven-baked bread, but crisp and fresh. The stew was savory, although I found it difficult to identify any individual ingredient, and especially good when eaten with the *pita.* Once we had begun to eat, the others joined in, slowly and silently. There was no dinner conversation. Several glasses of sweet warm tea helped to wash the heavy victuals down.

When we all had finished, the pan and the brass pot were given to the Salukis, who licked them clean. It would be the only cleaning they would get; when the dogs were no longer interested in them, the utensils were put away for the next meal. Cigarettes were distributed after dinner—not the Time brand but scraggly hand-rolled ones filled with tobacco from a pouch belonging to one of the Arishiya. The cigarettes smelled unmistakably like marijuana, although the filler could have been just powerful Turkish tobacco. I was offered one and tried to smoke it, my first cigarette in ten years. It had no more effect on me than my pipe tobacco does.

A general drowsiness overtook everyone but Salim and Bailey, who were energetically discussing Bedouin poetry and oral law. Salim's keen memory for legal-precept rhymes and other verse prompted Bailey to write down by the light of the candle everything Salim said. The others, their eyes half closed, seemed intoxicated by the recitations (and, perhaps, their cigarettes), repeating and caressing the rhyming syllables—*ee* and *aydee* and *eesh* and *eem* —their faces full of wonder at how the poet came up with the exact rhyme and yet preserved the meaning. Salim's other verses not about the law were mainly poems of longing, courage, despair, and, oddly, loneliness. Every element of their life has a standard poetic symbol—war, revenge, the seasons, childbirth, death—and the poets who created these symbols are legendary heroes, known to all. Indeed, one of the loftiest hopes one Bedouin can wish another is for the birth of a poet in his family.

No audience was ever so rapt as this one. But at last, the listeners succumbed to sleep—first the children, wrapping themselves in threadbare blankets and rags; then the Arishiya, burrowing into their rough bedding taken from burlap sacks; then, one by one, the Bedouin men, a few even nodding off as they sat cross-legged before the failing fire; finally, I myself, crawling into my sleeping bag at nine o'clock, my feet pointing west away from the dawn. I lay supine, staring straight up at the stars, barely conscious of Salim's and Bailey's voices, of the reverberant Saluki repartee, of the snoring and coughing and flatulence and borborygmus of the sleepers, of the camels chewing cud, of an owl hooting, of a hawk whistling. I imagined being one of the Israelite host, camped here in the night rapture of Sinai with the flocks and friendly fellow Semites, pondering a new, stringent set of laws, a vague, unfulfilled promise, and a confusing God. This must have been the way it was, I thought as I fell asleep.

I don't remember how many times I woke up during the soft, sweet night, certainly more than five. The first time, I know, was occasioned by the sound of sand being brushed aside near me. Blinking awake, I saw Salim smoothing out a spot on the ground for Bailey's sleeping bag, the way a father might prepare a bed for his favorite son. Another time, a lip-smacking camel almost stepped on me. I was also jolted out of my dreams by flashes of light, which turned out to be those stroboscopic Sinai stars. Once, I saw a brilliant flaming meteor, or maybe a piece of a man-made satellite intrusively plunging to earth. The last time I awoke was to the first light of dawn. Facing west did not make for longer morning sleep at Ein El Furtaga. The burnt-orange reflection of the sun on the canyon walls was so strong, so splendid, that to close one's eyes again would have been a profanation.

It was just before five o'clock. A few of the others were stirring, and Salim, the last to retire, was already up and about, starting the campfire for breakfast. He nodded to me and smiled; I nodded and smiled back. We stood side by side and watched the bright orange dawn bring the wadi to life. Salim had spent just about every morning of his existence in this place, and yet his fascination with the new day was probably stronger than mine. The sounds of coughing and spitting by the other risers—smokers' hack, mostly— dissolved the lovely moment. I walked down to the unlocked Land-Rover to see if anything was missing. Everything was in order, even Bailey's pistol hidden under the front seat. An old man who had shared dinner with us the night before was at morning prayer— standing, kneeling, prostrating, standing, kneeling, prostrating, a solitary, mystical morning exercise. A Saluki nibbled at a fresh pile of camel dung, his breakfast. Nothing is wasted in the desert.

I watched the breakfast *pita* and tea being prepared—the *pita* as the night before, the tea and sugar in equal measures mixed with water and boiled in the blackened brass teapot. Bailey was awake and I saluted him with my first question of the day: Since Bedouins never seem to shave, why don't their beards progress beyond stubble? It was too early for an answer to such a question. "I don't know," he mumbled. There was a new face around the campfire, a tall, young Bedouin sporting a Rolex watch and missing two fingers on his left hand. He had arrived during the night with his camel, whose teeth were the cause of his missing fingers. Bedouins love Rolex watches as much as they distrust (but prize) camels. I observed his camel for a moment—that comical, stupid, vicious beast indispensable for transportation and, sometimes, food. After the age of six when their mouths are tough as leather, they can make do on almost any forage, even acacia buds. Their ability to go without fresh supplies of water is desert legend. They can endure boredom, hobbling, beatings, and their own smell with dumb stoicism, and then, when their owners least expect it, violently rebel —as unpredictable as the Middle East itself.

The breakfast was simple and invigorating, *pita* dipped in tea. The sun rose swiftly, and with it came a mixed chorus of birds, including the sand-colored thrush called the *bulbul* and, to everybody's pleasure, the cackling partridge. Bedouins welcomed the cackle of the partridge because it heralded spring. There is a crafty saying that, in effect, goes like this: When the partridge begins to cackle and neighbor visits neighbor and the embers of the fire last until the morning and the night is not too long, those who say they've looked for fresh pasture and not found it are liars. The partridge is cackling, the winter is over, and the camps are empty because there is new forage to be had.

Just after six o'clock and four glasses of tea, Bailey and I prepared to leave camp. We packed our gear, checked the Land-Rover, and filled our canteens at a spot where the stream reemerged from the ground, near a protective ledge. "You see that ledge," Bailey said. "A few years ago, I brought my wife and sons here at Passover. We set up camp and held our Seder at this very spot in the open. Salim slaughtered a paschal lamb and baked the real matzah, *pita,* and it was the greatest Seder since the original one. I'll never forget it. We had a magnificent experience."

Bailey and I walked back to Salim's booth and offered *shukrans* and handshakes all around. I wanted to offer something more substantial for my remarkable stay at Furtaga, but that was not done. Perhaps if I could arrange for a doctor to see the consumptive boy soon . . . no, I was being a missionary again.

FIVE

WE STRUCK OUT for Mount Sinai and St. Catherine's Monastery, from Ein El Furtaga a half-hour helicopter ride, perhaps, but a long tortuous trip through rough country by Land-Rover. On the map, the most direct route was through Wadi Ghazala, off Wadi Watir, to Ein Khudra (the alleged site of Hazeroth, meaning "fences," where the Israelites had once camped), but nobody was sure how clear the wadi road was. We reasoned that it would be quicker and safer to return to the coast road and head west into the interior over the more-traveled Wadi Saal.

And more-traveled it was. It seemed that every tourist in the Sinai was on the wadi road to Mount Sinai for the weekend: American Christian Bible-study groups in blue Egged tour buses, kibbutz children in trucks, some dauntless folk in ordinary cars (most of which were stalled at the side of the road with flat tires and overheated radiators), and a convoy of five GMC Carryall vans, operated by Johnny's Desert Tours, crammed with hardy, elderly Europeans. One of the Johnny's Desert Tours drivers recognized Bailey and stopped near us to talk. He said that he had already been to the Mount Sinai area and that it was inundated with tourists. Besides the ones coming overland, fifteen Arkia (the Israel domestic airline) flights had put in at the small Mount Sinai airport. All the sightseers had been turned away by the monks of St. Catherine's, who refused them permission even to enter the monastery grounds, let alone spend the night at the monastery hostel. Bailey and I wondered whether our letters of introduction to the monks would work. The more travelers we saw, the more we despaired.

110

The morning haze was quickly baked off by the sun and it was hot in the wide, windless wadi. Oblivious of the heat, however, was a Bible-study group sitting in a circle before Ein Khudra, reverently reading Old Testament passages and attentively listening to the tour leader's lecture on Hazeroth. He recounted the story, in Numbers 12, of how the Israelites stopped at Hazeroth, after suffering one of God's plagues for their greed and discontent. While there, Miriam and Aaron spoke against their brother Moses, "for he had married an Ethiopian woman." The Lord appeared before the slandering siblings in "the pillar of the cloud" and visited leprosy upon Miriam, until she was "white as snow." Moses interceded with God in Miriam's behalf, and after seven days she was cured and allowed back into the camp. Then the Israelites moved on to Kadesh Barnea. As the story was told, the Bible students read the passages before the sandstone rocks that might have once been the fences of Hazeroth, and their faces shone in the sun. I have rarely seen people look so transported, so radiant.

Ein Khudra is the site of a Bedouin legend, too. A crack in a rock near the water hole is called Bab El Rum, or "Christians' Gate." The Bedouins once believed that the crack was the entrance to a tunnel leading directly to Asia Minor (the home of the Christians) and that it had been closed by pro-Bedouin magic. This wadi was also the scene of a notable journey in the late eighteenth century by the Swiss explorer Johann Burckhardt, who was the victim of Bedouin treachery while attempting to reach Akaba from St. Catherine's. He was ambushed by an offshoot of the very tribe he had hired to protect him, the notorious Awlad Said. (Bailey quoted a Bedouin proverb concerning treachery in general and the Awlad Said in particular: "Indecency from an indecent family is not indecency.")

Wadi Saal is named for the acacia trees that grow abundantly about its broad floor. What with the dangerous acacia thorns (capable of puncturing a tire as surely as a six-inch spike), the paucity of shade, the tourist traffic, and Egyptian vultures (familiarly known as "Pharaoh's chickens") constantly circling overhead, it had none of the charm and beauty of Wadi Watir. It does possess a geological phenomenon, however, called *sawan wa elmaz,* or "flint with diamonds"—a stone looking like a curious dried fruit, which, when split open, reveals a dazzling cluster of quartz. Bedouins have been known to sell these stones to the credulous as rough diamonds. The wadi was also the location of an Israeli government-sponsored experiment in upgrading Bedouin agriculture with wells, cisterns, plastic pipes, and fenced-in plots available for those relatively few Bedouins who wish to till the soil. (A favorite Bedouin proverb still is "When the plow crosses the threshold, manhood departs." Major Jarvis, in his capacity as governor of Sinai between the World Wars, once tried to interest his charges in growing vegetables by what he called "backdoor methods." He issued an edict forbidding the planting of seed, whereupon the Bedouins perversely planted seed in every damp spot for a while. But a British-style agricultural show the major promoted was a disaster. The Bedouins dressed up their animals in rags and bought succulent vegetables from Cairo to put on display.) The Israeli experiment was the conception of a legendary civil administrator of the Sinai named Moshe Sela (whom everybody calls "Moshe Vehetzi"—"Moses and a Half"—because of his height). He became a Sinai legend as a result of his selfless dedication to Bedouin welfare and improvement. It was said that he could perform miracles, even when dealing with such a formidable force as the Israeli bureaucracy. We hoped to look him up at the Civil Administration Center near the monastery.

But first there was a mixed bag of sights to see: for instance, the Mount Sinai airport, a trig, modern airfield which would be a credit to any small American city, about twenty kilometers north of its namesake. Developed from an old military landing strip in a broad wadi, it had eight Arkia planes lined up on the tarmac, discharging and taking on passengers. The airport, more than anything else, was responsible for the latest invaders of the Sinai—the legions of tourists, who were making life miserable for the St. Catherine's monks —by reducing what was once a difficult safari into the Mount Sinai area to just a short flight from Tel Aviv or Jerusalem. The airport lies before the eruption of jagged, red-granite high peaks rising south of the Watiya Pass, the scene of the last great intertribal war, between the bellicose Sawalha and Aleigat tribes, in the tenth century. Control of the vital pass meant control over this south-central region of glorious heights and venerated holy places.

Not all the holy places are Christian and Jewish. South of the Watiya Pass and not far from St. Catherine's is the Tomb of Nebi Saleh, a plain, whitewashed, domed building often described as "The Mecca of Sinai." Just who Nebi Saleh was is still a moot point. The holiest saint for the south Sinai Bedouins—collectively spoken of as the Towara, or People of Tor (the Mountain)—may or may not have predated Islam. Professor Palmer believed that this righteous prophet was a charismatic sheikh, the progenitor of the Sawalha tribe, whose miracles (such as producing a she-camel from a rock near the Mount Sinai summit, the "footprint" of which is still evident) were adopted by Mohammed during his visit to the Sinai. The exploits of Nebi Saleh were confused with the deeds of Mohammed, as well as those of Moses and Elijah. It could be said that Nebi Saleh is a Bedouin distortion of the tales credited to all these holy men.

Whatever the case, the tomb itself has become the site of annual feasts held by the Towara tribes. The celebrating Bedouins cover themselves with dust from the tomb for good luck, sacrifice sheep, race camels to the ululating of the women, bury their dead and pray near the tomb, and, after all that, mount a *mesamerah,* or fantasia, with dancing, singing, hand-clapping, animal imitations, and a gargantuan feast often consisting of a roasted camel stuffed with a roasted sheep stuffed with a roasted goat. There was no celebration taking place at the tomb when I stopped by, but a few Bedouins were praying outside and placing humble offerings (bits of cloth, wild flowers, and candles) inside. As they entered the tomb, they recited the traditional prayer, "There is no God but Allah and Mohammed is His Prophet," and prostrated themselves before the shrouded catafalque facing Mecca, which indicated that whether or not Nebi Saleh predated Islam, he was certainly a Moslem now.

Passing buses crowded with sweaty, disappointed travelers returning to the airport from the closed monastery, and happier Israeli youngsters setting up tents in camping grounds, we bumped

The Plain of Raha, viewed from near St. Catherine's
Monastery. *Magnum.*

down the road toward Mount Sinai, the goal of countless thousands
since the Exodus. Before us was the Plain of Raha, the vast, baked
flats where the Israelites had camped and doubted and grumbled
while awaiting the theophany and law-giving from the Mount.
Could the Plain of Raha hold the entire Israelite host? Perhaps. But
could this arid stretch of sand and stone support them and their
livestock for more than a few days, without constant life-giving
miracles? And, for that matter, was this area the site of the true
Mount Sinai? The Exodus—one of the world's greatest and best-
known tales of survival, freedom, and revelation—was still a subject
of heated debate among scholars, the most contentious event in the

Old Testament. Who was where and with what and with whom can, and probably will, be argued till doomsday.

Apart from all the wilder speculations on Exodus wanderings, the theories can be broken down into two basic geographical concepts: the Southern, or traditional, Route and the Northern, or scientific, one. As every Sunday-school child knows, the Southern Route has Moses and the Israelites fleeing Egypt through the parted Red Sea, somewhere in the vicinity of the Bitter Lakes, near present-day Ismailia. After the sea waters closed in on their Egyptian pursuers, they proceeded southeast along the Sinai coast, past the springs of Marah and Elim, through the oases of the Wadi Firan, and then on to Mount Sinai, Hazeroth, Kadesh Barnea, and, decades later, the Promised Land. The Northern Route is the brainchild of the academics, the scientists, who reason that the Israelites crossed not the "Red Sea" but the "Reed Sea" (*Yam Suf,* in Hebrew). This, they argue, could well be the reedy, marshy El Tina Flats and the Bardawil Lagoon along the northern Mediterranean coast. The lagoon, especially, could be considered a separate sea because it is divided from the Mediterranean by a narrow, curving spit of sand along which the Israelites might have traveled. During severe storms, the sand spit is often breached by the Mediterranean, and the unwary —say, Egyptian soldiers riding in heavy chariots—would be engulfed and drowned. This would leave the Israelites free to roam through the dunes of northeastern Sinai to Gebel Halal (the Northern Route "Mount Sinai"), Kadesh Barnea, and, ultimately, Canaan.

The Northern Route theorists offer all sorts of logical points to back up their argument. For instance, manna and quail, which God provided for the hungry wanderers, are more plentiful in the north than in the south. Manna is thought to be the sweet, small, whitish deposit left on the ground after certain scale insects feed on the tamarisk tree. North Sinai Bedouins call it *mann* and still use it as a sweetener. Migrating quail fall from exhaustion on the strand near the Bardawil Lagoon after crossing the Mediterranean on their way from Europe to Africa. The fat, oily birds seem to be divinely delivered, and they are easily caught in nets by the Bedouins and sold as delicacies. Other points supporting the argument are that Moses would have avoided the Egyptian soldiers garrisoned at the Serabit El Khadim turquoise mines, only fifty miles from Mount Sinai; that the Lord's "pillar of a cloud" to guide the Israelites by day and the "pillar of fire" to guide them by night are common natural occurrences along the Mediterranean littoral in the spring, towering thunderheads moving west to east with night lightning; that just about every Exodus place-name has an equivalent geographic name in the north (even Gebel Halal can be construed to mean "Mountain of the Lawful"). To these arguments, the Southern Route traditionalists answer that theirs is the accepted route, more closely aligned with the biblical text, especially in place-names. Also, they say, the Bible clearly states that "God led them not through the way of the land of the Philistines"—the northern, Via Maris road—"although that was near; for God said, Lest peradventure the people repent when they see war, and they return to Egypt. But God led the people about, through the way of the wilderness of the Red Sea."

Perhaps the most unorthodox concept of the Exodus was suggested by Professor Zeev Meshel, the Tel Aviv University archeologist who explored the Judean center at El Kuntilla. "The Old Testament, as we know it today, is the work of different editors," Meshel had told me during a Jerusalem interview, "and these editors made the place-names very definite. One place-name we can absolutely identify is 'the way of the land of the Philistines,' because that is surely the Via Maris. But the Philistines didn't even exist during the time of the Exodus, so the reference to them is an anachronism. There were invading armies and caravans using that route then, which could have made trouble for the Israelites, but no Philistines. It is useless to identify biblical place-names." (The American biblical scholar Edward Robinson concurred: he wrote dryly, "A tolerably certain method of finding any place at will is to ask an Arab if its name exists. He is sure to answer yes, and to point out some point at hand as its location. In this way, I have no doubt, we might have found a Rephidim, or Marah, or any place we chose.")

Professor Meshel also suggested that the Israelites "stumbled" on the Promised Land, that while the Old Testament was being edited "the fixed aim to Canaan" was added as an embellishment. Therefore, there could have been many routes and many Mount Sinais. "It might have taken forty or four hundred years for them to find Canaan," Meshel said. "Old Egyptian records tell of tribes searching for water in dry years and emigrating in better times. Perhaps there were several exoduses from Egypt, each migration wandering in the desert until good land was found, like the Bed-

Sinai holy tomb. *Magnum.*

ouins do today. The Israelites were nomads in Sinai and their habits were similar to the Bedouins'."

The similarity between the Israelites and the Bedouins is what might be termed the Moses-Jethro link. According to the Bible, Moses, while a member of the Pharaoh's court, killed an Egyptian overseer who was beating a Hebrew slave. He fled for his life to the Sinai and there he met Jethro (also known as Reuel), the sheikh of sheikhs of the Midianite tribe, whose territory covered both the east and west sides of the Gulf of Akaba. He lived for years as a shepherd with Jethro and married Jethro's daughter, Zipporah. More importantly, he was imbued with the natural mysteries of the Sinai and the revelation of a single, all-powerful God, through the appearance at the base of Mount Horeb (an interchangeable biblical name for Mount Sinai) of the Burning Bush that was not consumed by flames. The voice of God spoke to him from the fire and instructed him to "bring forth my people the children of Israel out of Egypt." Faced with this awesome mission, Moses had to conceive a code of life for the survival of his people, burdened as they were with a slave mentality, once they had been delivered from bondage and were loose in the wilderness. This is where Jethro's influence came in. Jethro, through the years, had taught Moses the Bedouin rules for desert survival, tribal organization, and, some say, even the idea of monotheism. In a sense, Moses' Bedouin father-in-law was the prime earthly instrument in the Israelites' painful trek to freedom. Bailey saw yet a greater influence by Jethro on Moses. "When Moses led his basically urban, enslaved people into the Sinai, he had to mold them into a tough national entity," he told me. "If they were to survive, they would have to live by the rules of the desert. I believe that Moses learned these rules well from Jethro and adapted them into his own codes, as God-given. There are absolute parallels between Bedouin desert codes and the Mosaic laws of the Torah—the same complicated, detailed regulations for living in the most primitive circumstances. For instance, I found that the Mosaic instruction about what to do if two men are arguing and a pregnant woman comes by and the unborn child is harmed as a result is straight from Bedouin law. I'm doing a great deal of

work on these parallels to prove my point." And, of course, there
is the obvious link between Bedouin hospitality and the Mosaic
instruction that "the stranger that dwelleth with you shall be unto
you as one born among you, and thou shalt love him as thyself."

The contemporary Bedouins in the immediate Mount Sinai area
could hardly be more removed from Jethro's Midianites. They are
the Jebeliya (People of the Mountains), a tribe descended from one
hundred Wallachian slaves dispatched to the Sinai by Emperor
Justinian to serve the monks at St. Catherine's. Over the years, they
married Egyptian women and were converted to Islam; however,
they were never accepted by other Sinai Bedouins because they
were somehow different—not purely Arabian in looks or breeding,
loyal to the monks and not the Bedouin hierarchy, and too Westernized in thought and learning. As we drove by some Jebeliya on
our way to the Civil Administration Center, I noticed—or imagined
I noticed—a different look to them. They seemed taller than other
Bedouins and a few had brown hair and blue eyes. Adept at rough-
stone construction, they have built sturdy granaries on the moun-
tainsides. The majority of them live in tents throughout the region
or in the monastery itself. Intermingled with these stone granaries
are retreat houses owned by the monastery. A prominent convert
to the Greek Orthodox Church, the daughter of Nazi Field Marshal
Erwin Rommel ("The Desert Fox"), spends part of every year in
contemplation at one of these houses.

We arrived at the kibbutzlike compound of the Civil Administration Center, an outpost of modern Israel in the midst of antiquity.
The compound consisted of an office, barracks, mess hall, repair
shops, garage, school, clinic, and twenty-five extremely serious Israeli administrators and ten industrious Jebeliya mechanics, cooks,
and menial laborers. We asked to see Moshe Sela and learned that
he was no longer with the Civil Administration but had fallen
victim, at last, to the bureaucracy. A strikingly beautiful Israeli
woman named Leki (government and military personnel in sensitive areas usually disclose only their first names, for security reasons) was temporarily in charge since Sela's ouster. She and her

assistant, a dark-skinned Indian-born girl named Leah, agreed to talk to us, when they weren't shouting into the microphone of a cranky radio, which maintained sporadic communication between the center and the administrators in the field. (They were having particular difficulty raising somebody called "Rootie"—Ruthie, I assumed—and our entire conversation was punctuated by cries of "Rootie! Rootie!")

The first question for Leki that came to mind was, What's a beautiful woman like you doing in a place like this? The answer, given with just the hint of a flattered smile, was that she had lost her husband in the 1973 Yom Kippur War and wanted to get away from Israel proper. She had heard of the wonderful things Moshe Sela was doing for the Bedouins in the Sinai and decided to join the Civil Administration. "I love it here," she said, via Bailey's simultaneous translating. "We all do. We are very sensitive to the Bedouins' habits and culture. If we didn't get into the spirit and rhythm of this place, we couldn't live here. Our doctors, for example, are army reservists assigned here, and they never fail to end up loving the duty. They treat the Bedouins both at the clinic and, by four-wheel-drive trucks, in their encampments. If the Bedouins are very sick, or in hard childbirth, they are sent to an Elath or Tel Aviv hospital. Our agricultural officers, too, spend days in the field with the Bedouins, showing them how to dig reinforced wells and grow better crops. We help just the Bedouins, not the monks or anybody else, unless there's an emergency. You see"—she gestured toward a Jebeliya cook, dressed in jeans and sneakers, working in the nearby kitchen—"we hire Bedouins, so we provide jobs and help the economy, also."

I asked her about Moshe Sela, and the very mention of his name filled her with emotion. "Everything we have done here in the south Sinai at all our administration centers is due to him," she said. "Since 1968, he was many things to the Bedouins, including a kind friend, and he understood them. We have never had acts of sabotage or terror here, again thanks to him. Some people think we are too radically changing the Bedouin way of life by giving them good health, schooling, a better living, even electricity, but I don't think so. They have so little. They need so much help. How can it be wrong?"

The staff present at the compound was about to have lunch in the mess hall, and Bailey and I were invited to share it. The meal was better than the usual kibbutz fare: the famous Israeli Army "loaf" (pressed meatlike matter, not bad when heavily seasoned; Bailey had survived almost exclusively on "loaf" when he had served a four-month army-reserve stint at an isolated post), a fresh salad, pot roast and gravy, sliced white bread, pickled tomatoes ("Just like Zabar's," said one of the staff who had lived in New York), apples, and tea. We and the civil administrators sat at a long table, shuttling the various dishes to each other boardinghouse fashion. At separate tables were the Jebeliya workers (the only Bedouins I had ever seen eating off plates with knives and forks) and some English and French archeologists who, by arrangement, ate at the compound when they weren't digging at a nearby site. We all ate slowly and talked little, which is the best practice in the Sinai midday heat. One subject that came up for discussion was the latest news about an Israeli from Galilee nicknamed "Abu Musa" ("Father Moses") by the Bedouins. He was described as a saintly, charitable man who had taken on the unpaid task of visiting Bedouins being treated at Israeli hospitals in order to help them with their problems, ease their culture shock, and generally comfort them. As far as anybody could tell, he did this simply because he liked Bedouins.

An old man sat down at our table, a bit late for lunch. His name was Mayani and he had emigrated to Israel from Poland, becoming a master carpenter in Petah Tikva, a town outside of Tel Aviv. He said that Moshe Sela had talked him into working as the carpenter for the Civil Administration, also teaching Bedouins the trade, and that he had never regretted moving here, although his family in Petah Tikva thought he was crazy. His Yiddish-accented Hebrew seemed to brighten everyone, and the tempo of conversation and joking increased. After lunch, we all helped to clean up. Every morsel of spilled food was scrupulously removed, the tables were scrubbed, and soon the mess hall was spotless. Bedouin workers did the heavier K.P. chores, and I suspected that the example of diligent hygiene was partly for their benefit. It seemed to work. There were very few Sinai flies about. The only plague was the incessant, droning diesel generator in an adjacent building. Apart from the generator, it was a pleasant lunch. Leaving the compound, I said to Bailey, "You see, not all missionaries are bad."

Now it was time to mount a frontal assault on St. Catherine's. Those who had already tried and failed were making their way back down a rutted wadi road toward a Field School, like the one at Yamit, where they could spend the night. As the Land-Rover approached a stern-faced Jebeliya guard stationed at a thick chain strung across the road, I felt as if I were the latest extension of all the assaults on the fortress-monastery over the years. In the fourth century, the monks, anchorites, and pilgrims living in the vicinity of Empress Helena's chapel of the Burning Bush were beset by Bedouin raiders, as were their fellow believers in Firan. Ammonius, an Egyptian monk of the era, described in his journal how the "Ishmaelites" attacked the Sinai settlement, plundering, defiling, eating holy wafers, and murdering thirty-eight before being frightened off by a fire on Mount Sinai. Even Nubian nomads invaded from across the Red Sea and slaughtered forty-one Christians, but they were eradicated by the Bedouins, for they had been trespassing on tribal lands. One hermit, it was said, turned himself into a palm tree to escape the slaughter.

In order to stabilize his position in the Holy Land and protect the Christians, Emperor Justinian ordered the construction of a fortress to surround the Mount Sinai church and settlement in about 530. Five-foot-square granite blocks, many of them engraved with Maltese crosses, were stacked one upon the other to form the outer walls, and towers fitted with covered ramparts for bowmen were constructed by imported masons. A completely self-contained town was erected within the walls surrounding the approximately eight-thousand-square-yard area, and given the monastery's isolated location, it was considered a man-made wonder. The only trouble was that its site was at the base of Mount Sinai, a strategically unsound position for a fortress. According to Eutychius, a patriarch of Alexandria, the supervisor of the construction, one Doulas, had built the monastery at the base of the mountain for the plentiful water found there and to spare the inhabitants from spooky thunder and other heavenly phenomena witnessed at night on the peak. For his solicitous, if unmilitary, concern, Doulas was executed by Justinian, once the emperor heard about the blunder. Of course, all the Bedouin raiders had to do to harass the monastery was simply roll stones down the mountain right into the settlement. The Christians were still under siege much of the time.

Later, the church and monastery were rededicated to St. Catherine, who, as a young girl in fourth-century Alexandria, had been converted to Christianity by a Syrian monk. During the persecution of Christians by the Roman Emperor Maximian, she was tortured for her aggressive proselytizing by being strapped to revolving spiked wheels, which miraculously didn't tear her to pieces. (St. Catherine is the patron saint of wheelwrights.) She was, however, subsequently beheaded. After her elevation to sainthood, it was revealed to a Mount Sinai monk that her body had been borne by angels to the highest peak in the Sinai peninsula, just south of Mount Sinai. The monks climbed to the top of the peak and discovered her bones there along with a strange deposit of oil. They interred the bones near the altar of the Burning Bush and renamed both the monastery and the mountain peak in her honor. The bones allegedly continued to exude oil, which was collected by the monks, who considered it a powerful and holy panacea. A cult of the virgin and martyr Catherine swept Europe in the Middle Ages, and the monks of St. Catherine's were the recipients of lavish gifts from nobility, in return for some of her alleged finger bones and vials of the wondrous oil. Most of the priceless treasures in the monastery today date from the largesse associated with the cult, which waned somewhat in later years.

The Bedouins had an equally inventive version of how the monastery came to be dedicated. They told Professor Palmer that Nebi Musa (or Holy Moses, as it were) arrived in Sinai with the Israelites and, thankful for his deliverance from the Egyptians, decided to erect a house of worship to commemorate the event. The next morning, his chief mason found that all the tools had disappeared. Moses discovered the tools at the base of Mount Sinai. Heeding the omen, he laid the foundation for the monastery, which was completed by his daughter—none other than a woman named St. Catherine. The Bedouins also believed that the monastery was under the special protection of Heaven, and anyone with evil designs upon it would be punished. This belief has been encouraged by the monks, who have been known to outfit the Bedouins with crosses to be worn as protective charms.

During the explosion of Islam in the seventh century, the monastery was assailed by a new force, the Moslem hordes. Since the peninsula was, in effect, a province of the Hejaz, the Christians were barely tolerated and often oppressed. The Jebeliya were forcibly converted to Islam, along with a few less-committed Christians, and the monastery's outbuildings were destroyed. It was said that a mosque was constructed by the monks within the monastery walls in honor of Mohammed's alleged visit as a boy to the area, but more likely, as a means of protection against Moslem raiders. (The story was also spread by the monks that Mohammed had later issued to the monastery a firman of immunity from persecution.) Another version has it that Moslem troops were so impressed by the monks' courage in the face of certain annihilation that their sultan ordered the monastery spared, provided that a mosque be erected on the place where Mohammed had once set foot. Actually, the mosque was built in the early 1100s for Moslem soldiers sent to the Sinai to fight the Crusaders. But for most of the Crusades, the monastery was firmly under the shield of the Frankish knights, some of whose crests and names were carved on wooden doors and refectory walls. Indeed, St. Catherine's thrived, receiving generous gifts from European rulers. After the Kingdom of Jerusalem fell in 1187, Moslem permission was required for pilgrimages, but the monks enjoyed a ten-percent tax on all goods brought into El Tor, until the fifteenth century. Thereafter, the monastery became increasingly dependent on the Russian tsars, who subsidized the monks in return for religious relics and art.

By the time Napoleon conquered Egypt and the Sinai at the end of the eighteenth century, the monastery was in a sad state of disrepair and disuse. Napoleon offered protection to the monks and sent General Jean Kléber on an expedition to survey St. Catherine's, where the general found only six bedraggled monks and twenty-two lay brothers in attendance. Floods had destroyed the eastern wall and some of the buildings, and so Kléber dispatched Cairene masons to renovate the structure. But the French had their own problems in the Sinai and soon withdrew, leaving the monks again in a tenuous position. Through it all, though, the monastery stood—never captured by infidels, always hanging on, sometimes by the frailest of threads. And through it all, too, the pilgrims came, the tourists of their eras. In the sixth century, as many as eight hundred were there at one time, causing the two hundred or so monks to complain about feeding them all. Sickness and plague afflicted them, and those who arrived over the desert as penitents withstood remarkable suffering. In the Middle Ages, it was the custom for murderers doing penance to go on pilgrimages bound in fetters forged from their murder weapons. Two Breton brothers who had killed their uncle were thus fettered and sent on a pilgrimage to Rome, Jerusalem, and St. Catherine's. Like manufactured Siamese twins they arrived at the monastery, climbed Mount Sinai, and attempted to return to Brittany, still chained together. Whether or not they completed the round trip is not known.

Nowadays, the visitors were an international mix of travelers, fettered with cameras and camping gear, and the monks were more in despair than ever. The Jebeliya guard at the chain across the road shook his head vigorously when we tried to drive past. Bailey spoke to him in Arabic and showed him our letters of introduction to Archbishop Damianos, the head of the monastery and the Order of St. Catherine. It seemed to work. We were let through—a small but significant victory.

Just ahead at the end of the track was Gebel Maneijar, the place of the first meeting between God and Moses. A spot of green and a tiny white chapel marked what the monks believe is the location of the heavenly dialogue. Then, presenting itself like a scale model of a desert fort, complete with oasis garden and cypress trees, was the monastery, set on a slight rise from the wadi floor to the base of Mount Sinai. Against the sheer, irregular granite side of the mountain, every stone and fissure perfectly in focus under the brilliant sunlight of a cloudless blue sky, it seemed at once tiny and gigantic—a compact, enclosed town hiding behind towering stone barriers. Up close, only the tips of the campanile, the mosque, and the dormitory dome could be seen over the walls. We parked and walked up some outside stairs to the west gate, in a courtyard just above the garden. Not a person was in sight, not so much as a stray tourist. At last, we heard a voice call to us in Arabic. It was a Jebeliya porter leaning from a small window high up in the wall overlooking the gate. Bailey told him our purpose in being there —that we wished to spend the night at the monastery, see its treasures, visit with the monks, and climb Mount Sinai early in the morning. The Bedouin answered circumspectly that all the monks were at prayer and nobody would be available to discuss our requests until five o'clock. We said we'd wait.

With two hours to kill before we knew whether we would be welcome or not, I decided to climb the mountain across the wadi from the monastery for a better view of Mount Sinai. Bailey stretched out in the shade of the courtyard wall to rest for whatever circumstance lay ahead. The breeze was strong and refreshing once I had climbed out of the wadi. Halfway up the mountain, on a ledge polished smooth by wind and time, were a hidden spring and pool, surrounded by stunted palms. I washed my face and drank from the icy, sweet water of the spring. Within the one hundred and eighty degrees of view open to me from this vantage point was an enormous chunk of history and legend, a vast panorama of Western culture and thought—Gebel Maneijar to my left, Mount Sinai and the monastery just in front of me, and the broad Plain of Raha down the wadi to my right. How absurd and beautiful the monastery looked from up there! Always ridiculous from a military standpoint, it no longer pretended to be a fortress, its ramparts filled in with stone and its cannon long gone. Teetering piles of boulders, just waiting, it seemed, to become avalanches at the slightest nudge, were poised on the mountainside directly over the walled compound. Its existence was so fragile and incongruous. Yet, its very inappropriateness in this godly, wild setting was a testimonial to tenacity and faith.

Mount Sinai grew ominous in jagged silhouette against the setting sun. If this mountain wasn't the veritable site, it would nevertheless do. It had all the right elements: grandeur, beauty, mystery. "Horeb," "Gebel Musa," "Mount Sinai," "The Mountain of God," or simply "The Mountain"—these were the names given to the peak by Jews, Christians, and Arabs. It was the Christians who were intent on setting an exact geographical designation for the mountain of the legend. Up till the fifth century, the designation had been at nearby Gebel Serbal, but then pilgrims changed their minds in favor of the present, more lofty location because of Bedouin tales of eerie rumblings on Gebel Musa and expeditions to test the stories. An intrepid, rather liberated nun named Etheria took it upon herself to climb Gebel Musa in order to see if the biblical sites were feasible on that mountain, and her reports, more than anything else, brought about the geographical change. With the celebrity of the Burning Bush chapel at the base of Gebel Musa, it was fully accepted in Christian and Arab circles that the mountain was indeed the true Sinai. (The latest confirmation has come from an unexpected source, President Sadat of Egypt, who, during a heady moment in the erratic peace negotiating, announced plans for a Christian-Moslem-Jewish shrine to be built on the peak, once, of course, Israel ceded the peninsula to Egypt. He also invited Pope John Paul II to pray there and suggested that the treaty-signing ceremony take place on the summit. Begin vetoed the treaty-signing ceremony idea, for religious and, perhaps, physical reasons. "To climb up at dawn to the summit in the belief that it is the place where Moses received the Ten Commandments is artificial and not serious," he said. Mount Sinai will be returned to Egypt during the nine-month withdrawal phase.)

But what of the Jewish tradition of Mount Sinai, which, after all, promoted the legend in the first place? Strangely enough, the Jews have never set an exact location for the mountain, although most now accept Gebel Musa as the probable place. Its precise location

A view from Mount Sinai. *Magnum.*

really doesn't matter so much. What seems more important is the mystique attached to the mountain. In rabbinical lore, all Jewish souls, past, present, and future, were on Mount Sinai when God made the covenant with His Chosen People. Isaac Bashevis Singer put it another way, in his novel *Shosha:* a character says, "We are running away and Mount Sinai runs after us. This chase has made us sick and mad." Beyond the recitation in the Old Testament of events that occurred on the mountain—the announcement of the law-giving to Moses, the theatrical presentation of the Ten Commandments, the divine instruction in the laws of the Torah, the pagan manufacture of the golden calf, the smashing of the tablets by a furious Moses, the reinstitution of the tablets by a "horned" Moses (actually, a misinterpretation of the Hebrew word for "shone," which is similar to the word for "horned"; the Bible says that Moses's face shone when he came down from the mountain carrying the new tablets)—beyond all that, there is a cabalistic mystique about Mount Sinai, wherever it is. It holds that God chose Mount Sinai for His theophany over all others—especially Mount Tabor, Mount Carmel, and Mount Hermon—because no idols were ever upon it. (More hard-headed scholars have pointed out, however, that the trumpets, fire, smoke, and thunder observed by the Israelites on Mount Sinai have roots in pagan Semitic festivals, when idols were as plentiful as donkeys.) Mount Sinai and the Temple Mount in Jerusalem (Mount Moriah) were the two sacred places through whose virtue the world existed. The mystics said that after the coming of the Messiah, God would bring Sinai, Tabor, and Carmel together and all three mountains would sing His praises. Keeping with this rabbinical pathetic fallacy, Mount Hermon, weeping over its exclusion, was made by God the highest mountain in the Promised Land and presented with an enviable cap of snow as compensation. Its tears became the Jordan River. In short, Mount Sinai is to Jews not so much a place as an intangible symbol, in a sense as meaningful as the Holy Ghost is to Christians.

It was almost five o'clock, the hour of decision. I made my way down the mountain and around the back wall of the monastery, the side closest to Mount Sinai. The rarefied feeling of being in the presence of deathless history, which I had experienced up on the mountain, was dispelled by the trash heap I stumbled upon outside the back wall—a town dump of tin cans, liquor bottles, half-burned garbage, plastic containers, and such discarded odds and ends as a broken toilet seat and a split garden hose. It was as if a wild picnic had taken place in the shadow of holiness, saluting godhood with rubbish. Even here in the sanctity of the wilderness there was a waste-disposal problem. I walked on top of the wall over the monks' garden, a flourishing rectangle of greenery with cypresses, palms, fruit trees, grape vines, vegetables, flowers, and penned animals, including a peacock. An aqueduct brought water to the garden and telephone lines led in from the direction of the Israeli Field School. Both the newer and older garden stones were etched with graffiti in Greek, Arabic, and Hebrew, some, according to the engraved dates, more than a hundred years old. Tourists never change.

There was more activity in the courtyard than when I had left Bailey there, two hours earlier. Bailey was talking in English with a cherubic blond, blue-eyed German girl in her twenties and an older woman who was unmistakably her mother. They were Christiane and Elisabeth Rahmer, from Frankfurt am Main, and they were touring the Holy Land on a shoestring. They had taken a bus to Nuweiba, another bus to the Field School, and had hiked in to the monastery, assuming they would be welcomed by the monks. They had since been told by the porter, via Bailey's translation, that they would not be welcomed and that they should leave the premises. Their feet were bruised from walking down the wadi road in cheap plastic sandals. With no place to stay, with no more equipment than a water bottle and a small rucksack containing tins of food and a change of clothing, they were weary, scared, and confused. Christiane said she had spent a month at a foreigners' kibbutz in Israel five years before but had never run into anything like this. Bailey and I promised to see what we could do for them, if indeed we were allowed into the monastery ourselves. "We will appeal to the monks' Christian charity," I told them.

Resting near the huge metal-clad wooden gate was a party of well-dressed South Americans, who, Bailey informed me, were the Venezuelan Ambassador to Israel, his wife, children, and servants. The ambassador had used his influence to be assured of accommodations at the monastery and was cooling his heels, waiting for the gate to be opened. The delay, apparently, was due to the imminent arrival of a hiking troop of Israeli teen-agers, led by armed guides from the Field School, coming down the wadi road. Bailey spoke to the Jebeliya porter in the window again and learned that the monks would not open the gate until the Israelis withdrew. They arrived in the courtyard—laughing, singing, joshing, generally underdressed—and proceeded to listen inattentively to one of their guides lecture them on the history of St. Catherine's. As the lecturer droned on in Hebrew, we were all getting anxious, particularly the Venezuelans. At one point, Bailey spoke to an armed guide, explaining the delicate situation. The guide shrugged in the Israeli manner—as if to say "If they don't like us, to hell with them"—but in a few minutes he marched his troop off toward the Field School.

As soon as they were out of sight and earshot, we heard the sound of bars being removed from behind the gate, which then swung open to reveal a bearded young monk, clad in the dark gown and fezlike hat of the Greek Orthodox monastic orders. He motioned to the Venezuelans to enter and said in Arabic to Bailey that he would like to see our letters of introduction. Affecting an air of indifference and making sucking sounds through his teeth, he slowly read the letters, both of them in Greek, to Archbishop Damianos. When he had finished reading, he said that the Archbishop was away in Cairo. He would have to consult with the senior monk about our entry to the monastery. As for the German women, it was extremely doubtful that they could stay. He closed the gate and barred it. We told the Rahmers not to worry, that we would somehow find a place for them to spend the night, perhaps in the Land-Rover. The monk's pompous attitude had frightened and disturbed them, they said; they were pious Roman Catholics and were not used to such treatment from the clergy. They had scrimped and saved for this trip, and, up to now, everyone had been kind to them. "We do not understand," Elisabeth said. At six o'clock, the gate opened again and the young monk told Bailey and me that we could enter. What about the German women? He regarded them closely, as if they were camels for sale, while making that curious sucking sound. After a long moment, he nodded pontifically. They, too, could enter.

We quickly unloaded all we would need from the Land-Rover, since the gates would be locked for the night once we had gone into the monastery. Then, carrying our gear, we followed the young monk, single file, through the portal into a dark tunnel and up some stairs to a central courtyard. The interior of the monastery was lovely and complicated. Whitewashed buildings, each with a different function, strained against one another and the exterior walls for space. There was no architectural logic to the enclosed town, like the anarchic charm of a hillside Italian fishing village. Several Jebeliya Bedouins were about, speaking in Greek to a few monks. (I later learned that fewer than a dozen monks are at the monastery at any one time, not counting those who reside in seclusion at chapels in the mountains. An Israeli who has had many contacts with the monks since 1967 told me that duty at St. Catherine's is considered a kind of punishment for members of the order, and so the intellectual and moral qualities of the monks there are not exemplary. However, all the members of the order, whether they serve in Greece, Syria, Egypt, Rumania, or the Sinai, want to be interred in the St. Catherine's Monastery ossuary when they die.)

The young monk led us to a terrace outside the archbishop's sitting room, near the living quarters. Within the sitting room, we could see the Venezuelans having coffee and chatting with the senior monk. When they had finished their coffee, they were directed to motel-like rooms nearby, the Jebeliya carrying their luggage for them. At last, the senior monk approached us, as we huddled together like refugees on the terrace. His bony, ascetic face betrayed testiness at our presence. We were obviously a nuisance. "What are your requests?" he asked us, through the Arabic-speaking young monk. Bailey told him that we, including the German women, would like to stay the night in whatever accommodations were available, buy bread and any other obtainable food for dinner, climb Mount Sinai with a guide early in the morning, and then visit the church, Burning Bush chapel, library, and ossuary before leaving. Of course, we would pay for these services. An animated discussion in Greek between the two monks followed. It was difficult to tell which one was for us and which one was against us. Finally, the senior monk addressed us. He told us that we could spend the night in the dormitory, have dinner in the dining room with our own food (only bread, water, tea, and sugar would be supplied by the monks), climb the mountain with a Jebeliya guide at 3:30 A.M., and, perhaps, after the morning Mass, see the church, library, and ossuary. We thanked him, and he answered rather coldly in English, "Welcome."

An aged Bedouin led us across the compound to the dormitory, the biggest building within the walls. We followed him up three long flights of stairs. On one of the landings, a sign in English read:

ALTITUDE MONASTERY 5,012 feet
MOSES MOUNT 7,560 feet
ST CATHERINE MOUNT 8,576 feet
CAIRO–SUEZ 127 kms
SUEZ–MONASTERY 280 kms
CAIRO–MONASTERY 407 kms

Bailey and I were assigned to Room 23, a dingy, buggy cell on the top floor, but relieved we were to be there. The German women were given the room next door. We four were the only guests in the enormous dormitory, capable of holding several hundred people, as it had centuries ago. A large window overlooked the trash dump outside the back wall at the foot of the mountain. Faded blue paint covered the room's plaster walls, and a mirror, two cots, a writing desk, one chair, and a single bare light bulb hanging from the ceiling completed the furnishings. Seeing swarms of tiny bugs, I immediately thought of the Miracle of the Fleas. At one point in the monastery's early history, it was plagued by a virulent infestation of fleas, which drove the monks to escape en masse to the top of Mount Sinai. The Virgin Mary appeared before them and said that the monastery was now flealess. When they descended, they found that this was indeed true, and they later built a chapel on the mountain commemorating the wonderful event. Just to be on the safe side, though, I unrolled my sleeping bag over the cot.

The dormitory dining room—seedy, cavernous, and decorated with tacky religious murals—became the scene of a delightful impromptu dinner. The four of us, of course, felt somewhat slighted at not being asked to break bread in the refectory with the monks and the Venezuelans, but the two Jebeliya in the adjoining kitchen were gracious and supplied us with cool water, plastic spoons, salt, tea, sugar, and home-baked bread—a hybrid loaf of hard *pita* and chewy Greek bread. To that, Bailey and I added our own provi-

CLOCKWISE FROM ABOVE:

Jebeliyas in the courtyard at St. Catherine's. *Magnum.*

A view from St. Catherine's Monastery. *Magnum.*

A scene at St. Catherine's, by the Well of Moses. *Magnum.*

The door of the church at St. Catherine's. *Magnum.*

Monks at St. Catherine's. *Magnum.*

Part of the interior of St. Catherine's Monastery. *Magnum.*

sions of canned corn, peas, and fish, four oranges, and Scotch. The German women contributed all they had in the way of food—some nondescript processed cheese and something called "Paté Vegetal," a bland soybean concoction, palatable when spread on bread with plenty of salt. We were all hungry and thankful for what we had (the Germans were absolutely ecstatic, in fact), and the sharing of food and conversation put us in intimate good spirits, the kind people participating together in a spontaneous adventure know best.

The monks of St. Catherine's have had their critics before. Procopius spoke of their life as "a careful study of death," and Reverend D. A. Randall, the Thurberian Columbus, Ohio, clergyman who trekked through the Holy Land in the mid-1800s, wrote that he was "not very favorably impressed either with their intelligence or usefulness." Professor Palmer was most critical, stating that the monks demonstrated "no care for anything but indolence and rum." When he visited the monastery in the middle of the nineteenth century, he was shocked to discover that they wouldn't hold church services unless the pilgrims demanded them. He was, however, touched by their giving loaves of bread daily to the local Bedouins, through a covered window in the north wall. (The monks no longer lower the loaves to the Bedouins through the window, but they continue to give bread to any Arab who comes to the main gate and asks for it.) But, perhaps, some visitors to the monastery have been uncharitable toward the monks, I thought as I strolled alone about the congested parapets and walkways after dinner. Their life here certainly was not easy. All they probably wanted from this world was to be left in religious insularity, free from mundane cares. Yet, throughout the centuries they have had to put up with waves of Bedouin raiders, fanatic Moslems, Frankish knights, penitent pilgrims, alien warriors, and now brash Israeli youngsters and history-hungry tourists.

I wandered down the long stoa in front of the dormitory, observing such compromises with modern life as a well-equipped dispensary, including a dentist chair and drill, a room housing an electric generator (which, we were informed, would be shut down at nine o'clock), storerooms containing canned goods, fresh vegetables, blankets, mechanical tools, and fire extinguishers (a precaution taken since a 1971 blaze, which was put out, with the help of the Israeli Army, before any serious damage occurred). I passed the open door of a monk's cell and saw its occupant reading a Greek newspaper under a bare bulb, an old sewing machine at his side. The last light of day was failing fast. I climbed the parapet over the main, or north, gate, from which I could look down on the church and the mosque, both in the center of the compound. The church appeared simple enough from the outside—standard rectangular Byzantine design with wooden roof and sandstone Russian campanile—but I knew what riches adorned the interior. The mosque, with an unusual square minaret, was used by the Jebeliya during Ramadan and other important Moslem feast days. It was situated next to the church, its small dome respectfully lower than the top of the campanile. Nearby were the breaks in the wall for a boatswain's chair, which was once used to hoist pilgrims into the monastery without the danger of opening the gates to raiders, and the bread-dispensing window. Radical insularity was a thing of the past, whether the monks liked it or not.

In the darkness around me, three Jebeliya were kneeling on their prayer rugs, facing both the church and Mecca, which was about six hundred miles to the southeast. And looming over everything, against a blinding starlit sky, was the dark presence of Mount Sinai, the great reason for it all. I was ruminating on the paradoxes of the scene, when I heard a sharp voice behind me say in clear English, "Go to your room! Please go to your room now!" It was a monk I hadn't seen before, one who, apparently, was on some sort of guard duty that night, an ecclesiastic curfew warden. Like a child caught filching an extra piece of cake at summer camp, I obeyed. By the time I had mounted the stairs to my room, it was almost nine o'clock, lights-out. I half expected a flashlight-wielding counselor in shorts, T-shirt, and crew hat to come by, checking to see if I was in my bed before taps, here at Hostile Hostel. But it had been a long day, and in just six hours we would be up and climbing. Bailey was already asleep. Without a thought about fleas, I slipped into my sleeping bag and went out like the light bulb above my head.

The next thing I saw was a flashlight shining in my face. It was held not by a camp counselor but by our Jebeliya guide, who said something quietly in Arabic and then left to knock on the door of the German women. We were all out of bed, washed, and assembled in the dormitory dining room at 3:30 A.M., where we breakfasted on hot tea and bread, a fitting meal before a difficult climb. Stumbling through the monastery corridors and tunnels, we followed the flashlight beam of the guide (who introduced himself in English as Mahmoud) to the original wooden north-gate door, which he opened with an outsized brass key. Over the tall portal were two inscriptions, in Greek and Arabic, which, in English translation, read: "This holy monastery was erected on Mount Sinai at the place where the Lord spoke to Moses, by the humble Emperor of the Romans, Justinian, in his own eternal memory and in the memory of his wife, Theodora." Once beyond the gate, we turned east on the wadi road, starting the long, circuitous climb up the Pilgrims' Way to the peak of Mount Sinai. With luck, we would be on the peak at sunrise—a memorable sight, according to everybody who had ever made the climb.

There was a brisk, dry, chilly wind. Although the Pilgrims' Way was not steep at the beginning, it was a harrowing walk in the dark over the nearly invisible stones along the path. Mahmoud's flashlight offered little help, since he was in the lead followed by Bailey and me, with the German women taking up the rear. The only sound, besides the wind and our curses and grunts as we stumbled over stones, was the celestial peal of the monastery bells sounding matins. But soon, it was first light and the going was easier. Also, the path widened, wide enough for a small cart, and the surface was smoother. About one third of the way up, we realized that Elisabeth Rahmer had dropped far behind, and we took a break to give her time to catch up. The stars were still clear as beacons, which inspired Bailey to recite a Bedouin poem about the Big Dipper circling the North Star. Mahmoud, like every Bedouin I had met,

was entranced by the native verse, savoring each syllable and repeating the rhyming word with reverence. In the growing light, I
saw that he looked like a tall version of Jordan's King Hussein,
complete with trimmed moustache and piercing dark eyes. We
asked him about his life, and he told us that he had been born in
a tent in a nearby wadi and had been working for the monastery
since he was a little boy. He was literate in Arabic and he had
learned to speak Greek and a few words of English, all of which
could help him gain more profitable employment on the outside,
if he didn't feel obligated by tradition to work for less money at the
monastery. (He earned five hundred Israeli pounds a month—
about thirty-five dollars—plus room and board from the monks, as
opposed to a potential three thousand pounds a month in, say,
Elath.) His sense of loyalty and responsibility was impressive.

In the first glimmer of dawn, the Gulf of Akaba and the mountains of Saudi Arabia revealed themselves through the morning
mist, as we started up again on a steeper, winding grade. I found
it easier to climb if I consciously imitated Mahmoud's Bedouin gait,
that gliding, regular rhythm of relaxed legs and swinging arms. But
there was no way of exactly imitating him; he was born and raised
in these mountains, he had probably walked to the top of Mount
Sinai five hundred times, and he climbed like a goat. Keeping a
steady pace, we reached a cleft between the lesser and greater
peaks, where we rested again, staring in breathless silence at the
lightening view. The greater peak, a conic pinnacle from our perspective, seemed to be glowing, as if in an Italian Renaissance
religious painting or a bad Bette Davis movie. The eerie sight
drove us to reach the top before the full sun came up. The cleft
broadened into a flat valley with a lovely garden and spring, surrounded by palms and cypresses. In the center of the garden was
a small stone house, a shrine to the Prophet Elijah, who, the Bible
says, had his own dramatic encounter with God on the mountain,
after fleeing from the wrath of evil King Ahab and Jezebel. The
Lord told him to return to Israel and elect Elisha as his successor.
Elijah is a holy figure to the Moslems as well as to the Jews and
Christians, and the shrine and garden are well cared for by the

Jebeliya. The monks celebrate a Mass at the shrine at least once every year.

From the Elijah shrine to the pinnacle, the path became a stone staircase of three hundred lovingly chiseled steps, carved out of the rock centuries ago by the monks. As I negotiated the steep, long steps curving up to the peak, I felt sharp pains in my shins. It was as if one must suffer this final pain in order to reach the top, a last trial for the penitent pilgrim. I wondered how those penitents in fetters—and sometimes on bloody knees—had climbed these bone-jarring steps. The setting and the shining goal certainly must have spurred them on.

For further inspiration along the way there were two more spectacles: the footprint of either Mohammed's or Nebi Saleh's she-camel, depending on which legend you believed, and the palace of Abbas Pasha, a ruin clearly visible on a mountainside to the west. The camel footprint in the rock indeed looked like a camel's footprint, but as if molded of plaster of paris. A tiny booth covered it, with tufts of vegetation strewn about as offerings, signifying the continuity of life. Some cynics have said that the footprint was manufactured by an ancient monk to protect the monastery from superstitious Moslems. As for the palace of Abbas Pasha, the story is far more mundane. He was the profligate grandson of Mohammed Ali and a pasha of Egypt in 1849, who, because of his excesses, decided to retreat into the wilderness to recover his sanctity. He placed joints of meat on various Sinai mountains, on the theory that the one that lasted longest would mark the holiest spot on which to erect a palace. The meat was preserved best on Gebel Tiniye, but after a tortuous road was constructed and a grand palace half finished—the most back-breaking enterprise for Egyptian slaves since the building of the pyramids—Abbas Pasha changed his mind and elected to live on Mount Sinai itself, so he could be closer to Nebi Musa. Bedouin legend has it that he fought with Moses on the mountain and then cursed the entire region. In any case, Abbas Pasha gave up the idea of a desert retreat and returned to Cairo, where he was killed by a slave whom he had discovered dallying in his harem. What's left of the road and the palace stands as a bleak memorial to yet another tyrant's madness.

With aching shins and perspiration evaporating in the chill wind, sucking the thin air for whatever oxygen it offered, I arrived at the glowing peak—the traditional highest meeting place of man and God—just as the sun rose strong and warm. The five of us stood together in the rehabilitating sunlight on the smooth granite top, each basking in his own personal pride and exaltation at having made it. For a while, nobody spoke. The wind was too loud for conversation, even if we had wanted to talk. Here we five were by wild chance—two Germans (one of whom had lived through the Nazi regime), a Bedouin, an Israeli, and an American—catching our breath and warming our bodies in this most unlikely, and yet oddly appropriate, place on earth, the frontier of Heaven, the top of the world. I have never been imbued with any religious spirit and I did not feel any then. Rather, I felt a sense of nature and heritage, which perhaps is the same thing. If there was ever a mountain for God to address man, this was it. Whether one believed the religious myths or not didn't really seem to matter. There was something magical about being on top of Mount Sinai.

While I marveled at the crystalline beauty, Elisabeth and Christiane crossed themselves and sat down to rest on a ledge. Bailey recited a prayer in Hebrew to himself, the wind drowning out his voice, and Mahmoud walked over to a compact white mosque just beside, but slightly lower than, a small white Greek Orthodox chapel. (There wasn't so much as a Star of David on top of Mount Sinai. It occurred to me that Bailey and I were the only tangible Jewish presence there.) I followed Mahmoud and noticed that he scraped a marking near the mosque door with a stone, to show that he had been there that day and all was well. A chalked inscription in English on the door read: "God is still talking today. Listen!" There were other graffiti both inside and outside the mosque— names and dates in a variety of languages (somebody named "Schweitzer" made a particularly prominent mark)—and crosses and initials were carved into the rock all about the peak. Once a year, the Jebeliya sacrifice a sheep to Moses in the mosque. The stone chapel, with corrugated-iron roofing which rattled in the breeze, was locked, but I managed to boost myself up to a barred window and peer inside. Through the bars and broken glass I saw an old bureau, some cans, and frescoes of Christ on the cross, an angel receiving Christ, and Moses leading his people away from Pharaoh. A rock in the chapel is believed by the monks to be the exact spot where the tablet of the Ten Commandments was given to Moses. A shallow, narrow cave next to the chapel is supposedly the site where Moses covered his face from the glory of God and slept during his stay on the mountain; a depression in the cave rock is said to have been made by Moses' head. Between the chapel proper and the cave is a small room, where the monks eat and rest when they come up to the peak once a year to offer Mass. Neither the monks nor the Bedouins ever sleep overnight on the mountain; Mahmoud told us that they want to keep the peak clean and holy, but, he admitted, they are also leery of unearthly noises reportedly heard at night on Mount Sinai.

Steps led from the pinnacle to various isolated roosts on ledges, where hermits and pilgrims through the ages have sat in contemplation. I descended to one of these roosts, barely large enough for a single person to sit cross-legged, on the edge of an escarpment. The morning was now full-blown, the sun having burned off whatever haze there was and heated the stone under me. The wind was still strong but pleasant, not chilly. I had the dizzying sensation that I could make out every pebble on mountains miles away. Before me was the peak of Gebel Katharina, where St. Catherine's bones were discovered, one of the few mountains in the peninsula higher than Mount Sinai. Clearly visible were the chapel of St. Catherine and an Israeli Army post on the peak, with a radar antenna, the latter a sudden reminder of a less ethereal world. During the bitter cold of one winter in these mountains, two Israeli soldiers had died of exposure when their jeep broke down on the road leading to the top of Gebel Katharina. Snowstorms are not uncommon. The remains of Abbas Pasha's palace were in sharp focus, and again I wondered at the extraordinary folly of its construction on such a high, craggy mountain. To the north was the El Tih plateau, harsh and forbidding in the bright light, and farther away I thought I could make out Wadi Saal and Ein El Furtaga. Three black birds with white markings—a species of crow called *shahariya*—alighted on a rock near me. Like everything that morning on Mount Sinai, they seemed to have some mystical significance, though what they signified did not come to me in an intuitive flash. Perhaps the sign meant it was time to go. It was past seven o'clock, and I wanted to see as much of the monastery's treasures as I could before the monks sequestered themselves for their Sabbath.

After one last, lingering, 360-degree look around, we started down from the peak. Our plan was to take the direct stone-step route back to the monastery, thirty-seven hundred stairs hewn from the rock of a narrow, precipitous path leading from Elijah's shrine straight to the back wall of St. Catherine's. We stopped at the shrine to sample some of the sweet well water and wash our faces at a small pool. Again, Mahmoud scratched some marks on a building in the garden—this time, the initials of his full name, Mahmoud Mohammed Abdullah Abudullah. He stood back and beamed at his handiwork, proud of his literacy. Just below the shrine were the ruins of the Chapel of the Fleas and the cave in which a saintly monk named Stephanos had lived out his life in splendid isolation. At several archways built over the steps, Stephanos would examine for piety pilgrims making their way to the mountaintop and would hear their confessions. Eroded rocks along the way startled us with their natural sculpture, some like prehistoric monsters, others like mammoth Brancusis. The stone steps, widely spaced and dangerously smooth, took all our concentration to negotiate them. The charley horses they caused were torture. One, apparently, must suffer while both ascending and descending Mount Sinai; only at the top is there peace. But the view of the wild terrain, the sculptured rocks and caves, the thick archways, and, finally, straight below us, the toylike monastery were worth the pain and effort of this return route. We arrived back at the main gate at 8:45, exhausted and aching but elated and anxious to see more.

A wondrous change of attitude had taken place while we were gone. The monks provided some hot tea and bread for us as soon as we entered the monastery and they pleasantly informed us that we could tour the premises with the Venezuelans at nine o'clock, beginning with the library. Why the change? we wondered. Had the Venezuelans interceded for us? Had the monks reread and reconsidered the letters of introduction? Was it because it was Sunday? Or was it because they would soon be rid of us? Whatever the reason, we were grateful.

At the gate to the library, sealed with a huge chain and padlock, were Father Paul, our guide on the tour, and all the Venezuelans, dressed as if they were attending the finest cathedral in Caracas. Father Paul unlocked the gate and led us into a large well-lit gallery crowded with icons, triptychs, panels, gilded doors, frescoes, and illuminated manuscripts, any one of which would have been a major acquisition by the Metropolitan Museum of Art. Another even larger room, sealed from us by a floor-to-ceiling wire fence, contained the approximately eight thousand ancient manuscripts and books belonging to the monastery, second only to the Vatican Library for precious texts in Greek, Syriac, Arabic, Slavonic, Latin, Persian, Coptic, Georgian, Ethiopian, and Armenian. (They had recently been catalogued and arranged by specialists from abroad and the room had the look of university library stacks, even boasting a fire-extinguishing sprinkler system.) The brilliance of the art, so casually displayed in that wilderness treasure trove, was staggering. One hundred and fifty icons (of the more than two thousand the monastery owns) were exhibited in the gallery, many of them dating from the sixth century and painted in the encaustic, or heated-colored-wax-on-wood, technique. The earliest ones—including the magnificent "Christ Pantocrator"—had survived the Byzantine iconoclastic movement because the remote St. Catherine's Monastery was so isolated from the iconoclast emperors; their value today is inestimable. Of the other works, the most arresting was a fresco of Moses, behind gilded portals in a small chapel dedicated to him, off to the side of the gallery.

Just a few of the monastery's precious manuscripts were on display in the glass cases, the fifth-century Codex Syriacus (a Syriac text of the Gospels) being the most important of these. The monks have been extremely sensitive about showing off their wealth of manuscripts ever since the notorious Codex Sinaiticus affair of 1859. That famous document—a fourth-century Greek manuscript of the Old and New Testaments commissioned by Constantine the Great and sent by Justinian to his favorite charity, the monastery—helped confirm and revise all other biblical texts. In 1859, the German theologian and scholar Konstantin von Tischendorf visited the monastery and was permitted to examine the rare manuscript leaves. He asked if he could show the remarkable pages to his patron, Tsar Alexander II, and the trusting monks agreed. Another version has it that von Tischendorf saw the monks using the leaves to start a fire, and, aghast, he saved the pages from destruction. Whatever the case, he took the manuscript away from Sinai, leaving behind a duly signed receipt. An English translation of the document was framed on the wall of the monastery library, under the title "How the Monastery Lost Its Codex Sinaiticus." It read:

> September 16, 1859
>
> I, the undersigned Konstantin von Tischendorf, presently on a mission to the Near East, by order of Alexander, Emperor of All Russias, testify by the present writing that the Holy Confraternity of Mount Sinai, in accordance with the letter of His Excellency Ambassador Lobanov, has handed over to me as a loan an ancient manuscript of the Old and New Testaments, being the property of the aforementioned monastery and containing 346 folia and a small fragment. These I shall take with me to St. Petersburg in order that I may collate the copy previously made by me with the original of the time of the manuscript's publication. The manuscript has been entrusted to me under the conditions stipulated in the aforementioned letter of Mr. Lobanov, dated September 10, 1859, and carrying the number 510. This manuscript I promise to return undamaged and in good state of preservation to the Holy Confraternity of Sinai at its earliest request.
>
> (signed)
> Konstantin von Tischendorf

Needless to say, the monks of St. Catherine's never saw the Codex Sinaiticus again. Russia kept it as a national treasure in the

Imperial Library at St. Petersburg. But in 1933, the Soviet government, desperate for foreign currency, sold it to the British for one hundred thousand pounds, half of which was raised by donations from ordinary Britons and schoolchildren. Ever since, the leaves have been in the British Museum. The monks were still understandably bitter about what Father Paul called "the theft," as the framed Tischendorf receipt indicated. An attempt was recently made to retrieve the Codex Sinaiticus from the British through UNESCO, the United Nations agency that deals in such matters, but, according to Father Paul, "the British want too much pounds sterling." Why, I asked him, didn't the monks sell an icon or two and use the money to buy back the Codex? Father Paul shrugged. "It is our Codex, anyway," he said.

The monks' nervousness over showing the monastery's manuscript and book collection was reflected in Father Paul's firm denial of our request to see the stacks, locked up behind the steel fencing. That room, we were told, was accessible to only the most trustworthy scholars, under strict supervision. I had previously learned that the stacks contained such literary oddities as an Arabic translation of the Book of Job, the Psalms in miniature script, a writ bearing the seal of Mohammed, documents of protection and repair of the monastery signed by General Kléber and Napoleon, and, according to Professor Palmer, a book called *Jane Shore, a Tragedie for Drury Lane Theatre.* Some Bedouins still believe that rain in the mountains is caused by the opening and shutting of a magic book that the Lord gave to Moses on Mount Sinai. They are convinced that the book is in the library, and that the monks, at their discretion, can bring about floods by leaving it open. During one flood decades ago, an irate Bedouin fired his rifle at the monastery after his livestock were drowned.

Our next stop on the guided tour was the church. A few other monks joined us and Father Paul. With great ceremony they produced outsized keys and opened the tall, intricately carved sixth-century doors, made of Lebanon cedar and remarkably well preserved by the dry climate. An inscription over the doors, from Psalm 118, read: "This gate of the Lord, into which the righteous shall enter." None of us, righteous or not, was prepared for the splendor. Beyond the narthex panels, erected by Crusader knights and carved with their crests, was the enormous vaulted nave with a hanging forest of silver and gold chandeliers, a handsome mosaic floor, a gilded ceiling with portraits of Christ, side chapels, dozens of icons of all ages and subjects (including Moses), monks' wooden seats along the main aisle, and seven-foot brass candlesticks cast in Nineveh. Two rows of six gigantic monolithic granite columns, painted white, extended down the length of the nave, each representing a month of the year and affixed with appropriate icons of saints venerated during its particular month. As we walked, hushed and overwhelmed, down the center of the nave, the monks kept a wary eye on us, looking, I imagined, for a potential von Tischendorf. At the iconostasis, the richly adorned wooden partition before the altar, the monks formed a protective wall between us and the icons.

Behind the iconostasis was a semidomed apse, the underside of the dome covered with a sixth-century mosaic of the Transfiguration of Jesus, whose glowing presence was flanked by that of Moses and Elijah, with Peter, John, and James beneath them, as the Transfiguration is described in the Gospel According to St. Matthew. Surrounding the mosaic were medallions of Old Testament prophets and New Testament apostles. On a vertical wall above the semidome were depictions of, supposedly, Justinian and his wife, Theodora, and more panels showing angels offering gifts and Moses receiving the Law and confronting the Burning Bush. The effect of this concentrated, ecumenical mosaic was stunning. And under it all was the catafalque holding the remains of St. Catherine and the altar laden with silver candlesticks and crucifixes. Only our stiff necks and the prompting of the monks made us move on to the Chapel of the Burning Bush, the original church built by Empress Helena, just behind the apse.

"Draw not nigh hither: put off thy shoes from off thy feet, for the place whereon thou standest is holy ground," the Lord said to Moses from the flames of the Burning Bush, according to the Book of Exodus. Heeding this injunction, the monks demanded that we remove our shoes in the anteroom of the small chapel, explaining that it was the holiest spot in the monastery. (Since my shoes still had the holy dust of Mount Sinai on them, I considered this unnecessary, but I didn't argue.) A large, red CO_2 fire extinguisher stood in the anteroom, lending a neat touch of irony to the scene. Was there fear of the Burning Bush igniting again? The actual site of the bush contained no bush at all, but rather a silver plaque laid in stone. Four small marble pillars supported a diminutive altar over the plaque, and around the chapel were wall tiles, more icons, mosaics, a censer, candlesticks, and Persian rugs. A lit candle over the bush site perhaps gave some justification for the fire extinguisher. It is said that a window over the altar catches the sunlight only one day a year—on March 23—allowing the chapel to be naturally, and mysteriously, illuminated. The monks seemed to be disappointed that none of us was especially affected by the chapel and its lore, even when they showed us the living descendants of the Burning Bush just outside the back wall of the church (the roots begin under the altar). Indeed, there were three green bramble bushes growing there, which the Venezuelans called *zarzamora*, a common plant in Venezuela. The monks claimed that these bushes were the only examples of the species in the Sinai and that transplantings outside the monastery have always failed. However, botanists have identified them as shrubs of the Colutea genus, plentiful enough in the hills of the Negev and northeastern Sinai.

Near the bushes was a well covered with wooden planks, which Father Paul said was the Well of Midian, where Moses encountered the seven daughters of Jethro after his first flight from Egypt. Father Paul's narration of the tale inspired Bailey to tell the Bedouin version: Moses ran from Egypt into the wilderness of Sinai and came upon the Well of Midian. He sat under a tree and slept, but was awakened by some girls who wanted to water their flocks. They couldn't lift the stone cover of the well, however, until Moses helped them. The girls watered their animals and went to their father, Jethro, and told him about the kind Egyptian, whereupon Jethro sent one of them back to find the good man and invite him to his tent. She discovered Moses still at the well and told him that

Jethro wanted to see him. Moses agreed to come and followed the girl. Along the way, the wind lifted her gown over her legs and Moses saw her bare flesh, an abomination among Bedouins. But Moses preserved her honor by instructing the girl to walk behind him, so that he could not view the wind's caprice—which is why all Bedouin women walk behind men to this day. (An apocryphal story, which made the rounds after the Arab-Israeli wars, held that the Bedouins reversed the traditional male-female walking positions because of land mines; in point of fact, no Bedouin woman has ever been seen walking in front of a man.) We were all amused by Bailey's story, with the notable exception of Father Paul, who quickly insisted that we had just enough time left to visit the ossuary.

Beside the white charnel house in the garden, alive with singing birds and buzzing insects, was a tiny, conventional cemetery. Because of the difficulty of digging graves in the rocky ground and the number of monks from the St. Catherine's order who must be buried at the monastery, bodies are disinterred from the cemetery after five years or so and the remains deposited in the ossuary. We were led into a spacious, airless room, fitted out with two coal-bin-sized cages. In one cage were hundreds of sandstone-colored skulls, piled one upon another to form a ghastly hillock; the second, larger cage held a hideous assortment of bones—ulnae, tibiae, phalanges, vertebral columns—in a massive anatomical jumble. It was as if a tornado had hit a medical school. In niches along the walls were the more orderly bones and skulls of various archbishops, tidily packed away in their individual recesses for the ages. But the most chilling sight was a full skeleton, dressed in formal dark-purple embroidered monk's robes and cowl, propped in a sitting position, its head shyly, questioningly atilt. The finger bones, with bits of dried flesh and nails still adhering, clutched a staff and a rosary, and the feet, ding-toed, protruded from the bottom of the robe. It was the well-preserved remains of Stephanos, the saintly monk who had lived alone near Elijah's shrine and had examined pilgrims for piety. Because of his virtue and sanctity, he was given the singular honor of "guarding," in appropriate costume, the dead, ever since his

The ossuary at St. Catherine's Monastery. *Magnum.*

own death in 580. After staring at Stephanos for a while, I became less appalled by him. His inquiring posture, so typical of what he must have been like in life as he heard the weary pilgrims' confessions, seemed to be asking what business I had here. At last, I had no convincing answer, and I joined the others, who were more or less fleeing into the bright sunlight outside.

Strangely enough, the visit to the ossuary did not diminish our appetite. In fact, we were ravenous. When Bailey, the Germans, and I returned to the dormitory dining room, we found that the monks had sent over cans of sardines and baked beans and some bread. While devouring these welcome rations, we concluded that the monks had been seized with guilt over their behavior of the previous day and were trying to make amends. Later, when they refused any payment for our stay, we were sure of it. Just past noon, we packed our gear, said our good-byes (the Venezuelans actually seemed sorry to see us go), tipped Mahmoud, and, with the German women, piled into the Land-Rover. Bailey and I still felt responsible for the Germans' welfare, but since we were scheduled to head northwest to Firan and the turquoise mines at Serabit El Khadim, the best we could do was drop them near the Civil Administration Center, where they might catch a ride to Nuweiba or Elath. Once again like two innocent waifs in the wilderness, they were left to their own meager devices. It was a sad farewell. The four of us had gone through a lot together. Watching them forlornly waving in the dust, we drove up the road by the tomb of Nebi Saleh to the Watiya Pass, then west along the Wadi El Sheikh (named for Nebi Saleh) toward Firan. We had already lived through a hard ten-hour day and we had, at the very least, another grueling ten hours ahead.

SIX

THE CENTRAL SECTOR of any given geographical entity has always
struck me, perhaps unfairly, as the least appealing, and the middle
of the Sinai peninsula was no exception. The quality of the terrain
changed quickly from mountainous grandeur to dry, sloping plains
rising from a rubbly wadi to the tops of unremarkable limestone
and granite hills. The going was hot and laborious. Only the appearance of a natural phenomenon that the Bedouins call "Moses'
Seat" broke the dull sameness. A recess in a rock that indeed looked
like a rough-cut Brobdingnagian throne, the seat is thought by
some persons to be the site of Rephidim, where Moses, annoyed
at his grumbling followers ("What shall I do unto this people? they
be almost ready to stone me," he cried rabbinically to God), was
instructed to strike a rock and produce fresh water to slake the
complaints. Also at Rephidim, the Israelites were set upon by the
Amalekites, a bellicose band of nomads. Joshua was appointed to
lead the inexperienced Israelites in a counterattack, which was directed by Moses from a hill. "And it came to pass, when Moses held
up his hand, that Israel prevailed: and when he let down his hand,
Amalek prevailed"—but his arms grew heavy, and so a stone
throne was placed under him for added support during the daylong
battle, which the Israelites thus won. Moslems believe that the
actual impression of Moses' body is on this holy rock along Wadi
El Sheikh, and some Jewish mystics hold that anyone who sees it
should give thanksgiving and praise to the Almighty. Bailey and I
took turns sitting on the throne, irreverently raising and lowering
our hands.

152

If it were possible to pinpoint a true Rephidim (and some biblical
scholars have spent years trying to do just that), it more likely
would be at Firan, about thirty kilometers to the west, since the
Amalekites would have been protecting the wells there against the
foreign intruders. Dubbed the "Pearl of the Sinai" by Victorian
explorers, Firan is a fruitful wadi-oasis bounded by the geological
spectacle of towering red-granite walls. Water, palms, tamarisks,
and rich soil are plentiful, all of which have made the region invalu-
able to anyone who happened by through the centuries of Sinai
history. Besides the Amalekites and the Israelites, those who happened by were, of course, various indigenous Bedouin tribes and
the comparative newcomers, the Christian hermits and pilgrims.
The first Christians to make their way into the green wadi considered nearby Mount Serbal to be the original Mount Sinai. They
created a monastic city at Firam in the fourth century, building huts
and enlarging the caves in the wadi walls. These caves, resembling
mouse holes from the valley floor, may have given the place its
name. According to Professor Palmer, Wadi Firan meant "Valley
of the Mice"—although he conceded that it might also be an Arabic
version of the biblical Paran (Arabs pronounce the letter *p* as *f*).
The ruins of the monastic city, and its crumbling church and garden, are still watched over by a solitary monk from St. Catherine's
Monastery, which has title to the land. But it is the Bedouins who
have taken back for their own purposes most of what was rightfully
theirs in the first place.

We had hoped to see Firan, then double back along Wadi El
Sheikh to another track, Wadi Beirak, which coursed vaguely
northwest toward Serabit El Khadim. But we were running late
(the road was rougher than Bailey had expected) and when we
stopped for cold drinks at a Jebeliya booth next to a veritable jungle
of a *bustan,* I decided that a visit to Firan was out of the question.
The only way we could see Firan would be to spend the night there,
missing out on an early-morning climb to the mines atop Serabit—
one of my prime objectives in the Sinai. Spending the night at Firan
was precisely what Bailey wanted to do; there were Bedouin friends
of his whom he wanted to interview at the oasis. Bailey was miffed.

I was adamant. We were both very tired. It was inevitable that two men thrown together for twenty-four hours a day in difficult circumstances would have at least one conflict of temperament. Unhappily, it was at that place and at that time.

Bailey had never been in Wadi Beirak before (one of the few tracks in the Sinai he did not know like his own living room), but a Bedouin at the Jebeliya booth needed a ride up the wadi and volunteered to give us expert directions. It was a good thing he came along, because the entrance to the wadi was so cunningly concealed by boulders and brush that we never would have found it by ourselves. After the first half hour of a grinding trek up the valley floor, I was sorry that I had overruled Bailey and not agreed to go on to Firan. It was too late to turn back, though. We were in the badlands, the worstlands—ugly, treacherous stone rubble and loose sand, empty of any sign of even desert life, unbearably hot as we crept along in four-wheel drive. In moody silence, we bounced and tossed and strained through every kilometer. The hostility of the terrain matched our common temper. Ominous vultures circled overhead, a redundant reminder of what was in store for us if we broke down. The distant, grayish El Tih complemented the unfriendly landscape. (A bartender at Fink's restaurant in Jerusalem had told me a few days before that he had been stationed in the El Tih region for more than a month, on reserve duty. "It is the absolute bottom," he said, pointing both his thumbs down.) To add to the general misery, small whirlwinds spun the loose sand into our faces, an indication that a khamsin was possibly due, but it was too hot to close the car windows. I felt a sudden paralyzing cramp in my right hand and realized that it was from gripping the window strut so tightly. As I tried to flex my hand, I saw that my knuckles were bone white. Maybe, I thought, we shouldn't have been quite so irreverent at Moses' Seat.

The Bedouin hitchhiker abruptly asked to be let out. In all likelihood, he couldn't stand the electric tension between the two strange Occidentals. Whatever the reason, he simply walked off into nowhere, without giving us any more useful information about what lay ahead. What lay ahead was more of the same but on rising ground. We were climbing, slowly but unmistakably, out of the desert floor. Bailey, struggling, sighing, and sweating, spotted a long strip of greenish flintstone off the track and cut over to it. Being able to shift out of four-wheel drive seemed to cheer him slightly. "Pray for more flintstone," he said, his first real words in more than an hour. "We can make time on flintstone. But if we don't reach Serabit by nightfall, we're in big trouble." He rubbed his lower abdomen and winced. "My liver's killing me. I never should have climbed Mount Sinai this morning." I felt guilty and apologized to him. He sank into morose silence again.

At last came a change of scenery and a sign of life. Red peaks rose in the distant northwest—Serabit had to be one of them, according to our maps—and racing toward us on the flintstone was a yellow jeep pickup truck full of Bedouins. An odd ritual, like a meeting of strangers in the Old West, ensued. Both vehicles went slowly past each other, stopped, and then backed up until the drivers were face to face. With no quick draws in the offing, Bailey and the Bedouin driver traded *salamats*. The Bedouin came unexpectedly to the point: he wanted three aspirin to quiet a splitting headache. (So Bedouins get headaches like the rest of us.) I dug into my rucksack and found my aspirin bottle. I gave him six tablets, three extra for good luck and for some good directions to Serabit. He told Bailey that the encampment of a Bedouin named Barakat, who supervised the Serabit area for the Israeli government, was about twenty kilometers farther up the wadi, but we must turn off to get to it. How would we spot the turnoff? It was hard to describe, he said. We exchanged thanks and pressed on. If anything, the encounter had dispirited us more.

The terrain changed once again. The flintstone strip ended and was replaced by boulders and more loose sand, looking like a desolate, meteorite-strewn plain on the moon. There was that lunar connection again—Sin, the Babylonian Moon God, and Sinai. Acacia trees popped up here and there, and between dodging the boulders and the acacia spikes, our speed was down to about ten kilometers an hour. A flat tire would finish us for the day. Only the peaks in the distance and traces of copper ore in the rocks (Serabit had copper mines, also) promised hope.

In this dismal wadi one hundred and fifty years ago, a famous battle was fought between troops and Bedouins, a punitive expedition by the Egyptians against the Towara. It was the last Bedouin stand against the Egyptians, and the results were inconclusive. Today, the setting was just right for a bloody battle: the sun, a pale white disc in the haze and dust of a gathering khamsin, an atmosphere hot and still, a sense of death and despair in everything. For a moment, the small white stones seemed to be skulls of long-expired warriors. A sheikh's tomb and adjacent cemetery did not brighten the scene.

I had been staring at the odometer, cheering on every new kilometer that registered. When we had traveled twenty kilometers from the point where we had met the Bedouins in the yellow pickup truck, there was still no hint of a turnoff and, indeed, the red mountains seemed no closer. Had we gone by the vague turnoff? Were we north of Serabit? Neither of us was sure. We were riding on pure intuition and a frightening stretch of loose sand, which brought us to the edge of panic. As we churned onward in four-wheel drive, barely making headway, burning up our fuel reserves while seemingly going nowhere, near total exhaustion, I felt myself breaking. "Let's go back and look for the turnoff," I said. "We must have passed it."

Bailey scanned the glowering horizon. "No," he said, "we'll never find anything in this light. We'll go on. Something will turn up. It always does." He was right, of course. A little Bedouin girl, maybe six years old, appeared out of the gloom, coaxing a herd of sheep and goats home. We were as thrilled to see her as if we had happened upon a Travelers Aid Society office. She was shy to the point of speechlessness, but Bailey managed to learn the whereabouts of her parents' tent, with the help of some sugar wafers and gentle talk. While he hiked to the tent, two hundred yards away, I tried out my few words of Arabic with her, but I might as well have been a Venusian, as far as she was concerned. She hid behind the animals, which were almost as tall as she was, her array of bright jewelry and colorful clothes giving her away. She had probably been tending the family livestock ever since she was old enough to walk, an amazing responsibility for a small child but one that Bedouins take as a simple fact of life. Soon, Bailey returned, smiling for the first time since we had left Wadi El Sheikh. The turnoff to Serabit was just a few kilometers up the track, the girl's parents had told him, and, what's more, a hard-packed gravel plain lay just ahead. With any luck, we would reach Serabit before dark. In gratitude, we gave the girl all our remaining sugar wafers and roared off.

"You see," Bailey said, once we were speeding along on the gravel plain, past striated monadnocks and looming mountains, "there's always a Bedouin around when you need one. It's the old *inshallah* principle in desert life, to trust in fate. God will somehow provide, and if He doesn't, well, that's His will." Brightening with the break in tension and a second wind, he went on to say that in situations like the one we were in you must make the best preparations you can but you must also put yourself in the hands of a superior force. "I'm certainly no Moslem, but I've come to believe *inshallah*. When I first went into the Sinai, I used to ask Bedouins if there were snakes around. They told me, 'Don't worry. If Allah sends snakes, he sends snakes. You can't go to sleep every night and worry about snakes. There are certainly snakes in the desert, but one must sleep. *Inshallah*.' And I would often make appointments with different Bedouins to interview them but they wouldn't show up. So after a while, I learned to seek out the Bedouins who were around and sometimes I'd get better information, priceless and unexpected. It doesn't pay to get worked up. If one thing won't happen, another will. *Inshallah*. Just last February, my wife and I went on vacation to Cyprus. We were sitting in the hotel lobby, waiting for our car to be delivered so we could go sightseeing. As we were about to get into the car, I thought I'd go back into the lobby and visit the head, because I probably wouldn't get another chance for several hours. My wife said, 'No, you're always going to the bathroom at the wrong time. Get in the car.' So I got in the car and we drove off. A few minutes later, Palestinian terrorists burst into the lobby and assassinated Yousef El Sebai, the editor of

the Egyptian newspaper *Al Ahram,* and they took a lot of hostages.
Can you imagine what they would have done to me, an Israeli, if
I had been in that lobby? *Inshallah* again."

As if to prove his argument further, we happened on a Bedouin
tent, from which an old man emerged and indicated the Serabit
turnoff, down a sandy hill a kilometer ahead. With some slipping
and sliding in the powdery sand, we rolled into Barakat's camp, a
community of a few tents and stone houses nestled together in a
bleak, uninviting valley, just as the pale sun vanished behind the
mountains to the west and the khamsin, on cue, swirled into a
full-fledged sandstorm. To our surprise, there was an Israeli campsite nearby, filled with touring youngsters who had come to Serabit
by bus over the better road from the west. We found Barakat's
house but no Barakat. His wife, a vivacious, talkative woman, told
us that he would be away till morning but—and this stunned Bailey
and me—she would be honored to give us some tea and prepare
dinner for us. She said we could sleep in one of the empty stone
houses, out of the storm. A Bedouin woman never invites strangers
into her house when her husband is away—a male relative, perhaps,
but never a stranger. Was women's lib coming to the Sinai? We
accepted thankfully. "We could have our heads handed to us when
Barakat comes home," Bailey whispered to me, as we sat down,
shoeless and cross-legged, on her carpet inside the house.

In the light of a glowing brazier, situated under a hole in the
corrugated-iron roof, I could see that Barakat's wife was exceptional. Aging but still beautiful (at least from her veil up), she
moved about with sureness and dispatch, shooing five adorable,
half-naked children away from her guests, giving housekeeping
orders to Nura, her teen-aged daughter, discouraging alarmed
neighbor women from peeking in the open doorway. While I
sipped the welcome hot tea and smoked my pipe, she unabashedly
asked me for some tobacco to make cigarettes with. (She smoked,
too!) I handed her my pouch, and she helped herself to just about
all the tobacco inside. One must meet generosity with generosity,
I thought, hoping I had enough tobacco in my rucksack to last me
till I returned to Jerusalem. Her hair was in a braided topknot,

signifying that she was married, and her black dress was adorned with tinkling pendent coins and turquoise jewelry. She coyly let her veil slip below her nose as she bustled about, readjusting it only when she was sure we had seen enough of her face. "Don't look at her too much," Bailey warned.

She was a flirt, like Sheikh Ibn Jazi's wife in El Arish, a not uncommon trait among Bedouin women. It was another Bedouin paradox—extreme female reticence (so strong that to photograph a woman is tantamount to making an indecent pass at her and insulting her husband) and explicit, earthy sexuality ("experts in the sack" was how Bailey put it). Bedouin women were called "ghastly" and "ugly" by early English explorers, who shrank from their tattooed faces and high body odors, and yet their natural beauty, especially in their smoldering dark eyes, could enthrall some Westerners. Those Victorian gentlemen were often of two minds about Bedouins in general. On the one hand, they tended to romanticize the desert dwellers as primitives with a native sophistication superior to Europeans'; on the other hand, they sometimes viewed them as congenital thieves still afflicted with the curse of Ishmael ("And he will be a wild man . . .").

While the women are a social cut below men—who, according to Islam, are the protectors and guardians of their honor—Moslem law also grants them rights to property, inheritance, and divorce. An Arab may have four wives but he must treat all with scrupulously equal attention. (He can rid himself of any one of them by repeating "I divorce my wife" three times. This divorce ceremony is also a Bedouin's method of swearing to a promise; by pronouncing the "three divorces," he pledges to keep his word or lose the wife in question.) A good, attractive wife is prized beyond all other possessions but she is nevertheless chattel, in the great scheme of things. An old Bedouin proverb is *El benat battaleb,"* or "Girls are good for nothing." In pre-Islamic days, Bedouins were known to bury alive some unneeded newborn females, as not worth the expense of feeding. Marriage is on a strictly commercial basis, arranged by the families. The prettier girls go for a higher price than the homelier ones, with the result that the beauties are often

married to richer, older men. A divorcée or widow, but not a
virgin, can object to a chosen mate. If a virgin runs off with a lover,
both can be executed by the families involved, although that practice is rare these days, even in fundamentalist Saudi Arabia.

The matter of rape illustrates how the Bedouin male generally
regards the female. As the shepherds and menial laborers, the
women must not be mistreated, so if they are raped, they can accuse
the culprits without corroborative proof. However, rape at night is
a comparatively minor offense since the woman should have been
home safe in the family tent; rape during the day is a far more
serious crime because the woman, alone with the flocks, was kept
from attending to her labors—a rather Marxist economic principle.
It is not easy to be a Bedouin female, but some, like Barakat's wife,
make the most of what there is.

After the tea, Nura led us stumbling through the darkness over
barbed wire and rocks, leaning into the wind-whipped sand, to a
sturdier stone house, where we would spend the night. Barakat's
wife had told us that we would be notified when dinner was ready,
and we sent back with Nura some canned goods to add to the stew.
The walls of the guest house, tight against the storm, were covered
with religious graffiti in Arabic—"Allah is great" and "There is no
God but Allah." I was feeling relieved and revived, thankful that
we were safe at Serabit and happy that Bailey and I were on good
terms once again. I unrolled my sleeping bag on the musty carpet
and took a few swigs from my Scotch bottle, fantastic medicine after
this day. Every so often, the head of a Bedouin woman would peer
in through the open doorway at us; we were obviously *the* event
of the settlement and today's gossip. I started to tell Bailey something but gave up when I heard him snoring softly. Within a minute, I was also asleep.

What seemed like ten seconds later, Barakat's wife appeared,
wearing a new bright-red dress, formally inviting us to her house
for dinner. We accepted with equal formality. She then vanished
and we staggered back to her house, still half asleep. With plangent
shouts, Barakat's wife discouraged the neighbor women from staring at us and kept the children in an orderly group near one wall

made of old boards and thatching, from which hung rags, clothes, a mirror, and some plastic bottles. A kerosene lamp dimly lit up the opposite corner of the room. The stew, concocted of canned lima beans, goulash soup, and Rumanian bully beef, was served to us in unwashed soup bowls, with, of course, sweet tea and freshly baked *pita*. While our hostess, on her knees, poured some water from a pitcher over our hands, her veil slipped off her face. She made no attempt to raise it again for the duration of the meal, perhaps to facilitate her eating. As she and her children ate together from the stewpot, Bailey and I wolfed down our food shamelessly. I was feeling a bit giddy and decided to tell Bailey a complicated joke, at which I alone laughed. "Don't laugh so hard," Bailey said. "They'll think you're making fun of them." I silenced myself with a sip of tea and a last swallow of *pita* with stew frosting.

Immediately after dinner, the younger children wrapped themselves in rags and blankets and went straight to sleep on the floor. Scraps of food were thrown to the goats, a few of which had wandered into the house. The dirty dishes and pot were put away for the next meal. Barakat's wife suggested that her daughter Nura be our guide for climbing to the mines in the morning. "She is only thirteen, but she climbs well and knows the way," the mother said. Nura, whose name means "light," glowed with a combination of pride and shyness. Then Nura's mother offered to sell us some small unpolished turquoise stones for one hundred Israeli pounds, which would also include the fee for Nura's help. We agreed to the arrangement and I handed her a hundred-pound note, which she stuffed into her dress. She produced a handful of irregular light-blue turquoises and I selected three. There was one other matter, Barakat's wife said. Another daughter had stomach cramps earlier that day and had gone to the Israeli campsite to ask for some medicine. Could Bailey drive over and fetch the girl? Bailey left with Barakat's wife in the Land-Rover, and I went to the guesthouse. About an hour later, he returned with the news that the girl had been treated by an Israeli nurse, who happened to be along on the tour, and that Barakat himself had come home and was not at all displeased by his wife's unusual hospitality. In fact, he was proud of her and he was honored to have entertained "Docto*rr* Bayl*ee*" and the American in his house. Thus assured that we wouldn't be beheaded in the middle of the night by a furious husband, we collapsed into the healing sleep of the spared.

In spite of my deep sleep, that curious built-in mental alarm clock we all seem to possess went off as dawn broke, at 5:15 A.M. It was a clear, cool morning, the khamsin having blown itself out, erasing the ugliness and murk of the previous day. The rich orange sunrise illuminating the inspiring peaks to the west of Serabit refreshed our bodies and spirits and we felt ready for a hard climb. I found myself humming "What a Diff'rence a Day Made" as we walked to Barakat's house for a breakfast of *pita* and tea. Barakat, a pleasant, gentle man, was beside himself with ebullient hospitality. We profusely thanked him and his wife (more retiring in her husband's presence), and, with Nura, we headed for the base of the mountain, a short drive away. Nura was revealed in the daylight as little more than a child—thirteen years old, as her mother had said, but with the frame of a scrawny girl four years her junior. In her black dress and cowl, her floppy sandals, she appeared eminently unsuited to be a mountain-climbing guide. Still, I thought, she knew the way.

As we approached the bottom of a stony trail winding up the jagged, bone-dry mountain, we came upon a squad of nine well-armed Israeli soldiers, munching oranges alongside an open Dodge military truck and a jeep. They told us that they were mostly reservists on duty at a central Sinai I.D.F. base and they were currently taking part in a combination training-and-cultural exercise—to patrol the area between their base and the Gulf of Suez coast and to explore the historical sites along the way, one of them being Serabit El Khadim. Lieutenant Micha, who led them, said in broken English that he was not sure of the best route to the Serabit mines and temple on top of the mountain, so we invited them to join us in our guided climb. They happily agreed—although there were some familiar draftee groans at the prospect of any physical exertion—and the lieutenant said that we could leave the Land-Rover here with the truck and jeep. He would assign two soldiers to stay behind and guard the vehicles, and they would rendezvous with us at the opposite side of the mountain, then drive Bailey back to pick up his Land-Rover. This plan would give the climbing soldiers some training in finding their way both up and down a mountain on different trails; the nonclimbing pair would gain experience in rendezvousing. The two chosen to stay behind couldn't stop grinning. "Have fun," they shouted after us. So led by a skinny Bedouin girl, Bailey and I and our armed escort of seven wise-cracking, griping infantrymen started up the angular, three-thousand-foot-high mountain.

It was as if I had somehow wandered into the third reel of one of those stereotypical Second World War movies, but with a change of setting and characters. The squad was a cross section of the Israeli Army: Lieutenant Micha (an educated sabra of European parentage, ambitious, cool, responsible); a Bombay-born private in his thirties (raunchy, loud, infatuated with anything American); a dark-skinned Moroccan Jew (moody, ill-at-ease, complaining); a sun-burned recent arrival from Rumania (sensitive, confused); a Bedouin tracker (distant, calm, with a long, thin acne-ed face under a thick poll); a short, blond teen-ager (nervous, fragile, suffering from vertigo); and, unbelievably, a corporal nicknamed "Texas" (the husband of a Dallas girl, née Mimi Bernstein; affable, pleased that his assigned weapon was a pistol and not one of the heavy M-16 automatic rifles the others were lugging). After the first fifteen minutes of the strenuous climb over loose rock in the warm morning sun, their banter slackened and was replaced by panting. Any misgivings I had entertained about Nura's mountaineering abilities were immediately forgotten. She climbed with the same sure, effortless, fluid movements of Mahmoud, the guide on Mount Sinai. Before long, her unflagging pace carried her well ahead of us. Two soldiers lagged far behind, and Bailey asked her to take a rest break so everybody could catch up. "Boy, if the Arabs could see this!" Bailey said. "The great Israeli Army panting along behind a little Bedouin girl." Nura, dignified throughout, broke into a soft smile when the stragglers trudged to the ledge where the rest of us were waiting. The view was stupendous—a sheer thousand-foot drop to the valley floor, from which sculptured monadnocks and furrowed cliffs rose dramatically. In the distance were smooth purple peaks before the Gulf of Suez. To the east sat the grim El Tih and the notorious Wadi Beirak—now looking so innocent—the scene of our horror of the previous day. How ridiculously easy it seemed from up there to find Serabit! Whether it was the inspiriting panorama or the nearness of the peak, we continued the climb with vigor, everybody keeping together. An hour later we reached the Egyptian Temple of Hathor at the top.

The temple complex was introduced by a sign in English and

Part of the temple at Serabit.

LEFT AND BELOW:
Sinai inscriptions at Serabit.

BOTTOM:
Steles at Serabit.

Hebrew, erected by the Israel government's Department of Antiquities, showing the plan of the pre-Exodus ruins. The sign was the only hint that modern visitors had been there before us. The hewn-sandstone ruins—sanctuaries, pylon, steles, porticoes, purification baths, courtyard, altar, and walls, covering about an acre—appeared to have been untouched by any force but time and weather since the Egyptians had abandoned the mines before the Ptolemies, although I knew full well that Petrie and other archeologists had removed several choice souvenirs (including the black statue of the slave which gave the place its name) to European museums. Indeed, the wealth of clearly marked hieroglyphs on the steles and cartouches gave me the sensation of strolling about an outdoor museum. The preservation was due to Serabit's lofty remoteness from war, vandals, less hardy archeologists, and voracious tourists. We walked slowly through the ruins, and I noticed that the Israeli soldiers were wide-eyed as they explored the sacred caves and tried to decipher the hieroglyphs.

The various inscriptions found in the Sinai generally fall into three categories: the hieroglyphs at Serabit, the alphabetic engravings in the revolutionary Proto-Sinaitic script (the link between hieroglyphic writing and the Phoenician alphabet), and the graffiti in various languages found along caravan tracks throughout the southern Sinai. The first category, all around us in the temple complex, included funerary inscriptions (Hathor was a Theban necropolis goddess, as well as the "Mistress of Turquoise"); entreaties to Osiris, God of the Dead, and other national gods; and reports on the difficult mining operations. The following are translations of two of the hieroglyphic tablets; the first was inscribed by Har-ur-ra, a faithful mine superintendent during the reign of a Twelfth Dynasty king, about 2000 B.C.:

> If your faces fail, the goddess Hathor will give you her arms to aid you in the work. Behold me, how I tarried there after I had left Egypt—my face sweated, my blood grew hot, I ordered the workmen working daily, and said unto them that there is still turquoise in the mine and the vein will be found in time. And it was so; the vein was found at last

and the mine yielded well. When I came to this land, aided by the king's genii, I began to labor strenuously. The troops came and entirely occupied it, so that none escaped therefrom. My face grew not frightened at the work; I toiled cheerfully; I brought abundance, yea abundance of turquoise and obtained yet more by my search. I did not miss a single vein.

The other, perhaps inscribed by a soldier, suggests that the writer was a precursor of Chairman Mao Tse-tung in his attitude toward the nobility of labor:

The mountains burnt like fire; the vein seemed exhausted; the overseer questioned the miners; the skilled workers who knew the mine replied, "There is turquoise to all eternity in the mountain," and at that moment it appeared.

But of far more scholarly importance are the Proto-Sinaitic engravings on the sandstone rock faces beyond the temple complex. These inscriptions were made by the miners, the Semitic slaves, who used a form of their native Proto-Canaanitic symbols as hieroglyph-inspired consonants to construct actual words, not just pictographs. Professor Joseph Naveh, a distinguished epigraphist at the Hebrew University, told me that no scholars were exactly sure how to read these Serabit engravings. "We do not know how many letters are in the alphabet and what they absolutely mean," he said. "Thousands of years ago, many Semites, the descendants of Abraham, worked for the Egyptians as slaves or, shall we say, people who must work for a stronger power even though they were as advanced culturally. They brought with them to the Serabit mines the clearest version we have of the Proto-Canaanitic script, but they did not invent it there, as some claim. The great value of their script was that it took the first consonantal sound of a particular pictograph and indicated the sound by a special mark. For example, the Canaanite word for 'house' began with a *b* sound, which was signified in the Proto-Sinaitic alphabet as a rectangular symbol called *beit,* which ultimately became the equivalent and name of the letter *b* in Semitic alphabets. *Beit,* coincidentally, means 'house' in Hebrew. So from the pictograph for 'house' came a consonant mark that could be used in many different ways to make many different new words. Instead of a person having to learn thousands of pictures meaning thousands of words, as in hieroglyphics and cuneiform symbols, he could learn a limited number of symbols and read and write an infinite amount of words. Reading and writing were no longer for special people, so the invention of this alphabet was the democratization of literacy. Out of it came the Phoenician, Greek, Hebrew, Latin, and English alphabets. One reason we are not precisely sure of what the Proto-Sinaitic engravings say is that there are no vowels, so we can only guess at the meaning of the words. It would be like coming across the English letters *mn;* it could mean 'man,' 'men,' 'min,' 'mon,' 'mun.' ''

The polyglot graffiti carved into rock faces along trading routes are the poor relation of the three categories of Sinai inscriptions, academically speaking. They vary from drawings of hunting scenes, native animals, crosses, and the menorah to such injunctions (reminiscent of Magic Marker scrawls on New York City subway cars) as "Remember Zailu, son of Wailu" or "Be mindful of Chalios, son of Zaidu" or "An evil race [the Bedouins?]. I, Lupus, a soldier, wrote this with my hand." Scratched in Aramaic, Kufic, Greek, and other European languages, they have given rise to all sorts of interpretations through the centuries. Cosmas, a sixth-century Alexandrian merchant, made a trip through the Sinai to India, and some Jews accompanying him on the journey told him that the inscriptions were the work of Moses and the Israelites. Cosmas was followed by a long parade of puzzled scholars, pilgrims, merchants, and explorers, who called the inscriptions everything from a sacred "song of Moses" to worthless scribblings, and wrote disputatious tracts about their opinions. (In the eighteenth century, an English bishop offered a five-hundred-pound prize to anyone who brought back copies of the holy graffiti, and the King of Denmark sent a scholar to decipher them.) Today, most experts consider them important only for what they might unintentionally reveal. However, Professor Avraham Negev, an authority on Nabateans, at the Hebrew University Archeological Institute, told me that just what some epigraphists found unimportant he found fascinating, especially the Aramaic inscriptions, which he believed to be the work of Nabatean travelers. "The inscriptions are mostly names," he said, "and the repetition of names tends to bore scholars. When I went into the Sinai in 1971, I made a full list of these names and investigated their meanings. They told me who passed by, what they were doing there, where they were from, where they were going, who were their enemies, what were their trades, their hopes, their dreams. In my research into the Nabateans, this information unlocked for me highly valuable data about their lives and culture. The inscriptions are anything but useless. They are history."

When we had taken our fill of the temple ruins, Nura, who had been sitting patiently on a block of sandstone, led us toward the mine adits, a few hundred yards down a trail from the peak. On the way we passed an extraordinary example of all three Sinai-inscription categories. At the top of a rock face was a rude cartouche, with hieroglyphs bordering figures of profiled Egyptians approaching an ankh-holding deity. Below the cartouche were two lines of Proto-Sinaitic engravings, and to the side were the graffiti "I. Crompton 1825" and some indistinct Semitic script. Lieutenant Micha thought he could make out the Hebrew word for "Miriam," which could have been either a reference to Moses' sister or evidence that someone named Miriam had wandered by at one point and wanted the event to be memorialized, as humans have done since the beginning of time. I asked Micha if he felt any special emotion, any connection with the past, as he examined the inscriptions. "No," he said. "It is all too old for me. But another matter is the Dead Sea Scrolls. When I see them in the Israel Museum, I can read the words, like modern Hebrew. Then I feel something strong." Would he be sorry if the Sinai was given back to Egypt? He thought the question over for a moment. "Yes and no," he finally said. "We fought for it many times, but it is not for us like the Galilee or Jerusalem. I agree to give back Sinai for a good peace, but maybe not Yamit and Sharm. Those we need."

We approached warily the first mine adit, a long, forbidding horizontal opening in the rock. There was a flurry of kidding about who would crawl inside and whether or not those who did would share any turquoise they found. "Texas" and I decided to enter the adit first. On our stomachs, we wormed our way through the shallow opening into a larger space, just big enough to move about in at a crouch. A thin slash of sunlight came through a crack in an interior wall, which could have been either natural or man-made. The floor was packed sand, littered with dry animal droppings. Traces of copper ore were in the walls, but no sign of turquoise. The mine had long since been exhausted, despite the hieroglyph author who wrote so optimistically, "There is turquoise to all eternity in the mountain." (A retired British officer named Macdonald tried mining turquoise near Serabit in the nineteenth century and went broke in the process.) It was difficult to imagine the slaves hunched together in this dusty cavern, picking away at the rock, searching for the elusive blue stones used to adorn Nilotic temples and Egyptian nobility. And yet, through all the misery, their minds were still keen enough to advance one of man's finest achievements, the alphabet.

"Texas" and I squeezed ourselves out of the mine and found the others in a much grander grotto nearby, which could easily have held fifty workers, leaving them plenty of room to use their tools. Six pillars, hewn from the rock, held up the ceiling and a primitive shaft brought both light and air to the mine. A disturbed bat flew erratically about, finally alighting in a niche too small for our explorations. Again, we found only animal droppings—no inscriptions, no turquoise.

Outside in the blessed fresh air, we sat around in a circle and ate oranges which the soldiers had brought with them. "Where is the turquoise?" somebody asked. Bailey said that some Bedouins claimed they knew of turquoise deposits at Maghara and Umm Bugma, ten kilometers southwest of Serabit, but they weren't telling how much was there. "So we won't be rich," a soldier muttered with mock resignation. I offered Nura a swig of Halazone-laced water from my canteen. She took a sip and made a sour face when she tasted the chlorine. Everybody laughed, including Nura. Despite the soldiers' lack of emotional connection with Serabit, they treated the area respectfully, burying their orange peels in the ground. They seemed embarrassed by a bullet hole we discovered in a hieroglyphic tablet; they hoped it was not made by an Israeli. It was just eleven days till Passover, and we all admitted that it was a little spooky to be so close to where Moses and the Hebrews might have passed about this time of year, three thousand years before. The Northern Route of the Exodus theorists argued that Moses wouldn't have brought his people near Serabit because of the Egyptian troops garrisoned there, but that speculation collapsed as I looked out over the terrain between the mines and the Gulf of Suez. The ridges and valleys were so thick and deep that Moses could have easily marched his host right under the noses of the Egyptians. Also, not more than a hundred soldiers were probably on duty at Serabit at any given time, hardly enough to stop the Hebrews.

Micha, Bailey, and Nura consulted a detailed military map and decided that a rocky trail on the north side of the mountain would be the best route to the scheduled rendezvous. We started down the plunging, rather dangerous path—which seemed in some stretches to be carved into the mountainside, similar to our descent from Mount Sinai—enjoying the view when we dared look up from our next steps. After edging along a particularly narrow outcropping, Micha noticed that one of his squad was no longer with us. He took a quick roll call and discovered that the absent soldier was the short, blond teen-ager who suffered from vertigo. Fearing the worst, the lieutenant and the Bedouin tracker worked their way back up the ledge to a bend in the trail. At last, they shouted to us that they had found the soldier, who was facing the rock wall, his back to the chasm behind him. He was paralyzed with vertigo, dizzy, nauseated, and embarrassed, and he refused to go on. They calmed him with gentle words, then blindfolded him and led him slowly down to where we were waiting. Green-faced and shivering, he said that he might be able to finish the descent, if someone held on to his arm. Nobody ridiculed him, for which he was grateful (I was sure that his humiliation in front of his friends and Nura was worse than his vertigo). Inching along, supported by the Bedouin tracker, he made it to the bottom of the mountain with the rest of us. "He will learn how to conquer this," Micha said, when we arrived at the rendezvous.

Under the shade of a few acacias, the two soldiers who had driven up the Dodge truck and jeep laid out lunch for everyone— sardines smeared on white bread, fresh tomatoes, carrots, oranges, and good water. It was only ten o'clock but we were all very hungry. The attitudes of the seven climbing soldiers and the two rendezvous soldiers were now reversed; the former kidded the latter for missing out on an exciting expedition, while the latter sulked. Nura and the Bedouin tracker each took their lunches to separate spots and ate in solitude. The others fell into universal post-workout army banter, invariably centered on sex. They had heard on the radio that the American aircraft carrier *Nimitz* was paying a goodwill visit to Haifa. "Every whore in Israel will be in Haifa now," said the soldier from Bombay, who went on to an- nounce that his dream in life was to cohabit with Elizabeth Taylor in America. "I will do to her what the Turks do," he said, demon- strating for the amusement of his fellows, some of whom were dozing in the shade. Bailey was driven back to our starting point that morning and returned shortly with the Land-Rover. We shook hands all around and wished each other luck. By eleven, we had delivered Nura to her house, taken tea with her parents, and were on our way again. As we headed toward Wadi Beirak, Bailey said, "Serabit was worth it, I guess."

"Inshallah," I replied.

SEVEN

IN THE DESERT, as I had learned, carefully laid schemes do not always work out. We had been planning to retrace our route over Wadi Beirak, visit Firan, and then attempt to reach Sharm El Sheikh, via the paved road along the Gulf of Suez, by nightfall. The little hill we had descended from Wadi Beirak at dusk on the previous day swelled to an Everest, as the tires whirred uselessly in its loose sand. Six times we tried, utilizing every combination of drives the Land-Rover offered, and each time we failed. There simply was no uphill traction in that gritty powder, and there was no reasonable way around it. We were defeated by a paltry rise after having scaled lofty mountains. *Inshallah* again. We junked our plan to visit Firan, turned around, and headed west on a solid road to Abu Zeneima, a port on the Gulf of Suez. The catch was that Abu Zeneima sits in the narrow southern part of the U.N. buffer zone, and the coastal road that runs by it can be used by Israeli vehicles only from three to six o'clock in the afternoon, twelve to three o'clock being reserved for Egyptian traffic. If we were delayed for some reason, we would never reach Sharm by nightfall.

Compared to the wadi tracks we had been over recently, the road to Abu Zeneima was the Connecticut Turnpike. It had been graded and tarred by the British in order to truck manganese ore from a now abandoned mine in the area to the Abu Zeneima harbor. Even after decades of war and little maintenance, a careful driver could make good time over it, if he slowed down to avoid plowing into the drifts of sand and the small landslides that occasionally appeared around corners. The edge of the parched El Tih massif was just to the north of us, with its escarpment of yellow and mouse-gray limestone and granite. Bailey had once traveled through El Tih by camel, since it is, to all intents and purposes, impenetrable by any other conveyance. He said it was a discouraging experience for both the travelers and the camels. Only the Tiyaha tribe of Bedouins were capable of scratching out an existence on the desolate plateau, and no other Bedouins covet their tribal territory.

Before long, the road degenerated into a narrow track between limestone cliffs, but we could still keep up our speed, as long as we didn't meet a car coming the other way. Fortunately, we didn't. After a tricky descent over a stretch of stone blocks, which reminded me of the steps in front of the New York Public Library, we entered a broad plain and sniffed the briny air of the sea. Some white barrels and an unattended barrier marked "UN Checkpoint 4" showed that we had passed into U.N. Buffer Zone 2-A, also called "Finnbatt" because it was policed by a battalion of Finnish soldiers under U.N. command. Straight ahead, like a shimmering mirage at the end of the road, was the Gulf of Suez, cobalt and calm in the hot early-afternoon sun. Beneath a blue-and-white U.N. flag stood a sandbagged sentry post, "UN Checkpoint 5," manned by a young, sullen Finnish soldier, his face scarred from sunburn. He leveled his bayonet-tipped rifle menacingly at us and in heavily accented English ordered us to park a few hundred yards back up the road in a sandy open space until three o'clock, when Israeli vehicles could use the coastal road. (It was just past one o'clock; we had made excellent time from Serabit.) Wasn't there a shadier place where we could wait? No. We had not bathed in several days and we smelled like she-camels in heat. Could we possibly swim at the beach along the gulf? No. We must wait in the car till three o'clock. No walking. No photography.

Resigned to a dismal two hours, we drove to the designated area, a broiling plain covered with bits of flintstone and Tuborg beer bottles. We decided to sweat out the time by having a light snack of canned fish, straightening out our gear, making minor repairs to the Land-Rover, reading, and (if the flies didn't devour us) perhaps napping. For the first time since I had been in the Sinai, I missed news of the outside world. Was the world still there? Where was this week's war, natural disaster, political crisis taking place? Did it really matter? I had to admit that it did, at that moment, anyway; I would have given anything for a radio tuned to the BBC World News Service. Another worry was our fuel supply. Because of all the gas we had wasted trying to get up that frustrating sandy rise near Serabit, we had barely enough fuel to make the next service station, at El Tor. If we ran out of gas within the U.N. zone, we could be in serious trouble. Despite those worries, the stifling heat, and the flies, we were in fairly good spirits, the tensions of the previous day's journey almost forgotten. I could just make out some Egyptian trucks and U.N. patrol cars on the coastal road, and occasionally a U.N. helicopter sputtered by above the shoreline, while the contrails of Israeli reconnaissance jets brushed the blue sky over the buffer zone.

At last, it was three o'clock. We rolled up to the barrier at the sentry post and asked the Finnish soldier, more sunburned than before, if we could go through. "No," he said once again, waving his rifle. "You cannot go till three-thirty. U.N. must use road till three-thirty." But he allowed us to park this time near the checkpoint. Two buses pulled up and unloaded about fifty Israeli children, who were on a tour of the Sinai from their Orthodox kibbutz in the north Negev. Like rabbits released from a hutch, the children scampered in all directions, and the flustered Finnish soldier telephoned for help to keep them in line. Soon, other sunburned Finns, dressed in shorts and sneakers, trotted from a Quonset hut nearby. With notable lack of success, they attempted to round up the exultant children. I was afraid the roundup might end in an unpleasant incident, so I produced a scuffed green tennis ball, which I had discovered while cleaning out the Land-Rover, and organized an impromptu game of good old American catch with the boys. For lads more used to soccer and basketball, they were pretty fair at throwing and catching high flies, although they insisted on catching the ball one-handed, as if it would have been a sin against God to use two hands. There they were, killing a half hour under the hot Sinai sun, a noisy bunch of skullcapped kids with braided side-locks playing a frenetic game of catch on the very sands their forefathers had roamed thousands of years ago, while incongruous Finns nervously watched. This latest Sinai culture clash concluded with oranges being distributed to one and all by the children's guides, and it was three-thirty.

The sentry, his mouth full of orange, raised the barrier and we drove through onto the coastal road, a good highway running between the gulf and some abandoned narrow-gauge railroad tracks. The shoreline was peaceful—gentle waves stroking the dunes, ships plowing north to the entrance of the Suez Canal, a handsome villa flying the U.N. flag on a bluff. The only sign of war was a wrecked locomotive, looking like a wounded beast dying in the sand.

The main business along the Suez coast is oil, which is why the official Egyptian flag of the Province of Sinai is a black derrick against a yellow background. We could see several oil rigs, returned to Egypt after Sinai II, sprouting offshore; others, farther south, from Abu Durba to El Tor, were still worked by the Israelis. The coastal wells had been developed for Egypt in 1964 by an Italian oil-exploration company, E.N.I., and, economically, they were Israel's richest prize in the 1967 Sinai conquest. Suez oil then fulfilled half of Israel's petroleum needs. A profitable industry had begun, with Israeli roughnecks, reminiscent of the hard-drinking, brawling workers in the Texas and Oklahoma oil fields, settling in the boom town of Abu Rudeis. Now, the Israeli roughnecks were working, with something less than certainty about their futures, in the newer boom town of El Tor, where the Alma field—expanded since the treaty negotiations and Iran crisis—was providing about twenty percent of Israel's normal oil consumption. (Israel has continued to pay fifty-percent royalties to E.N.I., just as Egypt had.)

Some geologists claim that the Gulf of Suez oil reserves probably continue north through the Sinai as far as the Mediterranean Sea,

An oil field near Abu Rudeis. *Magnum.*

which, if true, might someday create a junior Saudi Arabia out of the peninsula. The stakes are enormous, especially since Egypt, even without all her Gulf of Suez wells, is already an oil exporter, hoping to produce a million barrels a day by 1980. Citing international law, the Israeli government has stated that, even if it returns the peninsula to Egyptian sovereignty, it reserves the right to share in any Sinai oil, up to one half the distance across the gulf—another claim disputed by both Egypt and the United States. Still, the creation of a joint Israeli-Egyptian petroleum complex in the Sinai, along perhaps with nuclear-power and desalinization plants, could go a long way toward securing the peaceful future of the peninsula. What such an industrial plan would do to the ecology and Bedouin life in the wilderness is another matter. As usual, nobody asks the Bedouin what he thinks about it all.

The way things stand at present, Israel is scheduled to give up its precious wells near El Tor seven months after the peace-treaty signing. This, perhaps the most painful concession for the Israelis in the hard treaty bargaining, was negotiated right up to the last minute. In return for the wells, Egypt pledged "normal commercial sales of oil" to Israel, and, in a separate memorandum of agreement, the United States promised to supply Israel's petroleum needs for fifteen years, at world-market prices, if other sources of supply were suddenly "unavailable." Although these arrangements seem secure, Israel is understandably nervous about the deal.

The intricate gerrymandering sketched out by Henry Kissinger in his diplomatic shuttles of 1974 and 1975 was crazily evident from the start of our drive down the coastal road. From U.N. Checkpoint 6 the route, for Israeli vehicles, turned ninety degrees to the east onto a new road. We had left Buffer Zone 2-A and were skirting, on its perimeter, the Egyptian area around Abu Rudeis. Technically, we were back in Israel-occupied Sinai. (A guard at an I.D.F. checkpoint put down the book he was reading in the shade of a half-track, examined our papers, and said, "Welcome to Israel!") Just to our right was Egyptian territory—a flat, mined, scrubby dune leading to the gulf. We could see more wells, a tank farm, offshore loading buoys, piers, an airstrip, and some housing for the oil workers. After another I.D.F. checkpoint, we were back again in U.N. territory, Buffer Zone 2-B, just slightly wider than the road. Ten kilometers more and we came to a fork in the road —Israeli traffic to the left (inland and east), Egyptian traffic to the south (but only as far as the end of Buffer Zone 2-B, just north of Abu Durba). We were back in "Israel" again, near the Wadi Firan track (which we had originally wanted to take), and curving south toward El Tor. The geopolitical design was beyond the grandest dreams of a Massachusetts politician.

We were traveling through the harshest desert of the Sinai, according to the Victorian explorers—El Kaah, or "The Plain." The beauty and breezes of the gulf vanished and all around us were disagreeable, sickly yellow scrub and coarse sand, disorienting mirages, and war detritus. Only the distant purple peaks to the east and some oddly twisted combat debris (one strafed Egyptian truck exposed its slowly turning radiator fan, looking like a Calder sculpture) broke the monotony. Professor Palmer, particularly, had loathed El Kaah, and it was perverse destiny that he should have met his violent death near that wretched, parched plain. Like so many British explorers, he had an ulterior motive in coming to the Sinai: political intelligence and espionage. He was assigned by his government to persuade the Towara to side with the British in putting down an 1882 Egyptian revolt, and to that end he was carrying gold with which he meant to bribe the Bedouins. However, he and his party were turned upon and slaughtered by their renegade guides. Because of their service to the Crown, their recovered bodies were interred in St. Paul's Cathedral. (One of Palmer's party was his Egyptian-Jewish cook, Nissim, who is probably the only Jew buried in that exclusive repository.)

Adding to the sinister quality of El Kaah was the unsettling fact that we were reduced to our last five-gallon jerry can of gasoline. To get our minds off the fuel problem, Bailey told me about the Aleigat of the El Tor region, a happy-go-lucky tribe which will use any excuse to have an all-night party, with attendant singing, dancing, hand-clapping, and hash-smoking. These jolly Bedouins, however, once held a party that they have since come to regret. To

celebrate the Israelis' withdrawal from their area after the 1956 Sinai campaign, they feted the U.N. troops who replaced the Israelis, and in the course of the merrymaking, they recited a short poem. *"Tili al gush wa pasha khush"* went the rhyme, which means, roughly, "Now the paper tigers have left and the pashas have come in." But in 1967, the Israelis came thundering back to El Tor, and the Aleigat, fearing revenge by the Israelis for the taunting poem, fled to the hills in panic. Of course, the Israelis had no idea of what was going on; they had never heard about the rhymed ridicule, and even if they had, they would have been more amused than upset. Still, many of the Aleigat, afraid of phantom vengeance, stay clear of the Israelis.

Just when my computation of kilometers per gallon figured us to be working on our last gallon of our last jerry can, we reached a gravel plain pocked with small gardens owned by St. Catherine's Monastery. We passed Hammam Sidna Musa, the "Hot Baths of Lord Moses," natural hot sulphur springs that were used as a cure for rheumatism by both Bedouins and the Christian pilgrims who settled at El Tor when it was a gateway to Mount Sinai. Beyond the springs was the town of El Tor, whose fortunes had risen and fallen with history: a crowded quarantine station for hajjis, an active port for Red Sea fishermen and seafarers of the Orient trade, then a seldom-used caravansary after the Portuguese discovered the Cape of Good Hope route between Europe and the East, and currently an oil boom town with modern apartment houses, date-palm groves, shops, and (I observed with delight) a large, modern gas station.

We rolled up to a fuel pump, and while a Bedouin boy filled our tank and jerry cans, I strolled about, looking over the town. Against the sun setting behind the Egyptian mountains on the other side of the gulf, El Tor seemed to be a hodgepodge of structures and people, like a small El Arish—concrete houses, dilapidated shacks,

---

A camel and ravens in the desert of the southern Sinai. *Magnum.*

The coastal town of El Tor. *Magnum.*

oil-drilling equipment, government buildings, military barracks; Bedouins, Palestinian Arabs, Egyptians, Israelis. In front of the headquarters of the south Sinai military governor, some Bedouin elders had gathered, like schoolchildren outside the principal's office. The scene attracted me and I photographed it. The next thing I knew I was being arrested by an armed Israeli soldier, who marched me into the headquarters building. Bailey saw what had happened and followed. A sneering sergeant told me that I was in a restricted military zone and was not allowed to take photographs. He wanted my camera and all my film, but I refused to give either to him. I told him I was a journalist accredited by the Government Press Office in Jerusalem and I showed him my letters of introduction and press card. He stared at them blankly. I gave him telephone numbers of government officials to call. He insisted that I give him my camera and film. I again refused. Bailey spoke privately to the sergeant, who stood firm. The impasse was costing us precious driving hours and might have even cost me a night in a detention cell, but luckily the duty officer suddenly appeared, a Lieutenant Lazar, whom Bailey knew from earlier Sinai trips. The lieutenant settled the matter in ten seconds and we were on our way again, my camera, film, and pride intact. "Don't let it get you," Bailey said, as we drove into the pink dusk. "It's the old army game. The sergeant is ambitious. He was bucking for something—probably the lieutenant's job." Anyway, we had plenty of fuel, El Kaah looked almost beautiful in the dim rosy light, an antelope playfully raced us along the side of the road, and, all things being equal, Sharm El Sheikh was only two hours away.

The region of Sharm El Sheikh—the "Bay of the Sheikh," named for an unknown Bedouin chief—is actually a series of reef-bound bays at the southernmost tip of the peninsula. Apart from its critical position—maritime traffic coming up the Gulf of Akaba or the Gulf of Suez is at the mercy of coast artillery mounted on the headlands —the area was never much more than a place for fishermen to sort out their catches, which often included Red Sea sharks and barracuda. After the Israelis captured and held Sharm in 1967, they renamed it Ophira, in honor of King Solomon's trade through the adjacent Strait of Tiran with Ophir, a vague term for Africa. They also set about developing Sharm/Ophira into a beach resort and military base. For many urban Israelis it is what the Hamptons are to New Yorkers—on a vastly reduced scale, of course. When its bright lights riddled the desert night ahead, Bailey snickered, "Ah, the gold coast." While he approved of the need for an uncrowded seaside refuge far from the noise and congestion of Tel Aviv, he disliked what the development was doing to his Sinai, scarring the dramatic shoreline with hotels and enlisting the local Bedouins into menial service. I was sympathetic to his point of view, but, on the other hand, at that moment I would have sold my soul for a clean hotel room, a real bed, and a long, hot shower. Even though he wanted to stay with a Bedouin poet he knew there, he conceded that a little civilization wouldn't hurt either of us.

We drove past the bay at Ras Muhammad, with its scraggly coral reefs and mangroves, skirted Sharm El Sheikh proper, and pulled into the newest settlement of Naama (Hebrew for "pleasant"), where the Sharem Hotel was situated. The lobby was buzzing with honeymooning couples, Israelis arriving on bus excursions, and European tourists, many of them hippies. Most of the signs were in English ("Day charters on sailing yacht Shalom—Inquire within") and the décor was Late Motel Tasteless. We checked into a double room, whereupon Bailey stretched out on a bed and fell asleep, while I took a thirty-minute shower. Later, at the hotel bar, the Danish bartender told me (over my third bottle of Gold Star beer) that Breik Odeh Abu Abdullah, Sheikh of Sheikhs of the Muzeina tribe, was a regular customer there. "He comes in and drinks Scotch and beer," the bartender said. "His Bedouins who work here don't seem to mind. I think he is a hero to them—and to the Scandinavian girls. Everybody around here digs the girls. Like the tourists, most of what you see comes from the outside. In Sharm, we have only our own water."

The next morning I explored Naama, while Bailey drove off to visit his Bedouin poet friend. The crescent bay contained a fine-sand beach scooped out of the dunes, dotted with sunburned children, baked baskers, and the go-getters found in every developing international resort ("I figure we can get the thing started with just five hundred quid," I overheard an enterprising Englishman telling a bored Frenchman). Here and there were dihedral sun shades, bubble cabanas, souvenir stands, boutiques, snack bars, and a disco called the White Elephant. Glass-bottom excursion boats and craft for skin divers were waiting for passengers at a dock. Everything seemed to be air-conditioned; the hotel dining room alone had twenty cooling units. I wondered if the Egyptians truly understood what they would be inheriting when this region of the Sinai was given back to them (which, according to the peace treaty, is scheduled to occur by April, 1982).

As soon as Bailey had returned (with a new and prized tape

cassette of Bedouin poetry), we checked out of the hotel and prepared to head north on a daylong dash to Jerusalem. But one more
spectacle stopped us cold. Some El Arish merchants had driven
their truck onto the hotel grounds and were hawking fresh vegetables to passers-by. Two of the passers-by were young Swedish girls,
bursting out of the flimsiest of bikinis. "Oh, tomatoes!" one of the
girls shouted, climbing into the truck to examine the wares. "We
live by tomatoes." The Arishiya were beside themselves, so flustered by the nearness of these practically nude blondes that they just
about gave away their entire tomato inventory. There was no question of Levantine haggling, and the girls scurried off with their red
treasures. Bailey said in Arabic to one of the perspiring merchants,
"Give me your truck and I'll get you the girls." The merchant
collected himself and announced that he would not give his truck
for fifty such girls, that his wife at home was a far better woman.
"Talk about your Sinai culture clashes!" Bailey said to me as we
drove off. "The only better one I ever heard of than that was about
a Jewish girl from America who met a Bedouin working at a hotel
here. She married him, took him home, and now he's in the family
business."

The road north, along the Strait of Tiran and opposite the coral-
encrusted Saudi islands of Tiran and Sanafir, took us through the
military region of Sharm, past an airfield (also used for civilian
Arkia flights), a firing range, antiaircraft positions, minefields, and
isolated I.D.F. lookout posts. One very famous and now abandoned
military site on the bluffs over the shore was Ras Nasrani ("Headland of the Christian"), where Egyptian coastal artillery had once
commanded the strait at its narrowest point. The cannon emplace-
ments were captured twice by the Israelis in daring raids—the 1956
strike by General Abraham Yoffe's 9th Brigade, after the Egyptians
had blocked the strait to Israeli navigation, and again in 1967, after
the U.N. forces stationed there were ordered out by Nasser. Both
times the guns were spiked by the retreating Egyptians. It seemed
as if every visitor to the gun pits had scratched some graffiti on them
—"Shalom" was the most prevalent, although some choice dis-
paraging remarks were written about the Egyptian Army, too—and

the British-made cannon were still engraved with the seal of George V. (Most likely, the "Christian" in the headland's name was an Egyptian salute to the English; the Bedouins have always called the place Siha.) Just Bedouin fishermen man the site now, living in the wrecked barracks nearby and drying their nets on the beach littered with the trash of war. When we happened by, two Bedouins were putting the finishing touches on a crude soft-drink stand and they asked Bailey if he would paint a sign for them in English. "HAMDAM'S HAVE-A-DRINK" was decided upon as a catchy enough name, and so a new business was inaugurated in the Sinai.

We continued up the coast on a dirt road toward Nabk, where the northernmost mangrove shrubs in the world are located. These dense evergreen plants grow just offshore, projecting their roots above water and drawing air into the trunks. The strange clusters, like a New England forest rising from the sea, attract gulls and small fish to the natural lagoon they create, water more turquoise than the rest of the Gulf of Akaba. The gulf was unusually rough that day. Crosscurrents and wind-stirred whitecaps made the always tricky navigation channel appear even more threatening. A couple of derelict ships on the reefs, their hulls stripped of everything worth taking, attested to how dangerous the waters are.

Up ahead on the dirt track were uncleared minefields, so we cut inland through a wadi to the main paved road, the tallest Sinai peaks like a solid wall of red granite in front of us. We roared down the wadi, and more wild game than I had spotted so far came out to see what the excitement was. Rabbits, antelope, hedgehogs, and a fox scampered about. The animal that I most wanted to see in the Sinai—the ibex—still eluded me. It is now a rare and endangered species, what with indiscriminate hunting by Bedouins and sports- men (the Sinai mountains were popular with big-game hunters during the British raj) and with the recent wars. Just before the main road, we stopped at a small Civil Administration outpost,

---

A gun emplacement at Ras Nasrani, looking toward Tiran. *Magnum.*

A Bedouin at midday prayers, at Dahab, with Israeli tourist camps in the background. *Magnum.*

nothing more than huts containing a clinic and school, and adjacent water tanks for the Bedouin flocks. Some boys ran to the car and with surprising forwardness pleaded for handouts. Bailey gave them pieces of candy and asked them if they had watered their goats. "Girls water the goats," one said. "Boys go to school." As we started toward the main road, Bailey shouted to them, *"Tisrig wala tishad,"* another old Bedouin proverb which he quickly translated for my benefit: "Steal but don't beg."

We were back on the 9th Brigade Road the Israelis had completed in 1971, connecting Elath and Sharm El Sheikh, and we were making excellent time. Along this stretch, the road followed the natural course of the old Wadi Samaghi (named for the sap of the acacia tree) and cut through the stark granite walls of the Sharira Pass, where a monument stands in memory of two Israeli soldiers who were killed by an Egyptian mine. Clouds intermittently covered the sun, changing the craggy landscape from yellow in the shade to rose in the sunlight, like a geological chameleon. We planned to make a lunch stop at Dahab, another prosperous moshav-cum-hippies, like Neviot farther up the coast. From the amount of backpacking drifters we passed and the latest Sinai inscriptions ("Carol 1975"), it was obvious that we were entering Darkest Hippieland.

Dahab itself is a wadi delta. Its name means "golden," and some archeologists speculate that it was once the site of Dizahab, which is mentioned in the Bible as a station of the Israelites' wandering. There is solid evidence that Nabateans and Romans existed there, however, and Bedouins have long used the Dahab oasis for light agriculture and fishing. It is well named; there is a golden South Sea paradise look to the place. Around the broad, palm-dotted bay were camping grounds and a snack bar, segregated from the melon-growing moshav, and posted signs promoted everything from snorkeling to souvenirs. The hippies seemed slightly more wholesome than their counterparts at Neviot, although they had that same beaten, catatonic air about them. Over a high-priced lunch of hot dogs, French fries, salad, and Coke, I talked with Eva, a pretty twenty-six-year-old girl from Munich who had recently hennaed her hair and tattooed one arm. Eva said that she wanted to live in Dahab forever, unless she was given a job as a model in Tel Aviv. When I asked her what the attraction of Israel and the Sinai was for so many Germans, she answered blandly, "Germans have always liked the Jews." I credited her answer to youth or hashish, or perhaps both. It would have been interesting to discuss her statement further, but we had to move on.

Before long, Wadi Saal appeared, marking the point at which we had turned off the 9th Brigade Road to St. Catherine's Monastery three days earlier. Only three days! It seemed impossible. And there, not far ahead, was the Yair Crossroads and Zvi Swet's gas station. Swet was away in Jerusalem, arguing a complaint before government officials, but his wife, Ruth, was running things with her iron hand. She was waiting on a hefty, gray-haired man who was trying on a *galabiya* in her boutique. He turned out to be none other than General Abraham Yoffe, the former leader of the 9th Brigade and currently the head of the Nature Reserves Authority, returning from an inspection trip around the Sinai.

Taking a few moments from his shopping, General Yoffe told me that he was as proud of the work his government agency was doing as he was of his war record, which included leading an armored division through the Gidi and Mitla passes in 1967. He was especially pleased with the warm relationship between the Sinai Bedouins and the government. "We treat them right and always take into consideration their feelings," he said. "Since ten years ago, we spent a lot of money to better their lives. Some work for us and we pay them well. I am also the right hand of the Civil Administration. We are separate agencies, but we work together with the same aim. I remember what a Bedouin sheikh said to me after the Six Day War. I knew him in 1956, but I saw him again eleven years later and he recognized me. He said, 'Look, if we have Turkish or Egyptian or Israeli rule, it is nothing to us. They come and go. We knew in our history a lot of people here, but you Israelis have one thing better than the others—you don't interfere in our life. You accept us as we are.' This is true. We don't interfere. We try to do what we think is right, and after that, you can form your own opinion about it. Most Sinai Bedouins feel like that sheikh, and this is why we don't have any ill feelings—no mines on the road (and they could have put a lot of mines around here), no terrorism. They have enough work, health, schools, that sort of thing."

I asked Yoffe about government attempts to urbanize the Bedouins. "Not in the Sinai," he said. "If they want to be in tents, they can be in tents. If they want to live here one part of the year and another place later on, it's up to them. As for General Sharon's attempts to urbanize them in the Negev, in Israel proper, that's different. Whatever land belongs to the Bedouins in the Sinai, they own it and can do what they want on it." He held up a piece of his *galabiya* to the light and, with a grunt, approved of its quality. "Tourism here is a problem," he said. "We want tourists, both Israelis and outsiders, to come to the Sinai, to enjoy themselves, learn from it, but not destroy it. We try to fight against litter and scribbles. We even put a sign on a rock that says you can write your names and what-not here but don't write on monuments. However, we can't police everywhere. It's a problem all over the world." He paused. "If we are ever returning the Sinai to the Egyptians, I say we should return it in good condition."

The rest of the trip north to Elath and into the Arava was un-eventful. A two-day-old *International Herald Tribune* I bought in Elath showed that the world could be uneventful, too; nothing much had happened, and I felt silly about missing the news. It wasn't until we were stopped at an I.D.F. roadblock well into the dreary, darkening Arava that the world truly caught up with us. A helmeted soldier carefully checked our papers, recorded our names and license-plate number on his clipboard, and then ordered us to pull over to the side of the road and wait for enough vehicles to form a convoy. "Are you armed?" he asked Bailey. Bailey said he had a pistol. The soldier smiled thinly. Was anything wrong? "I wouldn't be here if there wasn't," the soldier said and walked to the car behind us.

While we waited for our convoy to form, Bailey speculated on what the trouble was. "There are two P.L.O. suicide squads still unaccounted for," he said. "We knew there were four; one was in the Cyprus incident and another shot up the bus north of Tel Aviv. Maybe our intelligence thinks one of the remaining two is around here someplace. It's possible they could have slipped over from Jordan." He placed the revolver on the front seat between us. A hell of a lot of good that will do us against Kalashnikovs and grenades, I thought. All the peace and beauty of the Sinai dissolved into the tension and fear of outlying Israel, caught up in its thirtieth year of terror and reprisal. The sun set quickly over the Negev hills —a dazzling sight, but I was sorry to see safer daylight disappear.

Finally, the assembled convoy, mostly big trucks and a few pri-vate cars, was waved through the roadblock. Its order soon deteriorated, as each driver tried to break his personal speed record to wherever he was headed. Israelis are far too individualistic to drive in convoys. Each headlight coming at us, each shadow by the road grew into a threat, a potential burst of gunfire. When I took my turn behind the wheel, I could feel my neck muscles lock. It was hot and still, but I perspired more than was necessary. Bailey, during one particularly lonely stretch of road just before the Dead Sea, suddenly recited the Bedouin rain-ceremony chant: "Oh, mother of rain, send us rain! Moisten the gown of the shepherd!" This, he explained, was chanted after a goat was sacrificed and its blood smeared about—not exactly the most cheering image. *Inshallah,* I thought, for maybe the twentieth time that week. What will be will be.

There were more roadblocks and more futile attempts to form convoys. The final roadblock was at the junction of the Jerusalem and Jericho roads, and once beyond it, we could feel the mountain breezes and see the glow in the sky of Jerusalem's lights. At last, climbing the Judean plateau, we could make out the silhouette of that glorious city, defying history, perched there forever, no matter what. "How doth the city sit solitary!" Jeremiah lamented, but I felt only giddy joy at the sight of it. We had come through, emotionally and physically spent but comparatively unscathed. I could not recall a time when I was more tired. At the main entrance to the Jerusalem Plaza, guests from some celebration were filing out and stopping to stare at the dusty, battered Land-Rover and its two dusty, battered occupants. It was almost eleven o'clock, Tuesday night, April 11. We had been gone since Friday morning, April 7, and we had traveled 1,830 tough, timeless kilometers. "Nice trip," Bailey said. I nodded. We shook hands and said good night.

EIGHT

I SPENT THE next four days in Jerusalem, recuperating and preparing for my remaining Sinai journeys—one to the U.N. buffer zone and the American early-warning stations, the other to the Egyptian-held part of the peninsula. My recuperation was somewhat complicated. After having lived and eaten with the Bedouins under conditions that would drive an American health inspector into premature retirement, I was astounded that I hadn't suffered even the slightest stomach disorder. But once back in Jerusalem, I accepted an invitation to a friend's house for a "real Jewish home-cooked dinner," and it was a full day before I recovered from that leaden repast. And after having climbed and descended precipitous mountains and hiked through broiling deserts without any physical complaint more serious than a charley horse, I was coaxed into joining a pickup basketball game at a Jerusalem schoolyard and promptly tore a muscle in my left shoulder.

There was another discouraging development. The American consul-general in Jerusalem, Michael Newlin, had been in touch with Cairo about my request to enter Egyptian Sinai directly from the U.N. zone; he informed me that permission had been denied "at the highest level," whatever that meant. So I would have to return to Israel from the U.N. zone, fly to Athens, and then change planes for a flight to Cairo—the equivalent of going from the East Side of Manhattan to the West Side via Hartford, Chicago, and Philadelphia, with a side trip from Philadelphia to Riverside Drive. Still, accommodations and Sinai traveling arrangements were promised, once I circuitously arrived in Cairo.

Although the United Nations had its hands full establishing its newborn peacekeeping force in Lebanon after the recent Israeli incursion into the south of that country, I had succeeded in gaining an interview with Lieutenant General Ensio Siilasvuo, Chief Coordinator of the United Nations Peace-Keeping Missions in the Middle East. The Finnish Army officer had first come to the Middle East in 1957, when he commanded the Finnish contingent of the U.N. Emergency Force in the Gaza area. Serving almost continuously under the U.N. flag since then, he has been chosen as the umpire for just about every important peace meeting between Arabs and Israelis, including the military negotiations at Kilometer 101 on the Cairo-Suez road, which brought about a separation of forces after the 1973 Yom Kippur War. As the representative of the U.N. Secretary-General and the overseer of the alphabet soup of acronymic U.N. agencies in the Middle East— UNEF (U.N. Emergency Force), UNTSO (U.N. Truce Supervision Organization), UNDOF (U.N. Disengagement Observer Force), and now UNIFIL (U.N. Interim Force in Lebanon)—he coordinated his multinational charges from the old British Mandate Government House, spectacularly overlooking Jerusalem from the Hill of Evil Counsel.

For a professional military man with such mighty responsibilities, General Siilasvuo is an affable, informal person, preferring to dress in a plain khaki sweater and trousers with the bare minimum of insignia. He has the square-jawed, slightly Asiatic cast to his face that the world has come to associate with Finns through photographs of Jean Sibelius. "The peacekeeping business in the Middle East has its ups and downs," he said, over strong coffee in his spacious office. "When opposing governments cooperate and support the U.N. forces—when they *want* a cease-fire to work—then peacekeeping is an easy matter. Otherwise, we are in trouble because the U.N. is always right in the middle. We think we are a

---

Dunes and an acacia tree in the southern Sinai. *Magnum.*

psychological deterrent by our very presence, but sometimes they fire on us, whether accidentally or not, and we go to the shelters. We are permitted to fire first only in self-defense, as in somebody obstructing a U.N. soldier, but we fire only as a last resort. My rule is that if we must shoot, then we have failed. When the 1973 war began in the Sinai, the Bar Lev Line did not hold as the Israelis thought it would, and the Egyptians came pouring through the gaps. The U.N. observers there were bombed and the Egyptians told us to go to Cairo. 'We don't want you looking at our backs,' they said. Some observers went to Cairo, some to Israel. We had to improvise quickly and we had casualties. There have been forty-two U.N. deaths in the Sinai alone since 1973, most of them from land-mine accidents, although a few, I believe, were intentional shootings. Now we are having casualties in Lebanon, and I am more worried because big powers are involved, like the French. Also, there are Soviet military observers in the Sinai, as well as Americans."

I asked the general what I could expect to find when I visited the U.N. troops on duty in the Sinai. "They are enthusiastic," he said. "They feel they are taking part in a historic event and are ambassadors of their countries. The conditions are harsh, but they acclimate to them. Also, there is just a six-month limit to their duty, and most of them are volunteers, with higher pay, and the Scandinavians are draftees, so the educational level is greater. English is the common language for the officers, but the ordinary soldiers usually speak just their own native language. This can make problems sometimes, but there is healthy competition in sports and to be the best soldiers. Political differences are no problem. The Poles are the first Communist troops under the U.N.—they provide logistic support in the Sinai with the Canadians—but they get along well. And everybody helps out the Bedouins with water and medical assistance. Some troops are fascinated by the local life.

"Of course, we are far from the beginning of a true world police force here, but we serve a very important function in providing a human barrier between enemies. Look, I have seen people as deep enemies, but when there is human contact, they are not enemies any

longer. The Kilometer 101 meetings were the first contacts between Egyptians and Israelis after the terrible war of 1973. The
Egyptian and Israeli generals got to like each other and progress
was made. The personal touch is important to peace. I saw this
happen many times. When Sadat came to Jerusalem, he went out
of his way to greet with warmth Ezer Weizman, who was in a
wheelchair because of an automobile accident. They talked for an
hour right off and became friends. That is what helps make peace."

My departure from the Jerusalem Plaza, at eight o'clock Sunday
morning, April 16, was a bit tonier than my previous leave-takings
with Bailey had been. I was better dressed, for one thing, I had all
my luggage with me (I would not be returning to Jerusalem this
time), and I was going off in style—in a white Volkswagen Dasher
station wagon with the large black letters "UN" painted on the
sides and roof. My itinerary called for me to be picked up at the
hotel by First Lieutenant Lars Alfon, a Swedish intelligence officer,
and his driver, Private Krister Cederberg, who would escort me
through the northern Sinai to Swedbatt, in U.N. Buffer Zone 1,
manned by a battalion of Swedish troops. After visits to outposts
and a briefing at Swedbatt Headquarters, I would be driven to
Ghanbatt, the central portion of Buffer Zone 1, garrisoned by
Ghanaian soldiers, who would then deposit me that night at the
Sinai Field Mission area of the American early-warning stations,
where I would stay for two days. (Between Ghanbatt and Finnbatt,
the narrow buffer zone starting at Abu Zeneima that I had traveled
through with Bailey, were Indbatt, an Indonesian battalion, and
patches of Israeli and Egyptian territories.) The itinerary was carefully spelled out in several languages by efficient military technicians, presumably leaving nothing to *inshallah.*

Lieutenant Alfon, a young English teacher in civilian life who was
completing his required military service with a six-month tour of
duty in the Sinai, explained the present tight situation of Swedbatt,
as we sped toward Gaza and the Via Maris coastal road. A reinforced company of 240 Swedish volunteers had just been trans-
ferred to Lebanon as the initial unit of UNIFIL. So far, one sergeant

had been killed and another wounded when their command car hit a land mine. Still, there were more volunteers for Lebanon duty than were needed, but the Swedish personnel in the buffer zone were making do at two-thirds their regular strength. We stopped at a roadside café just north of Gaza for buns and coffee, and the lieutenant greeted another Swedish officer, dressed like Alfon in starched khakis with "SVERIGE" patches on their left sleeves. He was on his way to Lebanon to deliver new cameras purchased earlier by the Swedish troops at their post exchange. "You see how crazy this all is," Alfon said. "We are in a deadly situation but the soldiers must have their new cameras."

Middle Eastern automotive tactics had infected Private Cederberg, a truck driver from Göteborg who had only eight more weeks left to fulfill his army obligation. With horn blaring, he raced through the jumble of Gaza, scattering donkeys, camels, goats, sheep, dogs, pedestrians, and all other vehicles from his blazing path. Only the children marching to school well off the road were safe. (The students going to school in the morning wear gray tunics and red pants; the afternoon shift wears gray tunics and blue pants.) Just past El Arish, where the desert began in earnest and sand had drifted over the road, Cederberg truly went on the attack, blasting the Dasher through each drift at speeds upward of seventy miles per hour. "It is the only way," Cederberg, a bad stutterer, apologized with some difficulty. Only way or not, we made remarkable time, reaching the marshy flats before the Bardawil Lagoon by late morning.

The Sabkhet El Bardawil—a vast, briny, shallow lake enclosed by a sand spit, which the Northern Theorists of the Exodus believe to be Moses' escape route from Egypt—was named for Baldwin II, a French King of Jerusalem from 1118 to 1131, "Bardawil" being an Arabic approximation of "Baldwin." After an expedition to free the northern Sinai from the Moslems, the King

Sabkhet El Bardawil. *Magnum.*

ate some tainted fish caught in the lagoon and died. (The Bedouin version of his demise was that Baldwin came to the area specifically to visit his Moslem girl friend, who was forced by the Saracens to steal Baldwin's magic cap, which made him invisible to his enemies. The girl stole the cap and Baldwin was killed the next day.) Many of his soldiers posted in the north Sinai intermarried with Bedouin women and converted to Islam after Jerusalem fell to the Saracens. Some adopted the name Bardawil, and to this day a few of the Bayathiyin and Suwarka fishermen on the shores of the lagoon have a European look to them. It tickled the British governor of Sinai, Major Jarvis, that two Bedouin smugglers named Bardawil had been arrested while Stanley Baldwin was Prime Minister of Great Britain.

The tainted fish that undid King Baldwin could have been one of the mullet that enter the lagoon by the thousands through breaks in the sand spit and are caught in fishermen's nets when they try to return to the Mediterranean. Their roe, called *bitarikh,* is extracted, dried in the sun, and sold for a good price as a purported aphrodisiac. Another plentiful fish is a species of flounder which, like its cousins, seems to be only half a fish; the Bedouins call it *samak Musa,* in honor of the holy man who parted the local waters and, inadvertently, they believe, some of the fish, in the process. When I had passed this way in 1969, during the War of Attrition, I stopped at a paramilitary outpost called Nahal Yam, where the rare and savory *ajuj* fish is caught and prepared in a small restaurant. It was one of the gastronomic high points of that trip to the Middle East, and I was sorry that we didn't have time to stop there now for an *ajuj* lunch. (Nahal Yam was also memorable as the place where, according to ecstatic news reports from Cairo, an Egyptian airborne commando raid had eradicated the Israeli soldiers present—supposedly at the very moment I was wolfing down the *ajuj.* There was more than the usual amount of Arab military-propaganda fantasy during the stalemated War of Attrition.)

The sky over the Mediterranean coast was overcast, giving the Bardawil Lagoon the gray, forbidding look of the Dead Sea. Some self-propelled guns were set up around Nahal Yam—the Israeli

Army on maneuvers as close as it could legally get to its enemy. We were approaching another extremely complicated gerrymandering of frontiers, the legacy of the meticulous territorial negotiations of Kissinger's Sinai II. First, there was Line K, beyond which only limited Israeli forces and armaments could be stationed up to Line J, the border of U.N. Buffer Zone 1. West of the twenty-four-mile-wide buffer zone were Line E and Line F, between which was the Egyptian limited-forces area, and beyond that lay the Suez Canal and Egypt proper. Even though we were on an official U.N. mission, getting past the I.D.F. checkpoint at Line K was the first hurdle. We were supposed to rendezvous with an Israeli escort officer who would accompany us over the seven-mile stretch to Line J, but since we were a few minutes late, the officer had left without us. A sergeant listlessly attempted to arrange a new rendezvous over his field telephone. We were instructed to wait by the side of the road. For close to an hour we waited, Lieutenant Alfon and Private Cederberg bridling. "We are not used to such treatment," the lieutenant said. "It must be because you are a journalist." It was true that others were permitted to pass with a minimum of delay —Canadian logistics trucks and Mercedes-Benz taxis filled with Bedouins heading east to visit relatives in the Sinai—but we were left stewing beside a desolate outpost in the dunes, just a shack and a water tower among stunted palms and creeping scarabs. Alfon was getting angrier by the minute. He demanded that the sergeant connect him with the officer in charge. The sergeant answered blankly that the telephones did not work well today. I recalled what an Israeli government official had told me about "Bedouinism" affecting troops who had been in the Sinai too long, that they became incapable of clear thinking and had difficulty improvising when something went awry—characteristics I had never observed in Bedouins themselves, by the way. I wondered if this muddled-brain syndrome, so unfairly named, hadn't infected the soldiers at this outpost.

Finally, the sergeant made contact with somebody at the other end of his field-telephone line. After a meandering conversation in Hebrew, he hung up and told us that we could drive to Line J without escort but we must promise not to take pictures. We promised and left, tires screeching and dust boiling behind us. I gathered from Private Cederberg's Swedish muttering that Israelis were not among his favorite nationalities. Just beyond the checkpoint was the bullet-pocked Bedouin hamlet of Bir El Abd, which had the misfortune of being directly in the path of every Sinai campaign throughout history. Yet, its mosque, school, and houses survived, much like its inhabitants, seemingly immune to time and bad luck. A nearby oil-drilling tower, sporting the optimistic sign "WESTERN DESERT INC. NO. 1," lent a Texas quality to the place. The Israelis were obviously testing the geological theory that Gulf of Suez oil ran underground as far as the north Sinai coast—without apparent success, however. At the Line-J I.D.F. checkpoint, we were expected, offered apologies for the delay, and quickly waved through. A sign painted in the U.N. colors of light blue and white read "WELCOME TO SWEDBATT."

Standing by the sign were the outpost commander, Second Lieutenant Elvhammar, Rifleman Sergeant Hogfeldt, and several other soldiers, including identical-twin sergeants named Burgfeldt—all attired in clean green fatigues and U.N.-blue forage caps. With stiff, Swedish formality, like government officials in an Ingmar Bergman movie, they conducted me on a tour of their home in the desert. U.N. CP 567 was a small tent village, with the exceptions of a more permanent water tower and wooden enlisted-men's barracks roofed with corrugated iron. Everything was as ordered and antiseptic as it could be in such a dusty, hot wilderness. Even a poster of a nude girl in the barracks seemed somehow pristine. Automatic weapons were carefully placed in racks (recoilless rifles are the heaviest arms the U.N. is allowed) and a straight line of white barrels, marking the J Line, disappeared into the dunes.

"We are in constant communication with patrols and other observation posts by radio and telephone lines," Lieutenant Elvhammar said.

"Except when the Bedouins cut the cables," Sergeant Hogfeldt interrupted. "I think they do it mostly as a prank. The children like to see our soldiers come out and repair the lines. When the repair unit comes, the Bedouins invite them to tea in their nearest tent or hut. It amuses them to see us, people from another planet, so to speak, fixing the wires, and it helps to break up our days here, although it is a bother always repairing. We hired Bedouin cable guards, who have three Egyptian pounds taken from their salaries every time a cable is cut. So far, they have received no salaries, so many cables are cut. I do not think they patrol the cables much."

The electric generator, used only at night, was shared with the Israeli checkpoint just across Line J, and the fresh water was supplied by the Israelis. "We have very good relations with the Israelis," the lieutenant said. "We exchange tea and coffee and *shaloms* with them. Also, we play football on the harder sand with them. Occasionally they win." Everybody laughed tightly. "For hot water, we let a water tank sit in the sun. It works. You see, there are all the comforts of home." Again, everybody laughed.

At lunch in the spotless mess tent, I was told that the food came in equal amounts from Egypt and Israel, with the one-beer-a-day ration being neutral Löwenbräu. They were proud of their cook, the only one of the ten soldiers stationed at CP 567 with exceptional culinary talent. The justifiably praised cook served up immense platters of well-seasoned eggs and ham (the ham from a little-known kibbutz where pigs are raised and slaughtered contrary to Jewish dietary laws), crisp home-fried potatoes, apple strudel, coffee, and Swedish hardtack. As we ate and sipped Löwenbräu, the men of CP 567 relaxed. They seemed pleased to have some company, some new faces. A battery-powered radio was turned on and blared music from *Hair,* via Abie Nathan's peace-ship radio station anchored off the Sinai coast. They told me that they cherished their tape cassettes of the popular Swedish rock group Abba and other canned entertainment sent from home, such as (much giggling) blue movies. Besides playing football with the Israelis across the way, they passed their off-duty hours jogging and weight lifting, and they were permitted fifteen days off during their six-month tour, which they spent on organized trips to Israel, Egypt, Jordan, or Syria. "Some of us got a trip to Lebanon, too," a sergeant said, "but not a vacation." (Nervous laughter.)

Lunch was pronounced finished when a canteen truck arrived at
the Israeli checkpoint. It came twice a week, and the Swedes were
invited over to buy soft drinks and personal items. They ran across
the J Line and queued in front of the truck with the Israeli soldiers.
Two events in one day! As we drove off for Baluza, the site of
ancient Pelusium and the present-day Swedbatt Headquarters, they
seemed wistful that one of the events had ended so quickly. "At
some of the Swedbatt posts in the desert," Lieutenant Alfon said,
"there are just five men, and things are not so civilized—no Israeli
companionship, no special treats, just roughing it."

Along the road, we saw a series of Bedouin settlements and
villages, most of which were familiar to me from my 1969 trip
through the north Sinai. The big difference now was that the Bayathiyin Bedouins living there, without fear of sporadic Egyptian
artillery fire every time a tank or truck raised a cloud of dust, were
no longer under Israeli jurisdiction. Since Sinai II was imple-
mented, they have been within the expanded U.N. buffer zone,
with the Egyptian government handling their administrative needs.
At El Khirba, for instance, the Egyptian and Sinai flags flew over
the new school, decorated with murals depicting idealized combat
scenes from the 1973 Yom Kippur War. The civilian teachers came
from Cairo for three weeks out of every month, and the health,
water, and housing services were administered by other Egyptian
civilians, headed by a retired general. It was not unlike the Israeli
civil-administration procedure in the rest of the Sinai. The quality
of construction and care was considered high by Egyptian stan-
dards, and the Bedouins were generally content. Since 1975, the
four thousand or so Bayathiyin had been permitted to cross freely
both the Egyptian and Israeli lines, selling their Bardawil fish and
trapped quail wherever the price was best and visiting relatives
wherever they happened to be. From their point of view, it was the
most convenient arrangement in a world they didn't especially want
to understand, a world that seemed never to leave them alone in
their rightful land. If there is a curse on the Sinai Bedouin, it is the
curse of occupation.

The United Nations, for its part, also saw to the needs of the

Bayathiyin. It facilitated their passage across the lines, fenced off newly discovered mine fields, helped put out fires in Bedouin shacks (unsuccessfully, as a rule; one recent hootch fire at El Khirba consumed the flimsy construction and its inhabitants in seconds, before the Swedish troops could arrive with their extinguishers), and contributed to the local economy by purchasing such items as polished brass shell casings, which the Bedouins enchased with stippling.

The windshield of the Dasher showed a few drops of rain, little more than congealed mist, as we approached Baluza, a few kilometers down the road. It was the first precipitation I had ever seen in the Sinai, and it wasn't much. Perversely, the air was still hot and dry. What was left of the Bardawil Lagoon, now just a brackish pond, lay beyond the roadbed of the old Allenby Railroad, its ties and tracks long since torn up to support the bunkers of the Bar Lev Line. At the gate of Swedbatt Headquarters, a sentry snapped to attention and presented a smart rifle salute as we drove through, a startling display of military discipline as opposed to the casualness of the I.D.F. The headquarters complex looked the same as it had in 1969 when it was an Israeli Army base: dun Quonset huts, tents, radio-aerial tower, outlying dunes dotted with Bedouin habitations. Only the flags were different and the airstrip ("Baluza International Airport," according to a sign) was enlarged so that it could handle aircraft as big as the C-130 cargo plane.

Nine years before, I had been briefed at Baluza by a thirty-five-year-old colonel named Yossi, who spent an emotional hour debunking fantastic war communiqués coming out of Cairo. This time, the briefing was conducted by the Swedbatt commander, Colonel Lindgren, and his aide, Major Ekman, both natty and formal in their pressed khakis. I was ushered into the colonel's office by Lieutenant Alfon, who then departed, his escort responsibility completed. Under crossed U.N. and Swedish flags and photographs of the King and Queen of Sweden, the colonel and the major launched their no-nonsense discourse with maps, charts, and a slide machine. The Swedbatt mission, they told me, was (1) to be present in the buffer zone, (2) to prevent movements of Egyptian and Israeli forces, (3) to observe and report any breaches of the truce agreement, and (4) to observe and report any changes in troops and equipment in the limited-forces zones. (Under the terms of the 1979 peace treaty, the U.N. mission would stay relatively the same. As each phase of the Israeli withdrawal was completed, U.N. troops and observers would be invited into narrow, impromptu buffer zones separating the limited Egyptian and Israeli forces, until the final Sinai-Israel frontier is established in 1982. If, because of one veto or another, the U.N. Security Council failed to approve these complicated arrangements, then the United States was committed "to take those steps necessary to insure the establishment and maintenance of an acceptable alternative multinational force," according to a Carter-to-Begin-and-Sadat side letter.) Besides the Swedes, Ghanaians, Finns, and Indonesians, there were the Poles, who handled road- and mine-clearing; the Canadians, who provided food, water, and maintenance; and the Australians, who flew patrol helicopters out of Ismailia. "Our mission has been good so far," the colonel said. "We have had cooperation from the Israelis and Egyptians, and most of the incidents we have reported have been the result of mistakes, sometimes even ours. Of course, it is not so easy to perform our mission with a third of our soldiers in Lebanon now, but by canceling leaves we can make do. We hope the others will be back soon."

The colonel and the major were both officers in the Swedish regular army, but all the other personnel of the three rifle companies that made up Swedbatt were draftee reservists. Officers and men alike served for just six months in UNEF, and since it was first established in 1956, forty thousand had volunteered. "It is good training for our soldiers here—very different from Sweden, of course," the major told me. "The khamsin depresses the men and sunburn can be a problem, but we warn them to take it easy and be careful. Having draftees—professional plumbers, electricians, and so forth—it makes life better for all, including the Bedouins."

I asked them about the Bedouin caprice of cutting U.N. telephone lines. "Ah, you have heard about that," the colonel said. "Yes, it can be a problem, like the unexploded mines and shells.

I think they cut the cables to use for clotheslines, maybe. Who knows? It's their desert. Their fishermen are now allowed into the restricted sea zone and there is some smuggling over the water. Most of it is on land, though. When we catch them, we just send them back in the direction they came from. They are prohibited from going south of what we call the Green Line, about halfway down our area, but they go anyway. That, too, can be a problem. You will probably see them when you go to CP 571 in the south with Captain Ravheden."

Captain Ravheden, the bearded commander of Swedbatt's Second Rifle Company, drove me in his white four-wheel-drive Volvo command car due south on an arrow-straight supply road. He was a customs officer in civilian life, and soon he was scheduled to return home to help train the replacement troops for Swedbatt, before completing his army service. As we plowed through the intermittent sand drifts, the captain cursed the Poles in a combination of Swedish and English. The Poles were in charge of clearing the roads as well as the minefields, and Ravheden wasn't impressed with their efficiency in either task, although he said that he sympathized with their difficulties. "The antitank and antipersonnel mines are very thick around here, where the big battles of 1967 and 1973 were fought," he shouted, over the whine of the Volvo's engine. "And, as you can see, it is mostly dunes here. The sand blows around, burying the mines under maybe three feet one day and leaving them exposed the next. Also, along the coast the waves sometimes wash the mines inland. Yesterday on this road, we saw some smoke from an explosion. We investigated and figured out that a loose camel had stepped on a mine and run off. The carcass will turn up one day. The antitank mines do not explode if a camel or person steps on them, but the antipersonnel mines will. The Bedouins have a sixth sense about the mines, but still accidents happen."

Fewer Bedouins were to be seen as we traveled farther south, but, as Colonel Lindgren had said, some went below the Green Line to forage their animals. They even have some illegal settlements in the restricted region, which they abandon when the U.N.

comes by on patrol. "You will see, from now on whenever we pass Bedouins they will always be heading north," Ravheden told me. "When they hear a car coming, they turn around and walk north until the car goes by; then they reverse direction and go south again to where there is grass. Even the camels know to turn north when a car comes. When we catch them, we must call in interpreters. It is all very confusing." Sure enough, a few kilometers later, two Bedouins and a herd of camels passed us, looking innocent as orphans as they trudged north. When they thought we were no longer noticing them, they turned around. Ravheden smiled and sighed.

The classic Sahara landscape, with dunes so steep and virginal that one longed for a pair of skis, became increasingly littered with war debris—tank treads, shell casings, burned-out trucks, jerry cans, barbed wire, bits of mangled steel. We turned east onto a crossroad which led to CP 571, one of the small, less-civilized outposts that Lieutenant Alfon had told me about. This was the Ismailia road made famous in 1973 when hell-bent Israeli reinforcements poured down it toward the Suez Canal, ultimately crossing the canal and entrapping the Egyptian Third Army in the Sinai. Tiny red flags on sticks, like a poppy field in the dunes, marked an orderly pattern of antipersonnel mines recently discovered by the Poles. We stopped to examine one of them up close, the deadly black knob of the mine protruding from the sand next to the red flag. The ugly potential of instant death scattered about this wilderness was chilling. Could there ever be a long enough peace, or at least an absence of war, to erase it all? "Just a few days ago," Ravheden said, breaking our gloomy silence, "the Poles found some skeletons not far off this road. The wind had blown away the sand covering them. An Israeli group came to check them and said they were not theirs, so now we will send the bones to Egypt for identification. They might have been there since 1967. Who knows? It is a dangerous world."

I didn't stay long at CP 571, manned by a handful of forlorn Swedish soldiers. The sergeant injured in the road-mine accident in Lebanon had been previously on duty there, his cot and locker still in place. It was past five o'clock, and I was overdue at Ghanbatt Headquarters for another briefing, before being driven to the Sinai Field Mission Base Camp. The itinerary called for Private Cederberg to take me to Ghanbatt in his Volkswagen Dasher from CP 571. Cederberg, grumpier than ever, was waiting at the appointed place, and after a short tour of the bleak tents and corrugated-iron huts of the outpost, we roared off to the south. Again, the men seemed sad to see a new face disappear so quickly.

Ghanbatt and the Sinai Field Mission were in a bulge of the buffer zone enclosing the two key passes, Gidi and Mitla, which coursed through the otherwise unnavigable central Sinai. Ghanbatt Headquarters was along the Mitla Pass, the more southerly of the two, and the S.F.M. Base Camp was near the Gidi. The American early-warning stations and the Egyptian and Israeli surveillance posts were situated on heights forming a rough rectangle around the passes. The roads connecting all these points were subject to sand drifts and ruts, which did not brighten Private Cederberg's mood. From our idle conversation, I learned that Cederberg not only disliked Israelis but Egyptians, Bedouins, Ghanaians, and every grain of sand and rock in the Sinai with equal passion. Only the prospect of his imminent return to civilian life in Göteborg, and the girl he would soon marry there, kept him alive, he said. Not even the dispersing overcast, just in time for a wondrous sunset, cheered him. When we reached the Ghanbatt territory, an appropriately warm African light surrounded us, the sun a bright yellow Necco wafer hovering over the western hills.

As far as Cederberg was concerned, our experience at the first Ghanbatt checkpoint proved beyond a doubt that the Ghanaians deserved his contempt. The guards, two gigantic blacks with tribal scars on their cheeks, had apparently not been alerted to our arrival, and the fact that we were in a U.N. car did not convince them of our legitimate purpose. They pointed their automatic weapons at us and shouted ferociously in Pidgin English, ignoring every credential we presented. One of them kept us at gunpoint while the other went to get the corporal in charge. "Damn people!" Cederberg sputtered. "They are new here and they are afraid of making mistakes. Punishment for them is very bad. They are not volunteers like us. Wild animals!" At last, the corporal, still wet from a shower, appeared in his undershorts. He questioned us closely, forcing us to repeat at least five times our purpose in going to Ghanbatt. I asked him to telephone his headquarters, where they were expecting us, but he refused. "No good," he said, which could have meant either that the field telephone was out of order or that he was afraid to bother his superiors. However, after a short but animated conference, the three soldiers suddenly stepped back three paces, saluted smartly, and waved us through. I felt as if I were living out a scene in Evelyn Waugh's *Black Mischief*—but then I had learned to expect anything in the Sinai.

Even though it had been almost five years since the last Sinai war, the Mitla Pass was still the world's greatest junkyard, an unsolved jigsaw puzzle of military scrap lining the road as far as the eye could see. The gathering darkness made the scene all the more grotesque and depressing. In the middle of the detritus was Ghanbatt Head-quarters, a hodgepodge of barracks and tents and soldiers rushing to their evening meal with clanging mess kits. We were met by Lieutenant Colonel Mark Achel, the Ghanbatt commanding officer, who listened with sympathy to my explanation of why we were late. Tapping his swagger stick against his left palm, he questioned a young aide, who accepted the blame for the mix-up at the checkpoint. The aide looked pleadingly at me and apologized. His discomfort was doubled because he was to be the briefing officer. But first, soothing cold beer was offered all around, and Cederberg, after downing his in ten seconds flat, saluted and left for Swedbatt, a happy man at last.

The briefing itself—anything but brief—was a painful and stilted exercise by the young aide, whose nervous English was almost incomprehensible to my ears. As Colonel Achel beat a soft tattoo on his knee with his swagger stick, the aide, using maps, charts, and overlays, lovingly described every checkpoint, position, and, it seemed, rock in Ghanbatt. I was due at the S.F.M. Base Camp for dinner, and I could tell by one of the maps that it was a good hour's drive away. Yet, I felt sorry for the poor fellow (my visit had surely

not made his day any brighter), and I sat as patiently as I could until
he had finished his lecture, forty minutes later. What I managed to
glean from the briefing, and from additional information provided
by the colonel, was that Ghanbatt was responsible for the security
of the S.F.M. but not for the Egyptian and Israeli surveillance posts,
called E-1 and J-1, respectively. Each surveillance station looked
after its own security and was allowed a maximum of 250 lightly
armed personnel, who were checked by S.F.M. liaison officers regularly. "Although my unit has been here only a short time," the
colonel said, "everything has been smooth for Ghanbatt. All abide
by the rules. No frictions. Cordial relations with everyone. Ghanbatt is the crucial U.N. area. Here at the strategic passes and the
S.F.M., if anything happens, well . . ." The colonel laughed. "Our
biggest troubles have been with the camels and the Bedouins," he
went on. "We see the camels all the time but seldom the Bedouins.
We are supposed to drive them north above the Green Line, but,
to be honest, we find it a little difficult. We are not sure where the
mines are, and to drive them across open country could be disastrous. We have been told there is no such thing as a wild camel, that
always there is a Bedouin nearby who owns it. Sometimes, we spot
a Bedouin on the open sand and we set out to drive him away.
Then, you don't see him anymore, only his camel. It is amazing to
us. Last Saturday, a camel blew up. If the Bedouin owner was with
it, he would have blown up, too. But he wasn't there."

Finally, at seven-thirty, I was given a lift in another white U.N.
Dasher station wagon to the S.F.M. Base Camp. Lieutenant Korso
was the escort officer and Private Akweke was the driver. They told
me that even though the Sinai was much drier than Ghana and the
dust bothered them, they were proud to help keep the peace. (Also,
I later heard, the Ghanaians receive a fifty-dollar-a-month bonus for
serving in the Sinai and automatically become members of the
palace guard when they return home after their tours of duty.) The
night was windy and clear, and the drive north to the Gidi Pass was
mysteriously beautiful, lunar and wild. The distant lights of the
S.F.M. Base Camp, high on a hill called Umm Khisheib north of
the Gidi, were tantalizing, especially so since the car was stalling out

from condensation in its fuel line. With erratic stopping and starting, we slowly gained the top of the hill, more than two thousand
feet high, and approached a floodlit security fence surrounding
what looked like the set for the climax of *Close Encounters of the Third
Kind.* At a final Ghanbatt checkpoint, a guard carefully examined
our papers, taking nobody, not even his own comrades, for granted.
The guard telephoned the Base Camp security office that all was in
order and a huge electrically operated gate swung open. We drove
through, and there before me was the grandfather of all Sinai
culture shocks.

Back in Jerusalem, I had met Owen Roberts, the Deputy Director of the Sinai Field Mission, who searched for a description of
what I would see when I arrived at the S.F.M. Base Camp. "It's like,
it's like—" he said, his eyes squinting in visualization, "if you took
an enormous cookie cutter, picked up a piece of a Dallas suburb,
and plunked it down in the middle of the Sinai desert." His image
was apt. The Base Camp was an instant Texas town, somehow
transplanted by the vagaries of world events to a wilderness on the
other side of the earth, where the interests of Israelis and Egyptians
were guarded by Americans, who in turn were guarded by Ghanaians. As I stared with glazed eyes and open mouth at my bustling
countrymen, dressed in bright orange pants and shirts, walking on
concrete pathways across a central gravel-and-sand quadrangle
bounded by modern beige buildings, red fire hydrants, lampposts,
and even a tennis court, a hefty man with glasses held out his hand
toward me. "Hi, there," he said. "I'm Jim Shepard. I'm your escort
for the next couple of days. I guess you'll want some food. The
dining room's officially closed right now, but we'll scare up something for you to eat. First, though, let me take you over to the
module where you'll be staying and you can dump your baggage
and wash up."

The module Shepard referred to was one of a complex of single-
story living units, which looked like nothing so much as a Texas
roadside motel, without the neon signs. Indeed, as Shepard explained, the modules *were* a prefabricated Holiday Inn once des-
tined for Florida. When Sinai II was signed and the need for an

S.F.M. Base Camp was pressing, the U.S. government bought up
the Holiday Inn, complete with furniture, and transported the entire thing by ship and flat-bed trucks to this hill over the Gidi Pass.
Inside, my module was decorated in standard Holiday Inn Traditional: adjustable air-conditioning, firm double beds, color-coor-
dinated drapes and bedspreads, small stove and sink, green touch-
tone telephone, multichannel Muzak, and vinyl-tiled bathroom—
with the exceptional additions of signs warning the occupants to
conserve water, a view through the large windows of the Sinai
desert, and ashtrays in the shape of Texas and marked with the
legend "E-SYSTEMS INC GREENVILLE DIVISION," the primary con-
tractor for the electronics equipment and the skilled personnel. Of
all the strange places I had camped in while roaming the Sinai, this
was by far the strangest. Ah, America, America! What other nation
on earth could have pulled this off?

Shepard led me from my module across the quadrangle to the
main building, which included the dining room. A public-address-
system announcer paged various personnel in the flat, oddly accented locutions of airline pilots. As soon as we entered the building, I was besieged by twangy salutations from the orange-suited
men and women lolling about the recreation area, listening to a
jukebox, reading, chatting, and playing pool, darts, Ping-Pong, or
TV games. A large bulletin board displayed notices about the
hobby shop, a photography contest, bingo games, organized
tours, movies *(The Goodbye Girl* and *Lisztomania),* plus posted
newspaper clippings of common interest and cute signs ("We
only have one Texas . . . Thank God"). The dining room—an
immense cafeteria featuring groaning boards heaped with potato
chips, soft drinks, fruit, candies, cookies, cakes, and the like—was
theoretically closed, but Shepard spoke to Ginger, a pleasant lady
in charge of the kitchen, who cheerfully whipped up an impromptu and delicious snack of two thick ham-and-cheese sand-
wiches, a fat wedge of cherry pie, and coffee.

While I munched, Shepard talked about life at the S.F.M. "One
of our big problems here is gaining weight," he said. "Eating is our
local pastime, just like in the States, only more so. I had to lose forty

pounds by restricting myself to only one real meal a day. We government people—I'm a liaison officer assigned to E-1 and J-1— we're supposed to pay one dollar for every meal here, since it's illegal for us to have free food, but the E-Systems folks eat free. And the food is damn good, though heavy on the Texas side. About seventy-five percent of us are from Texas, mostly the Dallas area, but there's a true cross section of America here—blacks, whites, older folks, girls, just about everyone."

I asked Shepard about himself, and he told me he was a native Californian, an old A.I.D. hand who had served in Ghana, Bangladesh, Ethiopia, and Washington ("D.C. was my worst assignment"). Tired of travel and separation from his wife in California, he was looking forward to retirement and to earning an advanced degree in social anthropology. (Families are not allowed at the S.F.M., although the director and deputy director house their wives in Cairo and Jerusalem, respectively.)

An E-Systems Texan, his neck draped with a Star of David and Hebrew charm pendants, joined us at our Formica table. While he polished off a container of milk, he complained about the fine sand that blew into the electric generators every day. "It's hell to keep them clean," he said. "There's sand all over the place, and you never get used to it." He also complained about a generally disliked colleague who was about to complete his S.F.M. duty. "I hate that guy and I won't be sorry to see him go." Shepard seemed slightly embarrassed by this airing of personal tensions so early in my visit. He suggested we drop in at the bar for a nightcap.

The bar was straight out of middle-class suburban Dallas. Beer and whiskey stimulated boisterous kidding and back-slapping friendliness, as well as some serious staring into glasses or at the mirror behind the shelves of bottles. A pert, buxom young barmaid (who ran the beauty parlor during the day) kept things orderly and companionable, remembering every drinker's name and preference. The watch-station technicians, I soon learned, were the aristocracy of the place; they were what the S.F.M. was built for and they worked the hardest. One of them, Alex Spann, a black E-Systems electronics expert, told me he was there for the money to further his education, the tax advantages, the travel, and "to be part of history." He had signed up for eighteen months. "We electronics observers work two long fourteen-hour days, then we get one day off, and that goes on for three weeks," he said. "After the three weeks, we get seven days off, and we can go anywhere in the world, just so long as we're back right on time, not a minute late or we catch hell."

Two liaison officers joined us, both of whom introduced themselves as "foreigners" from the Boston area. One was a wiry former Green Beret sergeant who had trained Montagnard tribesmen in Vietnam, and the other was a young man fresh out of Holy Cross, at the S.F.M. for only five weeks. They seemed reasonably content with their duty in the Sinai and felt that they were contributing to peace, although the former Green Beret missed his Montagnards. Another new arrival, a girl who had traveled to the S.F.M. via Egypt, said how disappointed she was by the surprising narrowness of the Suez Canal, which she had imagined to be a broad waterway. This prompted the telling of the latest S.F.M. joke: What's the difference between the Suez Canal and Bella Abzug? One is a busy ditch. With that, it was time to go to sleep. Shepard told me the schedule for the next day: breakfast at seven, then a briefing and demonstration of the electronic-sensor gadgetry, and later a grand tour of the watch stations around the passes. "It'll be a long day, I promise you," Shepard said. "When you get back to your module, leave a wake-up call with the telephone operator."

NINE

IN THE DAYLIGHT, my first impression of the S.F.M. Base Camp as a transplanted chunk of Texas still pertained, but instead of a Dallas suburb, it seemed more like a west Texas cattle town. Over breakfast (steamy sausages and eggs, coffee, and toast; chili, peppers, and tacos were also offered), Leamon "Ray" Hunt, who had been the S.F.M. director for ten months, told me that in all his years of being a "troubleshooter" for the State Department, working in the Sinai was his most rewarding experience. "It's a first-time thing for all of us," he said. "Nothing like the S.F.M. has ever been done before, one nation supervising a cease-fire." By virtue of his office, he wasn't required to wear the orange uniform, preferring a khaki short-sleeved shirt and corduroy trousers—a fitting costume for the active Foreign Service man he had been since he was twenty years old. "Being an Oklahoman, I guess I feel at home here. Actually, I'm pretty much at home anywhere in the Middle East, I've been around it so much."

After breakfast, we walked over to his well-secured office in the administration building, where Hunt talked about the S.F.M.'s past, present, and future. The S.F.M. is the overseas arm of the Sinai Support Mission, which reports directly to the President. When Congress voted it into existence after the Sinai II agreement was signed in September, 1975, a crash program was started to set up the early-warning watch stations and a primitive base camp. By February, 1976, when the Israelis evacuated the area, the S.F.M. was ready and operational, a monument to American efficiency and planning. "It cost twenty million dollars to get it going," Hunt said,

216

"and it takes about eleven or so million a year to maintain, but it's taxpayers' money well spent. There's been no criticism in the press or Congress because it's worth it to help keep the peace. Look at it this way: the yearly upkeep is about half the price of one F-14 jet fighter."

When a violation of the truce accords is observed, reports are instantly filed with the Egyptians, Israelis, Washington, and the U.N. On its own authority, the S.F.M. can order correction of the violation. "So far, nothing has happened that's made us really nervous," Hunt told me. "Both sides want the agreement to work, so it works. Most of the violations are accidental or silly ones, like straying reconnaissance flights or hiding prohibited weapons in the convoys to E-1 or J-1. Our liaison officers monitor the surveillance stations, searching and counting personnel and vehicles in the convoys, and they are permitted to go to whatever lengths are required to uphold the agreement. Of course, they must be diplomatic, sensitive, and professional, which is why many of them are State Department people. We don't ever ask for something unless we're ready to insist on it. We've had some Mexican standoffs. One was five hours long—over a box containing electronic gear in a convoy to J-1. The Israelis were testing us, setting a precedent. But it's usually nothing serious. We're still writing the book in this business. It's a choice, important assignment, despite the pressures."

Given its exalted position in the region, the S.F.M.'s relations with its neighbors were remarkably good. Purchases from the Egyptians and Israelis were scrupulously even-handed; food not flown in from America came from Israel and petroleum products were from Egypt. An S.F.M. refrigeration technician recently repaired the freezer at E-1 and saved all the frozen food stored there. One of the liaison officers was engaged to an Israeli girl, and the S.F.M. personnel usually travel to Israel on their days off. (They seemed to feel naturally at home with the Israelis, who are more American—indeed Texan—in their ways than the Egyptians.) A pickup S.F.M. rock band performed at the nearby Bir Gifgafa Air Force base, and the Israelis there helped out by supplying helicopters in medical emergencies. (Later that morning, I learned that an

S.F.M. office worker who had fallen down and hurt her head was rushed to the Bir Gifgafa military hospital for X-rays.) As for the U.N. troops, the Ghanaians, Swedes, Finns, and Indonesians were regular visitors to the enviable facilities of the S.F.M. (although "we're never invited often enough," Lieutenant Alfon had told me), and the Americans had also entertained other U.N. nationalities, including the Russian observers, who pretended to be unimpressed. There was very little contact with Bedouins, however. "I haven't seen a Bedouin here in ten months," Hunt said. "Once a sensor picked up the sound of a Bedouin riding on his camel in Mitla East. We called the U.N., but the Bedouin had disappeared. Their camels are a hell of a problem, though."

As of that morning, Monday, April 17, 1978, there were 152 persons on the S.F.M. roster: twenty-two government people ("U.S.G.," as they refer to themselves) and the rest E-Systems contract personnel. Of the 152, thirteen were women (between the ages of twenty-one and sixty-two), eleven were blacks, three were Spanish-Americans, and three were Jewish. None were of Arab, Moslem, or Oriental backgrounds. Their education ranged from the third-grade to the master's-degree level. Seventy-five percent were native Texans and seventy-five percent were Protestant. Catholic and Protestant services were held at the base once a month— a priest coming from Cairo and a minister coming from Tel Aviv —and, of course, Jewish services were handily available in Israel.

"Even though we're mostly Texans," Hunt said, "we're a fairly normal society in a highly abnormal situation. There is friction, naturally, but we've never had a fight, per se. Some arguments in the bar, maybe, but nothing really physical. Tensions are usually released during the seven-day leaves and on the tennis courts and in the gym. There has been no trouble whatsoever with minorities. The blacks don't necessarily stick together and everyone mixes well. As for the women, well, they're a civilizing influence. There's sexual pressure on them but no real problems. Although some of them are quite young and pretty, they tend to be like girls of an earlier generation—say, the 1930s. Sure, there are affairs, but mostly platonic relationships. Some have known each other ever since high school in Texas. Two couples who met here at the S.F.M. later married—after they left, of course. We're such a tight, patriotic community with a sense of mission that our people behave themselves. Even our most menial worker here is a kind of diplomat. Gripes are aired at town meetings. At the last one, the big complaint was about somebody's pet Saluki dog which was always underfoot. Also, anyone can be easily fired if he misbehaves. Drugs are grounds for immediate dismissal. Our work is too important for that stuff. There's a long waiting list of people in the States who want to work here. The average pay is fifteen hundred dollars a month—tax-free up to fifteen thousand dollars for five hundred and ten days, with thirty-seven days home leave allowed in that time. A cook, for instance, gets seventeen hundred a month. No unions. No overtime. But money isn't the whole story. We like being an important part of history. In a way, we're a Hollywood model of smalltown America—sort of nature imitating art."

And how about what the Israelis call "Bedouinism"? Hunt answered, "During the summer months, especially, you can see a zombie effect on our people, although the Texans are used to hot, dry weather. Still, everybody gets slowed down by the heat and isolation. Khamsins make us all edgy, so we're careful not to ruffle feathers. Privacy is respected, even holy, here."

And what of the future? Hunt thought over the question for a moment and said, "If a real, permanent peace is arranged, our role and the U.N. role should be phased out. But if there is gradual peace, I think the Egyptians and the Israelis would want us around for mutual confidence. Our technology and our very presence is the great stabilizing factor."

Hunt was right on both possibilities. The peace treaty called for a gradual withdrawal *and* a permanent peace, with the S.F.M. continuing its operations until the completion of the Israeli evacuation from the area east of the Gidi and Mitla passes (nine months after the signing of the treaty), at which point the S.F.M. mission would end, the instant Texas town vanishing into Egyptian Sinai. Egypt and Israel also requested that the U.S. Air Force continue its previously top-secret surveillance flights in Lockheed SR-71s over the

Sinai, until the final Israeli pullback. America would be involved in the execution of the peace treaty for years to come.

Just down the hall from Hunt's office was the electronic domain of Douglas Dodson, whose official title was Operations Manager, E-Systems, Inc., Greenville, Texas. Dodson was, unsurprisingly, a Texan by birth and nature, his short stature notwithstanding. His right arm had been amputated during his childhood. He was the grand old man of the S.F.M., having been assigned there on a temporary-duty basis from the beginning; two and a half years later, he was still there, running the entire intricate technical operation.

Using models of the sensor devices, he explained how they worked. "Most of these gadgets were perfected in Vietnam," he told me. "This here one is the MINISID, Miniature Seismic Intrusion Detector. These two tubes are buried in the ground, one tube for the battery and the other for a VHF radio transmitter and geophone. Only the thin antenna is above the ground. O.K. Now when the geophone senses something, it encodes the vibration in a digital format and says over the radio like, 'Hi, I'm Sensor Number Fifty-two and I got me an activation.' The signal comes to a receiver in the nearest watch station, and the receiver says to the operator, 'Ol' Fifty-two is sitting out there in the pass and he says he's gettin' run over.' That signal lights a light, toots a horn, and makes a mark on a chart recorder. It only activates every ten seconds, to conserve power, but the timing tells us a lot. If there are three straight activations in a row, we turn on the Acoustic Add-on Unit mike and listen in. Our boys can recognize from the sound they hear what the intrusion is. It's like having a guy sitting down there in the desert all the time working for you, only the guy's always awake and he doesn't need food or nothing, except a battery change once in a while. Some of the big batteries can last more than two years. In Vietnam, we had to move these things around, so we used small batteries just good for thirty days or so.

"Now, here we have the DIRID—the Directional Infrared Intrusion Detector—which is sort of two shotgun-barrel tubes on a tripod above ground that sense temperature changes between the background and any intruder. It's a passive optical device that can report both the presence and the direction of movement of the intruding object. Anything that passes in front of it is recorded, and because there are two tubes, it does its job twice, so we can tell which tube was affected first and figure out the direction. We use just three of these babies. Also, we got the SSCS, the Strain Sensitive Cable Sensor, that's placed on each end of every sensor field. It's an almost invisible cable laid in the dirt and across roads. Any pressure activates the cable and a transmitter. So that's how we keep tabs on every little footstep around here."

Dodson directed me into the adjacent Operations Center, a large room straight out of Cape Canaveral, crammed with humming radios, mysterious racks of electronic equipment, strung cables, telephones, teletype machines, flashing lights, and some very cool technicians. The center of the Center was a massive board with tiny lights marking every sensor device on a superimposed translucent map of the S.F.M. area. "When we get a hit," Dodson said, "the activated sensor not only reports to the nearest watch station, but to this board also. The light will start flashing very slowly, then faster and faster. After ten seconds, it's on solid. If it gets activated again, it starts flashing again, which means something else is coming by, and we can follow its direction by what lights go on the board. When other sensors farther off the road light up, we know the intruder is more than a Volkswagen. It could be a tank or a truck. Tanks are so noisy and heavy they'll hit every sensor we got. Also, tanks will stay on the sand, not the paved road, so the sensor lights will be lopsided. When you have experience in this game, you can tell just like a fingerprint what every hit is—camel, human, car, jeep, tank, truck, whatever. The human being is really the basis for all this; the sensors are just a tremendous aid. For instance, the sensor can't tell you the difference between a U.N. or Israeli or Egyptian jeep. The watch-station operator must be able to tell the difference. At night, he has a special night-sight scope that helps him."

I asked Dodson if he saw me coming last night. "We tracked you all the way from the time you entered Ghanbatt," he said, rather smugly. "All the sensors tripped in order, and we even knew your car was having trouble coming up the hill to the Base Camp. We knew who you were, so we didn't worry, but if you were in an Egyptian or Israeli vehicle, we would have checked with Ghanbatt CP Bravo near the main gate. We would've said, 'We got an unidentified heading for Bravo.' But we knew it was a U.N. vehicle. We track all the U.N. vehicles, if only for constant testing of the system as proof that it's working. By the way, you were also eyeballed by the boys in Alamo, Watch Station 3, which overlooks the Base Camp. We had you in our sights all the time." While Dodson spoke, a light began to pulsate, then another and another. He glanced at the board and said matter-of-factly, "U.N. vehicle. No sweat."

It was a warm, clear day, perfect for a tour of the S.F.M. Dodson, Shepard, and I set off in the standard company car, a white four-wheel-drive Chevrolet Blazer, equipped with a crackling radio (our position had to be periodically communicated to the watch stations and the Base Camp, just as if we were an aircraft flying cross-country) and emblazoned with the large black letters "SFM." I was impressed with how nimbly Dodson could drive the Blazer, point out the sights, and handle the radio, all with one arm. One of the sights, on a high hill just to the west of the Base Camp, was J-1, where Shepard had put in a lot of time as liaison officer. "That strategic point was captured by the Israelis in 1967 and has been in constant use ever since," Shepard said. "They have the very latest in electronic equipment and a terrific view of the Gulf of Suez and Egypt proper. E-1, to the east of the Base Camp looking toward Line K, has only been around for three years and the Egyptians there don't have such sophisticated equipment. We go to great lengths to make sure the supply convoys to E-1 and J-1 never meet on the same road. Special side roads were built

The Mitla Pass.

The Gidi Pass, and debris from the Six Day War. *Magnum.*

to each surveillance station—anything to prevent incidents."

The Blazer headed west through the Gidi Pass, skirting the original temporary Base Camp, now just a pile of trash and a tall antenna. The pass stretched out before us, a wide, rugged canyon rimmed by small purplish mountains. The legend "LOVE" was painted on an old, disused bunker along the road and in the distance we could count nine loose camels nosing about. Dodson radioed the position of the camels to the Operations Center. "There's got to be a Bedouin camel herder around here somewhere," Dodson said, "but we'll never find him." Wild game abounded, despite the mines, and those Texans at the watch stations, all of them good-ole-boy hunters, sometimes cry for a deer rifle when they spot some fat gazelle. Dodson stopped dead on a groove across the road that held one of the strain-sensitive cables. The Operations Center immediately called us and asked what was happening. Dodson radioed back that he was just seeing if they were on their toes. He pointed to a hair-thin antenna sticking up out of the sand nearby. "That MINISID there is telling them a hell of a lot about us," he said. "Spooky, isn't it?"

At the end of Gidi West, we turned south toward Mitla West and the first watch station we would visit, Caddo Mountain, about twenty-five kilometers away. (Many watch stations, surveillance stations, and checkpoints had Texas-style names: Watch Stations 1, 2, and 3 were Caddo Mountain, Rockwall, and Alamo, respectively; E-1 was Rodeo and J-1 was Quarterhorse; the checkpoints were Smokey, Sabine Mountain, Red River, and Lone Oak. I wondered aloud if there was any symbolism attached to the names. Not intentionally, I was told.) We were in junkyard country once again, the scrap heaps of war all around us. "There was a lot of cowboys and Indians going on around here," Dodson remarked. "Look over there, for instance. That's an old Israeli artillery emplacement and those black things sticking up are 175-mm. shells, all duds. It pains me, too, because they are American-made." We stopped for a moment to look at the war souvenirs—the dud shells, fuses, gunpowder pellets, mines, all of them potentially capable of going off. I tiptoed from rock to rock over the emplacement, strangely fas-

cinated by the concentration of ugly peril. Dodson was right; the
unexploded shells had American markings on them and were dated
1970, so they must have been used in the 1973 Yom Kippur War.
I picked up a rifle-cartridge casing as a memento and stuffed it in
my pocket.

Caddo Mountain, or Watch Station 1, lived up to its name,
topographically. Perched high on a steep hill, it was a two-room
prefabricated steel-and-concrete structure, in a style well known
in American prefabrication circles. A chain-link fence surrounded
the station, one side of which abutted a precipice. When the
watch-station personnel first arrived there, they amused themselves by collecting old tires and rolling them down the cliff, bet-
ting on which one traveled the farthest. We were greeted warmly
by the two orange-suited Texans on duty, one of whom had a
shock of hair almost the same color as his uniform. While we
sipped coffee, I jotted down a list of the furnishings and equipment: a kitchenette with a microwave oven, dining table, coffee
table, and pantry shelf holding canned snacks, fruit juices, coffee,
tea, and a family-size bottle of Maalox; a vacuum cleaner, dart-
board, and electric heater; a modern bathroom; a clock set to
Greenwich Mean Time, a powerful telescope, radios, portable
nightscope, teletype, graph recorder, binoculars, and maps; a pad-
locked glass gun case containing two AR-15 automatic rifles, two
shotguns, ammunition, and white-smoke grenades. A notice on
the face of the gun case read:

> Mitla West. In case of a life-threatening situation, break glass and
> remove the weapons. The selector switch for the AR-15 is located on
> the left middle portion of the rifle. The magazine-release button is
> located on the right middle portion of the rifle. The safety position for
> the 12-gauge shotgun is located on the top rear portion of the rear
> stock. All guns are loaded. While firing the AR-15, if it jams and you
> are unable to seed or chamber another round by cocking the bolt,
> extract the magazine, reinsert the magazine, and recock. All guns are
> loaded.

What is considered a "life-threatening situation" at the S.F.M.?
I asked the redhead. "Well," he drawled, "in case somebody is
crawling over the fence out there and he's got a gun, I guess."

"You don't want to make a mistake, however," Shepard inter-
posed quickly. "You don't break the glass without damn good
reason."

What if intruders come in strength? I asked. The redhead smiled
broadly and said, "We'll just sit back and say, 'Hi, there, fellas.
Want some coffee?' But if they're terrorists, we're supposed to use
our own good judgment. If there's no help nearby, none of our
vehicles in the vicinity, then I'd have my gun in my hand and I'd
shoot the first fellow over the fence. In a real invasion or war, I'd
bug out and try to get behind either the Israeli or Egyptian lines,
out of the crossfire."

Had there been any serious incidents recently? "The closest
thing to a serious violation," the other Texan said, "was an Israeli
jet buzzing the radio tower near the Base Camp five days ago. They
never explained why they did it. Either it was for fun, or they were
testing us, or maybe the pilot overshot the runway at the air base.
Anyway, we duly recorded it. Usually, it's quiet as a cemetery
around here. It can be boring as hell. To tell you the truth, I just
survive from one seven-day leave to another."

I was invited up onto the roof of the watch station, where the
big nightscope (Night Observation Device, Long Range) was
mounted. It intensifies available light fifty thousand times, and
when there was an unidentified hit after dark, one of the operators
would rush up to the roof to check it out. The scary piece of
equipment even picked out ships in the Gulf of Suez ("You can
read what it says on their stacks," Dodson said), presenting every
image in green tint. "The nightscope gives us a twenty-four-hour
visual-verification capacity," Dodson remarked, patting the machine affectionately.

We left Caddo Mountain and drove to Mitla East, past the Ghanbatt Headquarters, and then to Watch Station 2, or Rockwall (after
a county in northeastern Texas)—a twenty-kilometer ride. The
farther east we went, the narrower the pass became. "Now you can

see why this place is so damn important, why it's always called the *strategic* Mitla Pass," Dodson said. "A few soldiers can hold off a whole army from those hills just beside the road. Why, you can play cowboys and Indians all day long around here."

Rockwall was pretty much the same as Caddo Mountain, except that its location was at a touchy conjunction of forces. It was separated from the heavily fortified Israeli position on the high ground, a short distance away on Line K, by a flimsy Ghanaian outpost, manned by a few soldiers. I was told that recently the Israelis, who monitor all the S.F.M. radio channels, had overheard some American suspicions about a newly positioned I.D.F. heavy machine gun. Knowing that the watch-station operators were studying the weapon through their telescope, they obligingly unveiled its camouflage for a better view, the gun crew bowing with mock graciousness. The feeling among the operators at Rockwall—and also at Alamo, the third watch station I visited, to the north of Rockwall —was grudging respect and edginess toward the Israelis, who appeared to them as friendly antagonists, always probing, always testing, always slightly dangerous. ("We are watchdogs, referees, and, in a way, hostages," Owen Roberts, the S.F.M. deputy director, had told me in Jerusalem.) Because the Egyptian Army positions were far enough away from the watch stations to preclude such direct contact, this feeling of wariness did not apply to Egyptians. The fact, too, that the Israelis were so much like these Americans only compounded the ambivalence. This conflict of emotions affecting the doggedly neutral S.F.M. people was evident again during our ride over a rough but beautiful back road north to Alamo and the Base Camp. Like a professional tour guide, Dodson pointed out the sights: eight more loose camels dumbly grazing on broom, an abandoned oil rig, a stalagmite cavern bursting with pigeons, and, finally, the scattered remains of an Israeli Mirage jet that had crashed into a ridge next to the road during the 1973 war. He stared at the metal shreds of what once was a sleek fighter plane and said softly, "Jesus, I hope the poor son of a bitch got a chance to bail out."

Owen Roberts arrived from Jerusalem at the Base Camp in his

Blazer (license plate "SFM 2") about the time our Blazer pulled up
to the security fence. He was in a rush to report to Hunt, but he
told me that we were all going to meet for drinks at Hunt's module
and then have dinner together in the dining room. Since there was
an hour to spare, Shepard suggested that I take a quick tour of the
Base Camp, or "Hometown, U.S.A.," as one of the more waggish
technicians had referred to it. As further testimony to the remarkable talent of Americans for creating "civilization" anywhere on
earth, here are my notes of the quick tour:

Security-fence gatehouse. Sensitized fence. Anything touches it
sets off signal and armed guards investigate. Another perimeter
fence four hundred meters out has even more sensors. High-resolu-
tion TV cameras pick up anything in between fences.

Warehouse. Communication-maintenance shop. Carpenter's
shop. Vehicle-maintenance shop. Logistics office.

Water-purification plant. Sewage-treatment plant. Treated efflu-
ence held in reservoir and reused for watering flowers, stunted
pines, cedars in quadrangle.

Main generators. Supply all power. Must be kept at constant level
or delicate equipment damaged.

Hobby shop. Lapidary shop. Very popular hobby with personnel, since stalagmites, other odd minerals so common. Ham-radio
shop. Model-crafts shop. Leather shop. Electronics lab. Photography darkroom. Well-equipped gym. Laundry and dry-cleaning
shop. Two women work there full-time.

S.F.M. ambulance. Infirmary with medic.

Tennis and basketball courts. Volleyball. No swimming pool
planned.

Desert, after all.

Living modules. Up to four people to a module. Crowded, but
few complaints.

Library. Mostly technical magazines and books (*E-Systems, Ink,* a
house organ, and *State Department News,* another house organ).
Some racy paperbacks.

Beauty parlor and barber shop. Sign: "IF YOU FEEL THE URGE,
THINK OF YOUR WIFE."

Movie theater. Two 35-mm. projectors. Doubles as auditorium, dance hall. One movie every other night. Color TV on nonmovie nights. TV cassettes from USA provided by service. Nobody watches Egyptian or Israeli TV. Some have own TV sets in modules; jacks in rooms for closed-circuit connection.

PX. Everything from film to S.F.M. T-shirts. Black Label Scotch $2.75 the quart. Bought two quarts. Prettiest woman at S.F.M. runs PX. Three off-duty men just hanging around. Lots of Texas kidding. First real sign of normal sexual byplay. That's what's missing in this Orwellian place—male-female relations—and children! What good is efficient, self-contained city without children? More a plush concentration camp than "Hometown, U.S.A." Still, a concentration camp with a good reason for being.

Drinks and dinner with Hunt, Roberts, Shepard, and the rest of the S.F.M. upper echelon were informal and pleasant. Roberts told me that he was slated to drive directly to Cairo, via Ismailia, in the morning. (As a diplomat, no travel restrictions applied to him.) I, too, was leaving for Cairo in the morning, but via Tel Aviv and Athens. There we were, two Americans at an American base, both of us about to travel to the same destination, and, absurdly, we couldn't travel together. "That's the Middle East for you," Roberts said, shaking his head. (How many times had I heard that expression, accompanied by the same shaking of the head?) Shepard said that he had been alerted to large-scale Egyptian military maneuvers just across the canal, probably a pre-Passover signal to Israel that the Egyptians still had a standing army (indeed, the eleventh largest in the world). "I hope the maneuvers won't interfere with your plans to come back into the Sinai from Egypt," he said.

From that disconcerting bit of information, the conversation turned to the chances for war or peace in the area, specifically the Sinai. I offered the opinion that with all the current talk about Israeli settlements, Egyptian revanchism, strategic passes, U.N. buffer zones, and American early-warning stations, nobody—but nobody—had mentioned the Bedouins, the people who truly belonged in the peninsula and should, theoretically, have the most to say about its destiny. They all looked at me strangely, as if trying to decide whether I was a troublemaker or simply crazy. "I'm sure," Hunt said, with diplomatic even-handedness, "the Bedouins will adjust to whoever ultimately takes over the Sinai, as they always have." I let the matter drop.

During dinner, an aide approached Hunt and informed him that a grand total of seventy-nine camels was reported wandering about the S.F.M. area that day, a new record. (Dodson alone, on our tour of the watch stations, had reported seventeen.) Hunt was shocked, but there wasn't much he could do about the camel situation until Ghanbatt found a method of rounding them up and sending them north of the Green Line. The aide also said that the S.F.M. office worker who had injured her head in a fall that morning and been taken to the Bir Gifgafa military hospital was all right, her X-rays negative. However, an Israeli soldier at J-1 had also been injured that day and was being evacuated by helicopter to Bir Gifgafa. Hunt told the aide to advise the Egyptians at E-1 that a helicopter was due at J-1 on a medical mission and that there was nothing to worry about. "All in a day's work," said Hunt brightly. "This is where the action is."

I said my good-byes and thanks after dinner (I would be departing early in the morning by the daily S.F.M. courier van for Tel Aviv), and strolled across the quadrangle to my module. [A little more than one year later, on April 25, 1979, that very quadrangle would be the site of a formal and uneasy exchange of the ratified treaty documents between Egypt and Israel, with American officials in patronizing attendance.] This would be my last night in the Sinai, and it was exquisite—a cool breeze, a brilliant splash of stars, and a three-quarter moon bright enough to make the floodlights unnecessary. The thought occurred to me that the piece of "America" I was walking upon in the Sinai was merely the latest example of alien culture forced on this timeless land. They will come and they will go, but, somehow, the great and terrible wilderness will outwit them all.

From where I was standing at seven o'clock the following morning while I waited to board the S.F.M.–Tel Aviv courier van, it was just 110 miles to Cairo, as the crow flies. It was only eighteen miles to my ultimate destination, the Egyptian limited-forces zone on the western edge of the Sinai. Yet, I was about to embark on a seventeen-hundred-mile trip, most of it in the wrong direction, in order to get there. I glumly watched Roberts depart in his "SFM 2" Blazer for Cairo. He would arrive in about three hours, while I would be still on my way to Ben-Gurion Airport near Tel Aviv. The white, twelve-passenger Chevrolet van was on its regular morning run from the Base Camp to the Tel Aviv S.F.M. office, fittingly located in the Ramada Inn. Besides the driver and me, there were five others going off to Israel on leave, all of them full of high spirits, with the exception of a young black man whose head was buried in a book. The raunchy jokes and banter in the long cadences of Texas made me feel as if I were back in the army, riding with my platoon out to some firing range for a day's shooting.

At an I.D.F. checkpoint on Line J, just north of the Base Camp, we rendezvoused with an Israeli escort officer (looking as if he would be more at home holding forth on Henry James at a literary party), and he led the way in his jeep as far as Bir Gifgafa. That daily routine was part of the petty protocol established in these parts after Sinai II; like most protocol, it accomplished nothing, except to justify its own existence. I had a sense once again of Israel's military might when we passed through the Bir Gifgafa area, a huge depot for armor as well as a modern air base. The Israeli strategy since the nearly disastrous 1973 war was to leave the heavy equipment in the desert and bring the soldiers to it from Israel proper, so the Israelis, more than ever, viewed these Sinai bases as critical. Clearly, it would take a lot of diplomatic maneuvering and firm promises to persuade them to give them up.

Just such maneuvering and promises were made by Carter during the extended peace-treaty negotiations. The United States agreed to replace for Israel the four Sinai air bases with two in the Negev, at enormous and wasteful expense, most of it borne by the American taxpayers. A suggestion was advanced that Sadat lease the Sinai bases to Israel—much as the United States leases its Guantánamo naval station from Cuba—which would not only save millions of dollars but be a gesture of faith in the validity and permanency of the peace treaty; another suggestion was that the United States take over a Sinai airfield for its own military purposes in the Middle East. Both ideas failed to impress Sadat. The fact that under the treaty terms the evacuated Sinai bases would be used only by Egyptian civil aviation hasn't cheered Begin very much. Consequently, as much as a billion dollars may be poured into the Negev replacement bases, causing hard feelings among Americans and further rampant inflation for Israelis. But the cost is still cheaper and far less odious than another Sinai war.

While we drove northeast over an uninteresting gravel plain—uninteresting for anything but tank battles—I talked with the others. An older man with a European accent, a kind of father figure to the younger ones, told me that he was a Yugoslav who had emigrated to Tucson, Arizona, in 1961 and had worked for the Border Patrol, until he signed up to come to the S.F.M. as a watch-station operator. He had an Israeli girl friend in the Galilee and, in fact, was on his way there to spend Passover with the girl and her family. "If all goes well," he said, "we will be married in June, but I will still work for the S.F.M."

As the others respectfully kidded him about his imminent marriage, I asked the studious young black what he was reading. He held up the book and smiled when he saw my double take at the title—*Zohar, Basic Readings from the Kabbala.* How, I wondered, did he come to be so engrossed in that subject? "I was in the Special Forces in Vietnam," he said, "and while I was there I became interested in Eastern thought. I was born a Methodist in Cleveland, but I was attracted more and more to mysticism. So when I came over here—I'm a security guard at the S.F.M.—I went to Israel on leave and talked to rabbis about kabbala. I admit they didn't know what to make of me, but now I'm learning Hebrew and they're beginning to take me seriously.

"You see," he went on, warming to his subject, "I realized that I was supposed to be something special when I learned what the names my father gave me really mean. Raphael, my first name, means the angel protecting my day of birth. Setchiel, my middle name, means the angel protecting my hour of birth. My last name is Rodgers. The views I follow are a mystical approach to bring all the religions together for a better understanding of life, so there will be no more wars. I have faith, and my faith will guide me as the conduit between my studies and the world. My fiancée, Marschelle Lee—she's also from Cleveland, we grew up together—she just came to Israel and we're going to be married this week by a Lutheran minister. She shares my mystical views. We plan to live and study in Israel till 1983. But I'm not sure how long I'll stay with the S.F.M. The money's good but there's not enough time for my studies." I thanked him for allowing me to disturb his reading with my questions. He nodded and returned to his book.

Before long, we had reached the dunes south of El Arish. Bedouins were grazing livestock amid tamarisk, eucalyptus, pine, and palm trees. I recognized a crossroad that Bailey and I had passed more than two weeks ago, during my first trip into the Sinai. I had come full circle, and to add to the feeling of completeness, a towering thunderhead—a veritable biblical "pillar of a cloud"— sat beckoningly over the Mediterranean coast.

The driver announced that he would skirt Khan Yunis and Gaza because of a recent stoning incident. (Another driver had quit after his first day on the job, when a Palestinian Arab smashed his van's windshield with a rock.) Sometimes, the courier followed the Beersheba route to Tel Aviv, to vary the routine and confuse lurking terrorists, who considered any S.F.M. vehicle a fair target. Fortunately, there were no incidents during our trip, and soon we were on a modern divided highway, speeding up the coast to Tel Aviv. By eleven o'clock, I was let off at Ben-Gurion Airport. "Peace," Raphael Setchiel Rodgers said to me in parting, and then added, *"Shalom."*

TEN

I WAS BOOKED on an Olympic Airways flight scheduled to leave Tel Aviv at 2:25 P.M. and arrive in Athens two hours later, which would allow me less than one hour to change planes for another Olympic flight to Cairo. Arrangements had been made for a car and driver from the Egyptian State Information Service to meet me at the Cairo airport and take me to the suburb of Giza and the Mena House hotel, lately famous not only for its view of the Great Pyramids but also as the site of the Israeli-Egyptian peace talks a few months earlier. Even given the mileage of this route, I would still be in Cairo in time for a late dinner, if all went smoothly. But all rarely goes smoothly in the Middle East. The flight to Athens was delayed, which meant that I would almost certainly miss the connecting flight to Cairo. There was no efficient way to notify the Egyptian State Information Service from, of all places, Tel Aviv. I was resigned to spending a miserable night in the Athens airport, waiting for the first available plane to Cairo.

Finally, the Olympic jet took off and landed in Athens at eight o'clock. I rushed to the transients' check-in counter and told the girl on duty of my plight. She said that an Alitalia flight was leaving for Cairo in forty minutes. She booked me on that flight and promised to telex the Information Service, explaining the change of plans. Rushing through customs and airport security (the latter still notoriously lax, even after the Entebbe hijacking, which began in Athens), I boarded the Alitalia plane just as the door was about to be closed. The plane took off into the clear night, gaining altitude over the Cyclades and heading southeast, in the very direction I had

234

belatedly come from. The passengers were a disparate group: tipsy Egyptian students, dressed in loud leisure suits and Cuban heels, returning home from European universities; somber *fellahin*, fresh from their menial labors in Italy, bringing back desperately needed cash to their families; natty businessmen and diplomats; a Bible-tour party consisting of Tennessee Williams matrons; and, in first class, Persian Gulf sheikhs, wearing immaculate white *galabiyas* and *kaffiyehs*, off to taste the Cairo night life, I assumed. Each passenger unashamedly studied the faces around him, perhaps looking for signs of a possible hijacker. My seat companion, a well-barbered businessman, was particularly nervous. He tugged at his shirt collar and tapped his fingers against the attaché case balanced on his knees. He ordered a drink from the stewardess and, with a sigh, confided to me that he had been on a long trip. "I miss my home," he said. "All I think about is putting on my *galabiya* and sitting with my family."

I, too, was nervous—concerned about the telex message reaching the Information Service in time and worried about being detained at customs because of where I had spent the past three weeks. (What would they make of that expended cartridge casing I had picked up at the Israeli artillery emplacement?) I needn't have worried all that much. Cairo airport customs was a desultory formality, especially compared to Israeli security's meticulous baggage searches. There was no government driver to meet me—I had arrived almost four hours late and so, obviously, had the telex message—but an army of importunate cabbies was more than willing to speed me across the Nile through moonlit Cairo on the forty-five-minute ride to Giza. By midnight, I had collapsed into the oversized bed in my room at the Mena House, a luxurious but slightly seedy remnant of the British raj, now managed by Indians. It was seventeen hours since I had left the S.F.M. Base Camp, just 110 miles away. I was too tired to take much more than a glance at the Great Pyramid of Cheops alongside the hotel. At least, I was in Egypt, and tomorrow things were bound to be better.

That optimistic sentiment, I realized the next morning, was a contradiction in terms. Things almost never get better in Egypt. My

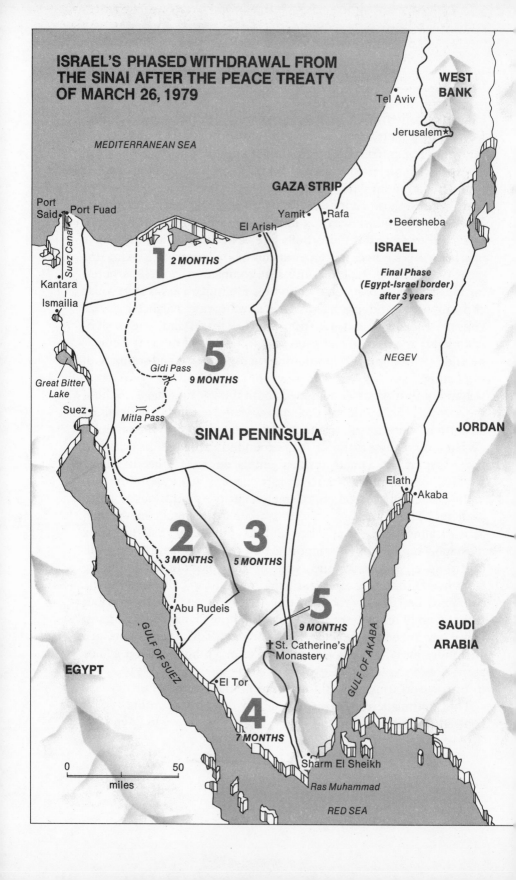

ISRAEL'S PHASED WITHDRAWAL FROM THE SINAI AFTER THE PEACE TREATY OF MARCH 26, 1979

MEDITERRANEAN SEA

WEST BANK

Tel Aviv

Jerusalem ★

GAZA STRIP

Port Said
Port Fuad

Yamit · · Rafa

El Arish

· Beersheba

ISRAEL

1 2 MONTHS

Final Phase (Egypt-Israel border) after 3 years

Kantara
Ismailia

NEGEV

5 9 MONTHS

Gidi Pass

Great Bitter Lake

Suez ·

Mitla Pass

SINAI PENINSULA

JORDAN

Elath
· Akaba

2 3 MONTHS

3 5 MONTHS

· Abu Rudeis

5 9 MONTHS

GULF OF SUEZ

† St. Catherine's Monastery

GULF OF AKABA

SAUDI ARABIA

EGYPT

· El Tor

4 7 MONTHS

0   50
miles

Sharm El Sheikh

Ras Muhammad

RED SEA

first order of business was to telephone Dr. Morsi Saad El Din, the Chairman of the State Information Service, and announce my tardy presence, apologize for standing up his driver, and find out what arrangements had been made for me to travel across the Suez Canal to Egyptian-held Sinai. However, the telephone in my room was stone-dead. I had heard that Cairo suffered from a chronic telephone problem, but I assumed that a dead room phone in one of the city's more opulent hotels was not a part of the nuisance. In the Byzantine lobby, the desk clerk told me that most of the guests' phones were out of order that morning, although one of the lobby phones seemed to be working. There was a queue of ten persons waiting to use that one operable phone—elegant English ladies of a certain age, wealthy Arabs in Bond Street suits, and Japanese and American businessmen. I joined the queue and watched in despair as, one by one, each person ahead of me shouted at the operator, waited several minutes, slammed down the receiver, and walked away muttering to himself.

An American standing in line behind me said that this lobby scene was "business—or rather nonbusiness—as usual. I'm in heavy machinery and I come here often. The phones almost never work right in this city. Nothing works right. After you're here for a while, you wonder why it took the Israelis six days to win that war."

"Well, how does anything ever get done?" I asked him.

"It doesn't," he said.

At last, my turn came. I gave the hotel operator the number of the State Information Service, and she said wearily that she'd try to get through. A few minutes later, she came back on the line to say that she was sorry but all the circuits seemed to be out of order in downtown Cairo. Like the others, I hung up muttering. The American in heavy machinery advised me to try "the Cairo shuffle." He went on to explain that when you want to get in touch with an individual and the phones aren't working, you take a taxi to his office or home. Meanwhile, that person may be trying to get in touch with you, so he takes a taxi or drives to your hotel or office. "You both usually cross paths in some traffic jam," he said, "and the whole day is shot. Office hours are only from eight till two, with

Fridays off. Nothing gets accomplished, except messages are left, and you make another stab at meeting the next day. The Cairo shuffle accounts for most of the horrible traffic and air pollution in the city, I think."

I took his advice (actually, it was the only thing to do) and ventured forth by taxi into the grand pandemonium of daytime Cairo. The State Information Service was in the heart of the downtown area, on the Sharia Talaat Harb, and inching along the boulevard leading from Giza to the city, I was immediately struck by the terrifying, seemingly hopeless troubles of the place. If every urban affliction on earth—with the possible exception of crime—were raised to the second power, there would be Cairo: poverty (beggars outnumber pedestrians on some sidewalks), congestion (Cairo may be the third most populous city in the world with more than eight million inhabitants in an area designed for three million; nobody knows for sure, since hordes of uncounted people live in such unlikely shelters as the tombs in the main cemetery), pollution (the varied skyline is bathed in a suffocating combination of dark-gray fumes and umber desert dust, suffused with the sweet putrefaction of the Nile, dung, flowers, and coffee), decay (slum buildings suddenly collapse under the weight of old age and neglect), and so on through each category—bureaucracy, insolvency, traffic, disease, filth, noise. Every obtuse cliché comes to mind with new meaning and intensity—"grinding poverty," "teeming masses," "wretched living conditions." Under ubiquitous billboards, murals, and posters of Sadat (Sadat smiling, stern, thoughtful, fatherly, brotherly, exemplary), crowds of women in black gowns formed outside shops, waiting to buy rumored new supplies of sugar, flour, and tea, the staples of Egyptian life. My cab driver pointed at the women and said, "That is why we need peace. There is never enough for all of us. With peace, Allah will make enough." The driver's point was well taken. Twenty-five percent of Egypt's income went toward defense, either for paying off war debts or for maintaining its swollen military establishment. With the average Egyptian worker earning less than the equivalent of two dollars a day and with one million unemployed nationwide, the government is compelled to subsidize from its depleted treasury the staples that the black-gowned women were waiting in line for, and it in turn must be subsidized by other countries. It is a humiliating and chancy predicament for a proud nation.

Even the government buildings were in an advanced condition of decay. The crumbling façade of the State Information Service was indistinguishable from the other crumbling façades jammed together on Sharia Talaat Harb, except for an Egyptian flag and a large bust of Nasser (the first representation of Sadat's once-worshipped predecessor I saw). At the entrance, six plainclothes security men checked my credentials, including a letter of introduction to Dr. Morsi Saad El Din, and one of them escorted me up to the top floor of the building in a tiny freight elevator. The passenger elevator was not working. I was led into a large office, where four girls, surrounded by useless telephones, were happily chatting. I introduced myself and explained the airport mix-up and my appearance at their office without calling first. They all giggled and smiled. "Is O.K.," one girl said. "The driver went home when you were not on the Olympic plane. We received no telex from Athens. Please have some coffee. Dr. Morsi will see you very soon, I'm sure."

I accepted a cup of thick, sweet Turkish coffee and watched the secretaries working and talking. They were positively bubbling with good humor. Nothing seemed to bother them—not the dead telephones, or the noise and fumes rising from the street outside the open window, or the bustling, shabby office. Through it all they smiled and giggled, giggled and smiled. A friend of mine who knew Egypt well once told me that its greatest national resource—more precious even than its Nilotic treasures—was the good humor and kindliness of the people. They are in love with life, which is perhaps why they are not successful warriors.

A few minutes later, when I met Dr. Morsi (as everyone seemed to call him), my friend's observation was reinforced. A sunny, open-faced man, he ushered visitors into and out of his office with unfailing warmth and grace. A poet and writer as well as a diplomat, Dr. Morsi had accompanied Sadat on the famous pilgrimage to

Jerusalem the previous November, charming just about everyone at the Israel Government Press Office. Before I left Jerusalem, all the press-office people there had instructed me to give their personal regards to Dr. Morsi, which I promptly did.

"How are my friends in Jerusalem?" Dr. Morsi asked, while waving good-bye to one caller and then gesturing to another to come in and sit down. "Tell me about them. Tell me about Israel. What are the people thinking?"

I told him that I had spent most of my time in the Sinai, but from what I had observed in Israel proper, there were mixed emotions about Sadat's initiative. He listened intently, as though I were telling him something he did not already know, and then he asked me about the Sinai. I said that the Sinai was in an even more confused state, but I was convinced that a fair peace settlement there, not excluding the Bedouins' rights, would go a long way to easing much of the tension in the Middle East. With Egypt and Israel at peace, war between other Arabs and Israelis would be out of the question for years to come and all the other regional and national problems would, perforce, be diminished. He nodded and said, "If only the opportunity is not missed. Such an opportunity will not come again for a long time."

Coffee was served, and one of the visitors, the Ambassador to Turkey who was home for consultations, walked out on the balcony to confer in private with Dr. Morsi. That, apparently, was how important business was conducted at the higher levels of the State Information Service. When Dr. Morsi returned to his desk, he told me that my request for visiting the Egyptian-held Sinai was still being processed but there was nothing to worry about. First, though, I must be accredited at the Press Center. One of his assistants, Fatima Fouad, would drive me there and help with the arrangements. "Give my best to America," he said, as I prepared to leave with Miss Fouad. "I loved New York when I was assigned there."

At the Press Center, in the Radio and Television Building on the east bank of the Nile, the telephones were working, but, as it turned out, that was the only encouraging note. Six frenetic male bureaucrats and Fatima Fouad tried to sort out the technicalities in getting me across the Suez Canal. While I was plied with three more cups of coffee—I was reeling with caffeine—they placed several calls and scurried back and forth to different offices in the building. Finally one of the men, who resembled Rudolph Valentino in his prime, returned breathlessly with the news that it would be impossible for me to travel to the U.N. buffer zone from Egypt. I explained that I had no intention of going to the buffer zone, that I had just been in the buffer zone; I simply wanted to cross the canal into Egyptian-held Sinai. "Ah," he said. "Then you will need the permission of the American Embassy." I said that the American Embassy already had given me its blessings. Still, he insisted, the embassy must give its permission directly to him.

A call was put through to an officer at the embassy, who chuckled when I explained the dilemma. "You don't need our approval to cross the canal," he said. "You need the Egyptian military's approval. It's the military that really runs things around here, despite what the civilians tell you." To satisfy the bureaucrats, he formally gave them the official American permission, anyway. The next step, I was informed, was to clear my request through the appropriate military office. "This will take time," Rudolph Valentino said. Meanwhile, he went on, Fatima Fouad would drive me back to my hotel and, later that afternoon, a Press Center escort officer named Mahmoud Gafar would be in touch with me, either by telephone or in person. "Don't worry," Miss Fouad told me. But I was very worried.

To test the desk clerk's theory that the guests' telephones were now working (but for in-hotel calls only) I rang up room service and ordered lunch. I decided to stay in my room that afternoon so I wouldn't fall victim to the Cairo shuffle and miss Mahmoud Gafar's telephone call or visit. I lunched on a thick club sandwich and a large bottle of tangy, but labelless, Egyptian beer. By four o'clock, two hours after most offices were closed for the day, there was still no word from Gafar. I tried the room telephone and it was dead. On a hunch, I went down to the lobby to check at the desk, and, sure enough, there was a handwritten message for me from

Gafar. He was sorry, the note said, but the permission to visit the Sinai hadn't come through yet. He would be by the hotel early the next morning with further news. That was all.

There was only one thing to do—see the pyramids. Like any other tourist in Egypt, I walked up the hill next to the hotel, trying vainly to dodge the aggressive guides with their camels and Arabian horses, which one could mount, for a price, to be photographed or to gallop around the Great Pyramid of Cheops. The stench, the sleeve-tugging, and the chaos were overpowering. Since I was accosted in English, I mumbled to one *fellah,* "Polski," whereupon he addressed me in fluent Polish. Even illiterate Egyptians possess natural linguistic skills, a result of being the laborers for so many nationalities. Polish—indeed, any language of a Communist state—does not light up their eyes, however.

The Giza Pyramids are probably the most famous tourist attraction in the world and they live up to their awesome reputation. Yet, for me, after having walked through the ruins of Serabit El Khadim in the stillness of the Sinai, these mysterious monuments seemed too awesome, too pat, almost as if they were put there solely for the tourists. A truck spraying DDT over the area shattered whatever illusion was left and I returned to the hotel.

Later that night, I watched an Egyptian soap opera on Cairo television. It was a standard family saga, but in Arabic with a Cairo middle-class setting: a disconsolate wife, a straying husband, a rebellious son. As in any soap opera, the surroundings were idealized, but most fanciful to me was the family telephone. It worked flawlessly. Following that was the news—mostly unedited film of Sadat touring the Red Sea region, inaugurating rural developments and receiving the praises of the provincials. In one shot of Sadat waving to cheering masses of local officials and citizens, I noticed that the only ones scarcely smiling were Bedouins.

At eight o'clock the next morning, I opened my door to a short, chunky, intense fellow, dressed in blue jeans and a sport shirt. It was Mahmoud Gafar. Perspiring and hanging his head like a little boy resigned to accepting punishment, he said that the military had refused permission for me to cross the canal for at least three days.

Since the next day was Friday, the Moslem Sabbath, the earliest I could travel to the Sinai would be Monday, assuming that the permission would finally be granted. "A general overruled Dr. Morsi," he explained sheepishly. "I am sorry." Had this anything to do with military maneuvers? "Perhaps," he said. I told Gafar that I was very disappointed, that I hadn't the time to sit around Cairo waiting to cross the canal on such a shaky promise. Was there nothing he or Dr. Morsi could do to help me? Suddenly, he brightened. "For sure," he said. (Gafar was one of many Egyptians who had adopted Sadat's favorite American locution.) "Downstairs is a Press Center car, with my driver Ramadan. We will take you as far as the western side of the canal and you can look at the Sinai from there. It is better than nothing."

I decided to settle for half a loaf, and so a few minutes later, Gafar and I were in the back seat of a Volkswagen Minibus, stuttering through the morning traffic under the guidance of Ramadan—a quintessential Middle Eastern driver, who used all his mettle, wile, and skill to advance his machine past one vehicle before attacking the next, successive tiny victories in an unending battle against time and space. Occasionally, he would touch a string of prayer beads dangling from the rear-view mirror. As we made fitful progress across a bridge over the felucca-speckled Nile, by the gargantuan Mohammed Ali Mosque and Saladin's Citadel, and then through Heliopolis (the Scarsdale of Cairo, where the guarded rich and powerful live in stunning contrast to the rest of the city), Gafar seemed to relax and grow voluble, his embarrassment eased somewhat. He told me that he was born in the Nile Delta village of Minouf, near Sadat's hometown of Mit Abul Kom. He attended Cairo University, where he majored in journalism and learned English, since then polished by his job at the Press Center. During the 1973 war, he was an infantry sergeant. He crossed the canal in the first wave and stormed the Bar Lev Line, emerging unharmed. "I was lucky," he said.

Once beyond Heliopolis and the airport, the green belt along the Nile dissolved into the stark desert that makes up ninety percent of Egypt—and is the source of ninety percent of Egypt's troubles,

in that the discouraging terrain and harsh life there drive the peasants to the capital. The traffic thinned and we entered the Cairo-
Suez Double Way, a straight, 134-kilometer road to the southernmost point of the canal. Gafar gestured at the flint-covered dunes
and gravel plains. "You can see for yourself our problem," he said.
"This is why the people flock to Cairo. At least there is hope of
making a living in the capital. We are trying to develop the desert
—factories are being built here, water pipes are being laid, electric
power, and so forth—but it is hard. Still, the people come to Cairo.
There is a section of the city called Shubra that almost equals the
entire population of Israel."

He went on to summarize what the Egyptians had already done
with the regained Sinai land and the canal region and what their
plans for the future were. The governor of the Sinai had established
an office in Kantara and from there he was administrating the
civilian services, some of which I had seen during my trip through
the U.N. buffer zone. In 1976, Sadat had launched his "Green
Revolution" in the Sinai—a sudden concern not only for the peninsula's Bedouins but for the thousands of *fellahin* he hoped would
emigrate there. Water was piped into the region from the old
sweet-water canal and trees were planted, with the promise of land
reclamation spreading eastward. So far, the revolution has been
more moss- than emerald-green, the major thrust of Egyptian interest and funds going toward the reconstruction of the Suez Canal
and its war-wrecked cities of Suez, Ismailia, Kantara, and Port Said.

After the canal was cleared (with the help of the American military) of sunken ships, mines, unexploded bombs, improvised
bridgehead-causeways and opened to maritime traffic in 1975, a
visionary Egyptian builder named Osman Ahmed Osman was appointed Minister of Housing and Reconstruction. He set to work
on a multibillion-dollar development scheme for the entire canal
area, encompassing such diverse projects as three two-lane tunnels
under the waterway, crash industrialization, free-trade zones, canal
expansion to handle bigger ships, tourist resorts, oil pipelines, and
massive housing construction. Osman's success in these monumen-
tal endeavors made him the Egyptian man of the hour, even upstag-

ing his close friend Sadat, until the latter's peace initiative of 1977.
(Posters and billboards of Osman were almost as plentiful in some
locations as those of the President.) The results of his efforts have
been compared to the building of the pyramids. The city of Suez,
almost completely destroyed by Israeli shelling and bombing, was
revitalized as a thriving oil and commercial port, with most of its
original 268,000 inhabitants returning to live in vast apartment
projects erected with Saudi and Persian Gulf financing. Liberal
conditions for foreign investments have already attracted new industry to Suez, including some American factories. Ismailia fared
better than Suez in the Egyptian-Israeli wars and its renaissance as
the headquarters of the Suez Canal Authority and as an agricultural
and commercial center has been easier. It, too, received Arab oil
money with which to reconstruct its housing and industry, and
some feel its future is brighter now than it was before 1967. The
canal traffic, Ismailia's major occupation, had practically equaled its
pre-1967 tonnage, earning a half-billion dollars a year in foreign
exchange at present rates, and as the canal was deepened and widened by a consortium of foreign dredging companies, its tonnage
would soon surpass any previous record. Construction of the first
highway tunnel, 141 feet below the canal, had begun at El Shatt and
was scheduled to be completed in 1980. It would probably go
further toward developing the Sinai—and bringing the peninsula
into the sovereign embrace of Greater Egypt—than anything else.

The northern, smaller canal city of Kantara suffered even more
war damage than Suez because it sits astride the waterway; Kantara
West received the brunt of the Israeli artillery while Kantara East
was pulverized by the Egyptian guns. (Kantara East was a ghost
town when I was there during the War of Attrition. Whatever life
existed was carried on within the deep bunkers of the Bar Lev Line,
with the exception of wild dogs and cats, many missing legs or tails,
roaming over the debris.) Consequently, Kantara had a difficult
time rebounding, although it made a good start as an administration
center. Its former residents trickled back to rebuild houses, and
when one of the transcanal tunnels is finished just south of the city,
it should prosper again. As for the notoriously sinful Port Said and

its sister-city Port Fuad just across the Mediterranean gate of the
canal, they were as sinful as ever. With the reopening of the canal,
Port Said sprang to life as a duty-free zone and a hotbed of smuggling. As many as fifty thousand Egyptians a day descended on the
urbanized sandbar at the northern tip of the canal to buy goods
ranging from watches to automobiles. At customs posts outside the
city, duty was supposed to be paid on the Port Said bargains, but
ingenious Egyptians figured out all sorts of methods to smuggle the
goods past the inspectors, several of whom were known to be
corruptible. The local economy and the growing population were
flourishing, and so was the black market of Port Said contraband
in other Egyptian cities. With tourists on cruise ships once again
stopping at the port for an evening's entertainment, its future and
fabled reputation seemed secure. After eight years of stagnation
while the canal was closed, Port Said was back in business.

The hot, flat desert between Cairo and Suez slowly lost any
pretense at civilian life. What habitations emerged from time to
time were army barracks, tent cities, and missile bases. Soldiers
were everywhere, drilling on dusty parade grounds, struggling
with smoky, overheated Russian and Czechoslovakian trucks, command cars, and tanks that were never designed for desert use, and
dozing in any available shade. Occasionally, we would see *fellahin*
constructing culverts, facing them with fine mosaics of hand-hewn
stones. In the stifling heat of noon, we passed the historic Kilometer
101 marker, where General Siilasvuo presided over the first Egyptian-Israeli disengagement talks after the 1973 war. Jagged, mauve
mountains appeared in the southeast and patches of scrub grew with
greater frequency. "It looks like the Sinai, doesn't it?" Gafar said.
"For sure, this desert is the same as the Sinai, the same land, but
with a man-made canal running through it. It is all Egypt."

Well, yes and no.

On the fringe of Suez began the new cities within the city,
named, and celebrated with gigantic billboard portraits, for their
benefactors, the late King Feisal of Saudi Arabia, the present Saudi
king, Khalid, and Prince Sabah of Kuwait. Each of them was a
well-planned, self-contained community with mosques, stores, and

pinkish limestone apartment buildings. Feisal City had just been completed and was already aswarm with new residents; the others, still under construction, would be even bigger than the four-thousand-apartment Feisal City. The sweet-water canal flowed between the highway and railroad tracks, on which chugged a diminutive train, with surplus passengers spilling over and clinging to the sides of the cars and engine, a common sight on Egyptian mass transportation. Economic activity was evident everywhere: oil refineries along the gulf; a "Misr-Irani" textile mill, a fertilizer plant, and a cement factory in various industrial parks; a busy *souk* along the main street, its shops and stands showing the international flavor of the port with such signs as "Bombay Bazaar," "Hotel d'Orient," and "Misr Beauty Saloon." But despite all the bustle and revitalization of Suez, the pervading quality was still one of war and destruction. Bombed-out buildings were a constant reminder of how much Suez had suffered since 1967, a few of the ruins in the process of restoration but most simply left amid their own rubble as ghostly monuments. But for the desert sun, the palms, and the sea breeze, Suez could have been a Ruhr Valley town just after the Second World War.

We drove slowly along a shell-pocked boulevard, under modern arches emblazoned with patriotic slogans, toward Port Tawfik, the southern entrance to the canal, where in 1869 Ferdinand de Lesseps arrived triumphantly from Port Said, having sailed aboard the first ship to navigate his incredible waterway. It is a shock to come upon the Suez Canal. To see huge ships moving as if by magic through a narrow channel cut into the desert, their superstructures visible above the dunes, muddles one's senses. More than a hundred years after its opening, the canal is still a miracle of engineering. The stone quay along the entryway had been restored, but it retained souvenirs of its hammering by Israeli guns. The stately old Green Island Hotel was totally gutted and scarred pedestals without their statues stood like grim sentries on the embankment. Some incongruous Bedouin tents were pitched in the rubble. A captured Israeli tank, its cannon pointing east, was part of an abstract propaganda sculpture, needlessly reminding passers-by of what recent violence had shaken the region. In the broad bay to the south of the entryway, ships awaited their turn to steam north, while fishermen's feluccas and Canal Authority launches wove among them. Beyond a sign reading "WELCOME BACK TO SUEZ CANAL," a freighter churned up the channel with alarming speed. As it passed, I noted the legend on its stern: "THOMAS LYNCH / MOBILE." Its wake hardly stirred an enormous blue Japanese dredger—the biggest dredger ever made, Gafar told me—deepening the canal. [On April 30, 1979—a little more than a year after I had seen the *Thomas Lynch* plow by—the first ship flying an Israeli flag, the freighter *Ashdod,* sailed through the canal. It was greeted by foghorns, sirens, spontaneous shouts of *"Salaam"* and *"Shalom,"* and a good deal of tight security. The right of free passage through the canal was guaranteed by the peace treaty, and the precedent set by the *Ashdod* meant that no longer would Israeli ships have to travel from the Red Sea to the Mediterranean by circumnavigating the continent of Africa.]

And just two hundred or so yards across the turquoise water was the Sinai, a grand yellow expanse a world away. Wide notches in its dune banks marked where the Egyptians had breached the Bar Lev Line with high-pressure streams of water. I could barely make out workers on the far side, excavating the dunes as part of a project to widen the canal. Gafar said that as an infantry sergeant he had crossed the canal and assaulted the Bar Lev Line just north of where we were standing. He stared at the smashed walls of sand and then turned away. I told him that nine years earlier I had peered from a camouflaged observation slit in a Bar Lev bunker over the canal toward Egypt, wondering what the view would be like from the other side. Now I knew. On the eastern horizon were the hazy hills of the Gidi and Mitla passes, where I had stood and looked toward Suez just two days before. I pointed out to Gafar what might have been Caddo Mountain, the S.F.M. Watch Station 1. "For sure," Gafar said, "it is a crazy world."

Gafar told me that he knew the best restaurant in Suez for fish, an old place that had come through the wars relatively untouched. It was right on the main street, which was crowded with *souk* shoppers and was ringing with the wails of Arabic music from ubiquitous radios. The restaurant, however, was almost empty, its thick, cool, whitewashed walls and slowly revolving ceiling fans a relief from the heat and din outside. I half expected to see Sydney Greenstreet, Peter Lorre, and Humphrey Bogart huddled together at a corner table. Since there were no fresh Gulf of Suez shrimp that day, Gafar, Ramadan, and I decided on fried *dalak* fish (somewhat like plaice), a lettuce-and-tomato salad, that good Egyptian beer, and Turkish coffee. To my astonishment, the meal was brought to our table accompanied by gratuitous platters of French fried potatoes and rice steeped in spicy gravy. Generosity was without question an Egyptian hallmark, and I complimented Gafar on the national trait. He smiled and said, "Maybe that is our biggest fault. Maybe we are too kind, too forgiving. To get by in this crazy world, for sure we will have to change. Take the Palestinians. We have been fighting their wars for decades, our men dying, our cities ruined, our economy upside down. So to thank us, they kill in Cyprus one of our greatest writers, Yousef El Sebai, the editor of *Al Ahram*—all because they do not like Sadat's initiative to give them peace and their own homeland. They have called Sadat names and threatened him. I think from now on we Egyptians must be more selfish."

While we devoured the superb lunch, I asked Gafar what he thought were the chances for success of Sadat's initiative, at that time frustrated by stalemate. "To look at it selfishly," he said, "only two countries really matter in the Middle East conflict— Egypt and Israel. Some of the others have great political passions and the oil countries have great money, but Egypt has the people and the civilization. That is something money cannot buy. If Israel gives up the Sinai and makes peace, then other good things will happen for the Arabs, I am sure. The Sinai should not be a big problem. It is not Israeli. It is Egyptian. If there is peace, the Israelis have nothing to fear from the Sinai."

I asked him if he, a Nile Delta native and now a Cairene, had any special personal feeling for the Sinai. "Truthfully, no," he said. "I would not want to live there. But to me it is still Egyptian soil. It

The mountains of the Sinai. *Magnum.*

belongs to us." But doesn't the peninsula really belong to the Sinai Bedouins? "The Bedouins were Egyptian before," he replied, "and they will be Egyptian again."

I repeated to Gafar what an Israeli intelligence officer had once told me: If Israel signs a peace treaty, it will be respected by any Israeli administration, no matter what happens to that country's leader, since it is a stable parliamentary democracy; however, Egypt is a nation governed by one man, at the pleasure of the military, and its assurances to abide by a treaty are questionable. (Indeed, the fact that an army officer overruled Dr. Morsi in the matter of my traveling to the Sinai seemed to substantiate this opinion.) Could Israel trust Egypt if something happened to Sadat and a little-known general was suddenly in power? "We are trying—Sadat is trying—to make a true democracy here," Gafar answered, "but it will take time. We are making progress. Maybe the question should be, Can we trust the Israelis after their past aggressions?" He put down his knife and fork and raised his palms in a papal gesture. "Whatever the case, we both need peace, and now it is the time to make peace. We *have* to trust each other."

Early the next morning—the eve of Passover—I left Egypt. My contemporary exodus was to Athens and New York. It struck me that the chaos at the Cairo airport might have resembled the confusion in the Pharaoh's court after the Hebrews had departed en masse. A brisk dawn wind had cleared the air, and as the plane circled Cairo I could distinctly see the Great Pyramids and the green strip along the Nile fanning into the delta. By the time the plane gained cruising altitude over the Mediterranean, the sun rising out of the Sinai illuminated the peninsula's sweeping, empty coastline, fading east into Gaza and Israel. From that lofty perspective, the Sinai seemed to be more a geographic keystone holding the Levantine arch together, rather than a wedge cleaving it. Perhaps, that could be the Sinai's ultimate destiny—to hold together the Middle East and give it a fresh start, the great historical battleground at last serving peace.

A loud cry for that tattered word "peace" had echoed from all quarters during my travels. I had come to the conclusion that the cry was sincere. Israel—debt-ridden, besieged, suffering the collective neurosis of a fortress state—desperately needed an era of tranquility; and with even more urgency, Egypt—untalented at war, a charity case, its people the victims of afflictions worse than God's ten plagues—looked to peace as its only salvation. The Sinai was the keystone and the key. If, under Egyptian sovereignty, the peninsula could be intelligently developed with clean industry, power facilities, desalinization plants, tourist resorts—perhaps sponsored by a latter-day Marshall Plan involving America, Europe, and, if they come to their senses, some oil-rich Arab nations—the mutual benefits to Egypt and Israel would be the firmest security possible, far more reliable than F-16 fighters and strategic passes. If new Sinai cities, like Yamit and Sharm El Sheikh, could be open to all nationalities, who would dare fire the first bellicose shot? And if, for once, the indigenous people of a newly developed land could simply be left alone to live their lives as they saw fit, free of petty, manufactured constraints, the humanitarian precedent would be a telling example to the world. The Sinai Bedouin, so blithely ignored in all the political maneuvering, has survived alien wars and occupation for thousands of years, but he may not survive the paving-over of the wilderness. It is a prospect the Bedouin has never had to face before, and should it come to pass, it would be a natural disaster. Peace is crucial, and the Sinai is crucial to peace. But so is the Bedouin, for he knows what the world has forgot: that our cultural roots are in the Sinai wilderness and if civilization is to flower, the roots must be tended and preserved.

Since the signing of the peace treaty, on March 26, 1979, peace in the Sinai has been officially declared. Israeli troops have already pulled back from a Mediterranean coastal strip to a point east of El Arish, and an old raj has returned to the peninsula. So far, there has been no great euphoria on either side. The hard labors of making a practicable peace are oddly cheerless and notoriously expensive. Distrust is still in the desert air like a khamsin. The same nagging, doubting questions continue to haunt the principals: What of Egypt after Sadat? Is some messianic general waiting in the wings, determined to drive the Israelis into the sea? Will the Arab confrontation states succeed in savaging Egypt and the treaty? Would edgy Israel launch a preëmptive attack? Can a "Carter Plan" revitalize the Egyptian economy? Or will America, without the encouragement and aid of the rest of the world, tire of funding and overseeing the enterprise? And then there are those seemingly insoluble issues of the Palestinians and Jerusalem.

Given the vagaries of the Middle East, the odds for an enduring peace are not favorable. But at least a start has been made—appropriately enough, in the Sinai. It may well be the last chance.

Index

Aaron, 47, 111
Abba, 203
Abbas I (Abbas Pasha), 140, 142
abd, 36
Abraham, 6, 167
Abu Aweigilla, 57, 58
Abu Durba, 176, 179
"Abu Musa," 121
Abu Rudeis, 25, 26, 176, 178
Abu Zuneima, 173, 197
Abzug, Bella, 215
Achel, Lt. Col. Mark, 210–11
Acre, 12, 14
Actisanes, 59
Africa, 1, 25, 36, 116, 183, 248
Agency for International
    Development, U.S. (A.I.D.), 214
Agriculture, Israel Ministry of, 36, 47
Ahab, 4, 139
Ahmed Fuad Pasha, 21
Air Force, U.S., 219
ajuj, 200
Akaba, 3n, 9, 11, 12, 13, 14, 15, 17,
    54, 89, 111
Akkad, 6
Al Ahram, 158, 249
Alamo (Watch Station 3), 222, 224,
    227
Albania, Albanians, 13, 59
Albright, William, 103–104
Aleigat tribe, 113, 179, 181
Alexander II, Tsar, 145
Alexandria, 10, 123, 168
Alfon, Lt. Lars, 197–98, 201, 204,
    205, 208, 218
Allenby, Edmund Henry Hynman,

1st Viscount Allenby, 17–18, 19
Allenby Railroad, 17, 24, 74, 78,
    205
Alma oil field, 176
Almaric I, 11
alphabet, 1, 8, 167–68, 170
Amalekites, 6, 152, 153
Ammonius, 122
Amram, 14
Anak, 46
anchorites, 10, 122
ancient history, of Sinai, 5–10, 39,
    59, 115–18, 123–24, 148, 166–69.
    See also Bible
Antiquities, Department of (Israel),
    166
Arabian peninsula, 1, 7
Arabic (language), 3n, 15, 17, 31,
    32, 41, 50, 53, 59, 60, 63, 66, 68,
    69, 72, 93, 96, 125, 126, 130,
    131, 132, 138, 139, 144, 146,
    153, 156, 160, 185, 198, 242
Arabists, 3n, 15. *See also* Bailey, Dr.
    Clinton
Arabs, 3n, 9, 10–11, 81, 91, 103,
    117, 159, 237; and Egyptian-Israeli
    treaty, 27, 28–29, 240, 249, 251,
    252; of El Arish, 20, 59, 62–67,
    68, 70–72, 77, 93, 94, 99, 104,
    105, 185; and Jews in Palestine,
    18, 21–22; nationalism of, 18–19,
    21, 23; and 1956 Sinai Campaign,
    23; Palestinian, 22, 23, 27, 28, 35,
    59, 77, 79, 182, 233, 249, 254;
    reaction to state of Israel, 22; and
    reconstruction of Suez Canal area,

Arabs *(cont.)*
    245; Sinai Bedouin contrasted to
    Saudi, 44, 103; and Six Day War,
    24; terrorists, 22, 76, 82, 157–58,
    233; town contrasted with
    Bedouin, 20, 103, 105; under
    Israeli government in Sinai, 25, 32,
    68, 72–74, 75, 76, 77, 87, 112,
    120–21, 155, 181, 183, 190; and
    War of Attrition, 24–25; of West
    Bank, 35, 82. *See also* Bedouins,
    Egypt, Islam
Arad, 83
Aramaic (language), 9, 168
Arava, 82, 191
Archeological Institute (Hebrew
    University), 169
archeology, and Sinai peninsula, 5–6,
    15, 38, 39, 114–17, 121, 166–69,
    189
arisha, 40, 41, 42, 52, 60, 88
Arishiya, 59, 68, 94, 97, 99, 104,
    105, 106, 107, 185. *See also* El
    Arish
Armenian (language), 144
Army, Israeli, 22–26, 39, 43–44,
    56–57, 58, 73, 87, 121, 137, 142,
    162–63, 185, 200–201, 205. *See
    also* Israel Defense Forces
Artom, David, 77–78
Ashkelon, 80
Asia Minor, 111
Assyria, 6, 8, 59
Athens, 193, 229, 234, 239, 252
atwa, 94
Auja El Hafir, 22, 32, 73
Awamra, Salim El, 44
Awlad Said, 111
Ayish (son of Suleiman Ibn Jazi),
    64–65, 66

Bab El Rum, 111
Babylonians, 8, 155
Badawi, 3n
Bailey, Dr. Clinton, 31–32, 34–36,
    37, 40–45, 47, 50–56, 58, 61–68,
    70–71, 72, 73, 74–75, 78–80, 81,
    83–84, 86–88, 90–91, 96, 99,
    100–101, 104–109, 110, 111, 118,
    120–22, 125–26, 130–33, 137,
    138, 141, 148, 149, 151, 152,
    153–63, 170–72, 174, 179,

    182–86, 188, 191–92, 197, 233
Bailey, Maya, 32, 157
Bailey, Michael, 74, 78, 79, 80
Baldwin, Stanley, 1st Earl Baldwin,
    200
Baldwin II, King, 198, 200
Balfour, Arthur James, 1st Earl of
    Balfour, 17
Balfour Declaration, 14, 17–18
Baluza, 204, 205
Bangladesh, 214
Bar Lev Line, 24, 25, 30, 196, 205,
    243, 245, 248
Bar-Yosef, Ofer, 5
Barakat, 155, 158, 160, 161–62
Bardawil Lagoon, 115, 198, 200,
    204, 205
Bayathiyin Bedouins, 200, 204–205
"Bedouinism," 201, 219
Bedouins, 5, 12, 14, 15, 29, 30, 31,
    40, 46, 49, 57, 60, 62, 78, 79, 83,
    84, 87, 89, 103, 109, 111, 115,
    122, 126, 153, 154, 155, 163,
    170, 171, 172, 178, 189, 200,
    209, 218, 224, 233, 240, 242,
    247; and agriculture, 35–37, 112,
    244; and ancient Israelites, 117–18,
    148, 149; astrology of, 97, 101,
    138; Bailey and, 31, 32, 41–45,
    49, 56, 62–67, 71, 72, 74–75, 83,
    87, 88–89, 96, 97, 99, 100–101,
    102, 105, 106–107, 138–39, 153,
    156–57, 159, 162, 183–85, 186,
    188; black, 36; and British
    administration of Sinai, 20–21,
    73–74; burial rites of, 55;
    contrasted with Palestinian Arabs,
    79; dining among, 66, 70–71,
    104–106, 113, 121, 161; education
    and, 105–106, 120, 188; of El Tih
    plateau, 4, 49, 174; of El Tor,
    179, 181–82; and future of Sinai,
    244, 253; and hajj, 11; as Israeli
    citizens, 35, 36; and Israeli
    government of Sinai, 25, 32,
    68–69, 72–74, 75, 76, 77, 87, 91,
    93, 112, 119–21, 181, 190, 201;
    marriage and family of, 42, 62–67,
    100, 105, 156–57, 158–62; of
    Mount Sinai area, 119–21, 122,
    124, 125, 126, 130, 132, 133,
    137, 138–39, 140, 141, 142, 146;

Negev encampments of, 36–37,
190; number in Sinai, 3, 20; oral
law of, 105, 106–107, 118; own
Sinai, 29, 190, 229–30, 252;
philosophy of existence, 103;
poetry of, 71, 96, 97, 101,
106–107, 138–39, 181, 185, 192;
pre-Islamic beliefs of, 101–102,
113; protocol of, 41–42, 44, 52,
55–56, 62, 66, 70–71, 99, 100,
103, 106, 119, 149; raid St.
Catherine's monastery, 122, 123,
124; and Sharm resort, 183, 184,
185; and Sinai warfare, 16, 17, 21,
36, 42–43, 156, 181, 202;
smuggling by, 21, 63, 69–70, 87,
200, 207; as spies, 16, 63, 68–69,
71; and tourism, 83, 112; tribal
strife among, 64, 86–87, 93–94,
112–13; and U.N. forces, 196,
202–203, 204, 206–208, 211;
urbanization of, 37, 190
Beersheba, 34, 35, 37, 39, 61, 233
Begin, Menachem, xii, 27–28, 61,
76, 88, 91, 127, 206, 232
beit, 167–68
Ben-Avi, Ittamar, 14
Ben-Gurion, David, 58
Berlioz, Hector, 100
Bernstein, Mimi, 163
Bethlehem, 34–35
Bible, 1, 4, 6, 8, 10, 14, 25, 32, 35,
39, 40, 44, 45–47, 82, 85, 111,
114–18, 127–29, 138, 139, 141,
142, 145, 146–48, 152–53, 189,
198
Bible-study groups, 110, 111, 235
Bir Asluj, 22, 32
Bir El Abd, 202
Bir Gifgafa Air Force Base, 217–18,
230, 231
bitarikh, 200
Bitter Lakes, 115
black goats, 37, 50
Bombay, 163, 172
Bosnia, 59
Boulders of Kadeis, 51, 52–53
Brancusi, Constantin, 143
Britain, 12, 59, 90, 94, 106, 146,
173; governs Sinai, 20–21, 44, 56,
70, 73–74, 75, 112, 186, 200;
hegemony in Egypt, 13–17, 18,

21, 29, 89, 235; 1906 boundary
line with Turks, 13–14, 37; and
1956 Sinai Campaign, 23; and
Palestine, 17–20, 21–22, 91;
supplies explorers of Sinai, 14–15,
30, 34, 39, 54, 159, 179
British Mandate Government House,
195
British Museum, 146
bulbul, 109
Burckhardt, Johann Ludwig, 111
Burgfeldt brothers, 202
Burning Bush, 4, 118; Chapel of, 10,
122, 123, 127, 132, 147–48, 149
bustans, 50, 99, 153
Byzantine Empire, 9–10, 36, 38, 39,
86, 137, 144

Caddo Mountain (Watch Station 1),
224–26, 227, 248
Cairo, 11, 12, 24, 27, 28, 62, 112,
131, 133, 140, 193, 195, 196,
200, 204, 205, 214, 218, 229,
231, 234–43, 244, 246, 252;
conditions in, 237–39, 242, 244
Cairo University, 243
Calcutta, 35
Caleb, 46
Camel Corps, 16, 20
Camp David talks, 27–28
Canaan, 45, 46, 47, 115, 117
Canada, Canadians, 89, 196, 201,
206
Carter, Jimmy, xii, 28, 206, 231, 254
Catherine, St., 10, 123–24, 142, 147
Cederberg, Private Krister, 197–98,
201–202, 209, 210
Chaldea, 6
Chapel of the Burning Bush: see
Burning Bush
Chapel of the Fleas, 133, 143
Châtillon, Renaud de, 86
Cheops, 7, 235, 242
"Christ Pantocrator," 144
Christianity, 9–10, 11–12, 30, 86,
111, 113, 119, 122–25, 127, 129,
130–33, 136–37, 139–40, 141–42,
143, 144–47, 153, 181, 186
"Christians' Gate," 111
Civil Administration, Israeli (of
Sinai), 112, 119–21, 151, 186,
190, 204

Codex Sinaiticus, 145–46
Codex Syriacus, 144
Colutea, 148
Congress, U.S., 216, 217
Constantine I (the Great), 9, 145
copper, 6, 7, 83, 155–56, 170
Coptic (language), 144
Coral Island, 11
Cosmas, 168
Cromer, Evelyn Baring, 1st Earl of, 13
Crusades, 11–12, 59, 62, 86, 124, 147
Cuba, 231
cuneiform, 168
Cyclades, 234
Cyprus, 157, 191, 249

Dahab, 189
Dahan, Col. Moshe, 67–69, 72–74
Damianos, Archbishop, 125, 131
Dayan, Moshe, 75–77
Dayan Fence, 75, 76, 77
Dead Sea, 32, 82, 192, 200
Dead Sea Scrolls, 82, 169
Denmark, 89, 168
"desert kites," 5
"desert rats," 59
desert trackers, 36, 51, 73, 74, 163, 171, 172
DIRID, 220–21
diya, 94
Dizahab, 189
Doar Hayom, 14
Dodson, Douglas, 220–27, 230
Doulas, 123
Druses, 72
Dumas, Alexandre, *père,* 15
dunes, 3, 29, 40, 75, 88, 115, 176, 178, 184, 201, 202, 205, 207, 208, 233, 244, 247, 248

E-1 (Egyptian surveillance station), 211, 214, 217, 222, 224, 230
E-Systems, Inc., 213, 214, 218, 220
Early Bronze Age, 5–6, 29
early-warning stations, 26, 31, 193, 209, 214, 216, 220–22, 224–27, 229, 230, 248
East Jerusalem, 81, 82
Edom, 82
Edomites, 6

Egypt, 1, 63, 69–70, 71, 87, 100, 119, 132, 140, 156, 173, 175, 190, 203, 215, 234–49, 252, 253, 254; administers territory of Bayathiyin Bedouins, 204; in ancient history of Sinai, 7–9, 59, 60, 115, 116, 117, 118, 123, 148, 198, 242; Army of, 22, 23, 24, 25, 39–40, 58, 67, 185, 208, 227, 229, 238, 243, 246, 252; British in, 13–21, 89, 179, 186, 235; controls Sinai, 7–8, 12, 21–23, 29, 69, 74, 185; and Crusades, 11–12; defense spending of, 238; and founding of Israel, 19–20, 21–22; French invasion of, 12–13, 124–25; nationalism in, 21, 23; in 1949 hostilities, 22, 39–40; in 1956 Sinai Campaign, 23, 87, 185; and Ottoman Empire, 12–13, 19, 89; and peace treaty with Israel, 27–29, 61, 74, 75, 76–78, 88, 94, 127, 176, 178, 184, 206, 219, 230, 231–32, 234, 248, 249, 252, 253–54; and reclamation of Sinai, 244; reconstruction of Canal area, 244–46; and Sinai Field Mission, 217, 219, 227, 230; Sinai surveillance post of, 26, 209, 211, 214, 217, 222, 224, 230; Sinai territory of (1978), 26, 31, 34, 176, 178, 193, 201, 229, 231, 237, 240, 244, 248; Sinai territory returning to (1979–82), 61, 78, 88, 127, 169, 178, 184, 191, 206, 219, 231–32, 249, 252, 253; and Six Day War, 24, 176, 185; Soviet aid to, 23, 25–26, 246; Suez oil of, 176, 178, 244, 247; temple and mines at Serabit El Khadim, 4, 7–8, 116, 151, 153, 156, 164, 166–72, 242; and War of Attrition, 22, 24, 200, 205, 245; and Yom Kippur War, 25–26, 196–97, 204, 208, 243, 246; and Zionist aspiration to north Sinai, 14
Egyptian Expeditionary Force, 16
Egyptian State Information Service, 234, 235, 237–40
Eighteenth Dynasty (Egypt), 7
Ein El Furtaga, 90, 96–109, 110, 143
Ein Gedi, 82

Ein Kadeirat, 44, 45, 46, 47, 49–51, 55
Ein Kadeis, 44–46, 51–55, 73
Ein Khudra, 110, 111
El Alamein, 21
El Arish, 9, 12, 13, 14, 16, 20, 22, 32, 42, 49, 51, 56, 57, 58–74, 77, 89, 93, 99, 104, 159, 181, 185, 198, 233, 253
El Arish Preparatory Boys School, 70
El Fatah, 23
El Kaah, 179, 183
El Khirba, 204, 205
El Kuntilla, 39, 47, 116
El Kuseima, 32, 40, 41, 42, 43–44, 49, 51, 55
El Shatt, 245
El Thamad, 13
El Tih plateau, 4, 49, 59, 68, 142, 154, 164, 173
El Tina Flats, 115
El Tor, 6, 124, 175, 176, 178, 179, 181–83
Elam, 6
Elath, 4, 23, 39, 64, 66, 83, 84, 86, 87, 90, 100, 104, 120, 139, 151, 188, 191
Elijah, 4, 113, 139–40, 143, 147, 149
Elim, 10, 115
Elisha, 139
E.N.I., 176
Entebbe hijacking, 234
Eothen (Kinglake), 15
Esau, 6
Etheria, 127
Ethiopia, Ethiopians, 59, 111, 144, 214
Etzion Geber, 85
Eutychius, 122
Exodus, 1, 4, 8, 10, 14, 15, 45–47, 128, 147–48, 152, 166; theories of, 40, 114–17, 171, 198
Eyalet of Beirut, 12
Eyalet of the Hejaz, 13

Fabri, Felix, 1, 3
Farouk I, 21
Feisal, King, 246
Feisal City, 247
fellahin, 235, 242, 244, 246

Field School, 75, 122, 130, 131
Filusiat, 9
Finland, Finns, 29, 174, 175–76, 195, 206, 218
Finnbatt, 174, 197
Fiord, The, 86
flash floods, 4, 96–97, 99, 146
Fouad, Fatima, 240–41
Fourth Geneva Convention, 29
France, 12–13, 17, 18, 23, 59, 86, 124–25, 196
Fuad I: see Ahmed Fuad Pasha

Gadna, 74, 79, 80
Gafar, Mahmoud, 241–43, 246, 248–49, 252
Galilee, 90, 121, 169, 232
Galss, 9
garden cities, 14
Gaza, 9, 11, 16–17, 39, 61, 79, 195, 197, 198, 233, 252
Gaza Strip, 3, 22, 23, 40, 74, 76
Gebel Halal, 40, 115–16
Gebel Katharina, 142
Gebel Maneijar, 125, 126
Gebel Musa, 4, 10, 127
Gebel Serbal, 10, 127, 153
Gebel Tiniye, 140
Geneva Convention: see Fourth Geneva Convention
Georgian (language), 144
Germany, 15–16, 21, 29, 37, 89, 130, 141, 189
Gezirat Fara'un, 11, 15, 85–86
Ghana, Ghanaians, 197, 206, 209–11, 212, 214, 218, 227
Ghanbatt, 197, 209–11, 212, 221, 222, 230
Gidi Pass, 4, 26, 190, 209, 211, 213, 219, 224, 248
Giza, 234, 235, 238, 242
Golan Heights, 25, 30
Gospel According to St. Matthew, 147
Gospels, 144
Göteborg, 198, 209
Governing Council (Yamit), 77
Government Press Office (Jerusalem), 182, 240
graffiti, along Sinai trading routes, 9, 166, 168, 169
Graye, 12, 86

Great Pyramids, 234, 235, 242, 252
Great Rift Valley, 82
Greater Egypt, 245
Greater Israel, 75. *See also* Israel;
    Sinai peninsula
Greece, Greeks, 8, 59, 132
Greek (language), 130, 131, 132,
    137, 138, 139, 144, 145, 168
Greek Orthodox Church, 31, 81,
    119, 131, 141. *See also* Christianity
Green Island Hotel, 247
Green Line, 207, 211, 230
Green Patrol, 36
"Green Revolution," 244
Greenville, Texas, 213, 220
Gulf of Akaba, 1, 4, 11, 13, 19, 23,
    24, 25, 83, 86, 118, 139, 183,
    186
Gulf of Suez, 3, 6, 7, 25, 162, 164,
    171, 173, 174, 176, 178, 183,
    202, 222, 226, 249
Gush Emunim, 82
Gypsaria, 39

Haga, 82
Haganah, 91
Haifa, 172
hajj, 11, 12, 89, 181
Halhul, 35
Hammam Sidna Musa, 181
*Handwriting of God in Egypt, Sinai and
    the Holy Land, The* (Randall), 15
Har-ur-ra, 166
hashish, 21, 69–70, 179, 189
Hathor (deity), 4, 7, 166
hawi, 102
Hazeroth, 110, 111
Hebrew (language), 6, 31, 35, 45,
    50, 68, 69, 72, 78, 93, 96, 115,
    121, 129, 130, 131, 166, 168,
    169, 184, 201, 232
Hebrew University (Jerusalem), 5,
    32, 84, 167, 168–69
Hebrews, early, 6, 7, 8, 10, 118,
    171. *See also* Bible; Israelites
Hebron, 35
Hejaz, 12, 13, 19, 64, 124
Helena, St., 9, 10, 122, 147
Heliopolis, 243
Herod the Great, 9
Herzl, Theodor, 14

hieroglyphics, 8, 166, 167, 168, 169,
    170, 171
Hill of Evil Counsel, 195
hippies, 66, 72, 89–90, 91, 184, 189
Hiram, 39
Hittites, 8, 59
Hogfeldt, Sergeant, 202
Holy Confraternity of Mount Sinai,
    145. *See also* St. Catherine's
    Monastery
Holy Cross, College of the, 215
"Hometown, U.S.A.," 228–29
Horites, 6
Howeitat tribe, 42
hudhud, 102
Hunt, Leamon "Ray," 216–20, 228,
    229–30
hunters: during British raj, 186; in
    prehistoric Sinai, 5
Hussein, King, 82, 139
Hyksos, 7

ibex, 186
Ibn Amir, Hassan, 44, 47, 49, 50,
    51–57
Ibn Jazi, Salim, 66, 99, 100, 104–
    109
Ibn Jazi, Suleiman, 42, 61, 62–67,
    68, 70–72, 99, 159
Ibn Khaldun, 103
Ibrahim Pasha, 13
icons, at St. Catherine's Monastery,
    144, 146, 147, 148
Igra (Labrador retriever), 100–101
*Impressions of Travel in Egypt and
    Arabia Petraea* (Dumas *père*), 15
Indbatt, 197
India, Indians, 13, 35, 120, 168,
    235
Indonesians, 197, 206, 218
inshallah, 157–58, 172, 173, 192,
    197
Institute for Desert Research, 58
International Herald Tribune, 191
Iran, 27–28, 176
Ishmael, 159
"Ishmaelites," 10, 122
Ishtar (deity), 6
Islam, 10–12, 42, 86, 93, 101, 102,
    103, 113, 119, 124, 136, 137,
    141, 152, 157, 159, 200

Ismailia, 24, 37, 76, 115, 206, 208, 229, 244, 245
Israel: and Bedouin citizens, 35, 36–37; conquers Sinai, 24–26, 36, 176, 183; military presence in Sinai, 31, 36, 43–44, 56–57, 58, 59, 61, 62, 67–70, 72–74, 78–79, 88, 142, 162–63, 178, 182–83, 185, 191–92, 200–202, 203, 204, 211, 217–18, 227, 230, 231; and 1956 Sinai Campaign, 22, 23, 87, 181, 185; and 1967 Six Day War, 5, 22, 24, 34, 36, 40, 91, 176, 181, 183, 185, 190, 222; and Palestinian Arabs, 22, 23, 27, 28, 35, 59, 77, 79, 254; peace treaty with Egypt, xii, 27–29, 36, 47, 61, 74, 75, 76–78, 88, 127, 176, 178, 184, 206, 219, 230, 231–32, 234, 240, 248, 249, 252, 253–54; pullback from Sinai, xii, 22, 28–29, 31, 61, 76–78, 88, 91, 94, 127, 169, 178, 184, 206, 219–20, 231–32, 249, 253; right of passage in Suez Canal, 248; settlements in Sinai, 25, 27, 28, 29, 47, 74–78, 183–84, 229, 253; and Sinai Arabs, 25, 66, 68, 72–74, 75, 76, 77, 105, 112, 119–21, 155, 181, 183, 190; and Sinai Field Mission, 217, 219, 226, 227, 230; and Sinai oil, 26, 40, 176, 178, 202; Sinai surveillance station of, 26, 209, 211, 214, 217, 222, 224, 230; Sinai territory of, 26, 27, 29, 31, 32, 36, 40–80, 178, 179–88, 191–92, 201–202, 203, 217–18, 231, 233; and War of Attrition, xi, 22, 24–25, 200, 205; and War of Independence, 22, 39–40; and West Bank tensions, 35, 82; and Yom Kippur War, xi, 22, 25–26, 36, 120, 195, 196–97, 204, 208, 224–25, 227, 231, 246
Israel Defense Forces (I.D.F.), 25, 36, 44, 57, 58, 62, 68, 69, 70, 72, 74, 77 78, 81, 88, 162–63, 178–79, 185, 191, 201, 202, 205, 227, 231
Israel Museum, 169
Israeli Consulate (N.Y.), 31

Israelites, 4, 8, 44, 45–46, 50, 55, 85, 107, 110, 111, 114–18, 123, 129, 152, 153, 168, 189, 252
Italy, 176, 235

J-1 (Israeli surveillance station), 211, 214, 217, 222, 224, 230
Jaffa, 86
Jaffa Gate, 17
James, St., 147
Jane Shore, 146
jarari, 55
Jarvis, Major Claude Scudamore, 20, 44, 56, 59, 112, 200
Jebeliya, 119–21, 122, 124, 125, 126, 130, 132, 133, 137, 138–39, 140, 141, 153
Jehovah, 1, 4, 6
Jeremiah, 192
Jericho, 81, 82, 116, 192
Jerusalem, 5, 11, 12, 13, 17, 19, 21, 32, 34, 58, 74, 78, 80, 91, 112, 116, 125, 129, 154, 158, 169, 182, 185, 192, 193, 195, 198, 200, 212, 214, 227; Carter in, 28; issue of, 28, 254; Sadat in, 27, 61, 76, 94, 197, 239–40
Jerusalem Plaza, 32, 34, 51, 80, 81, 192, 197
Jerusalem Post, 84
Jerusalem Temple, 39, 46
Jesus, 9, 142, 147
Jethro, 118, 119, 148–49
Jews: homeland for, 14, 17–19, 21–22; meaning of Mount Sinai to, 129; Orthodox, 34, 82, 175; at S.F.M. Base Camp, 218; Suleiman Ibn Jazi on, 66. *See also* Bible; Israel; Israelites
Jezebel, 4, 139
jihad, 24
Job, 40, 146
John, St., 147
John Paul II, Pope, 127
Jordan, 22, 23, 34, 49, 81, 82, 139, 191, 203
Jordan River, 9, 17, 47, 82, 129
Jordan Valley, 30
Joseph (husband of Mary), 9
Joshua, 46, 152
Judea, 39, 82, 116, 192

Justinian I, 10, 119, 122–23, 138,
  145, 147

kabbala, 232
Kadeir, 49
Kadeirat tribe, 49
Kadesh Barnea, 10, 32, 38, 44,
  45–47, 49, 50, 55, 85, 111, 115
kadus, 50, 54
Kagan, Arie, 75
Kantara, 9, 16, 20, 24, 94, 244, 245
katef, 40–41
Khalid, King, 246
khamsin, 74, 78, 79, 154, 156, 158,
  162, 206, 219, 251
Khan Yunis, 233
kibbutzim, 75, 83, 90, 110, 119,
  130, 175, 203
Kilometer 101 negotiations, 195,
  197, 246
kina, 75
Kingdom of Jerusalem, 11, 124
Kinglake, Alexander W., 15, 54
Kings, First Book of, 39
Kissinger, Henry A., 26, 178, 201
Kitchener, Horatio Herbert, 1st Earl
  Kitchener of Khartoum, 15–16
Kléber, General Jean Baptiste, 125,
  146
Knesset, 27
Koran, 64, 100
Korso, Lieutenant, 211
Kufic (language), 168
Kuwait, 246

Labor Party (Israel), 75
land mines, 47, 97, 149, 185, 186,
  189, 190, 196, 205, 206, 207,
  208, 211, 224
Late Pleistocene, 5
law-giving, the, 1, 4, 45, 107, 114,
  128, 147
Lawrence, T. E., 15, 17, 42, 53
League of Nations, 20
Leah (at Civil Administration
  Center), 120
Lebanon, 22, 68, 83, 195, 196,
  197–98, 203, 206, 208
Leki (at Civil Administration Center),
  119–20
Lesseps, Vicomte Ferdinand Marie
  de, 247

Levites, 45
Lindgren, Colonel, 205–207
Lloyd George, David, 1st Earl of
  Dwyfor, 18
Louis IX, 86

mafish hakuma, 21, 29
Maganna, 6
Maghara, 170
Mahmoud (Jebeliya guide), 138–39,
  141, 142, 151, 163
Majid (singer), 63–64, 65, 66, 67
Mamelukes, 12
mamour, 20
manganese, 173
mangroves, 186
manna, 115
manuscripts, at St. Catherine's
  Monastery, 144–46
Mao Tse-tung, 167
Marah, 115, 116
Marshall Plan, 253
Mary, the Blessed Virgin, 9, 10, 133
Masada, 82
Maximian, 123
Mecca, 11, 49, 86, 89, 101, 113,
  137
"Mecca of Sinai," the, 113
medical services, Israeli, 73, 218,
  230
Mediterranean Sea, 3, 6, 9, 14, 19,
  20, 59, 61, 70, 88, 115, 176, 200,
  233, 246, 248, 252, 253
Meinertzhagen, Col. Richard, 18–20
Meir, Golda, 75
Mena House (hotel), 234, 235
Mentu, 6, 8
mesamerah, 113
Meshel, Zeev, 39, 116–17
Mesopotamia, 19
Mesopotamian Semites, 6
Messiah, 129
Metropolitan Museum of Art, 144
Micha, Lieutenant, 162–63, 169,
  171–72
Middle East Institute (Columbia
  University), 32
Midianites, 7, 118, 119, 148
Military Government, Israeli (of
  Sinai), 31, 32, 67, 69, 72. *See*
  Israel; Israel Defense Forces
Milukhka, 6

mines, at Serabit El Khadim, 6, 7–8, 116, 151, 153, 156, 161–62, 166–67, 169–71
MINISID, 220, 224
Minouf, 243
Miracle of the Fleas, 133
Miriam, 47, 111, 169
Mit Abul Kom, 243
Mitla Pass, 4, 26, 190, 209, 210, 218, 219, 224–27, 248
Moabite Mountains, 32, 82
modules, living, 212–13, 215, 228, 229, 230
Mohammed, 49, 113, 124, 140, 146
Mohammed Ali, 13, 140
Mohammed Ali Mosque (Cairo), 243
monotheism, 1, 8, 118
Montagnards, 215
Morocco, 19, 68, 163
Morsi, Dr.: see Saad El Din, Dr. Morsi
Mosaic laws, 118–19
Moses, 4, 10, 45–47, 50, 51, 111, 113, 115–16, 118, 124, 125, 127–29, 138, 140–41, 144, 146, 147–49, 152, 168, 169, 171, 181, 198
"Moses' Seat," 152, 154
Moshav Kadesh Barnea, 47
moshavs, 76, 77, 83, 88, 89, 90, 189
Moslem Brotherhood, 49
mosques: on Mount Sinai, 141; at St. Catherine's Monastery, 124, 137
Mount Carmel, 129
Mount Cassius, 9
Mount Hermon, 129
Mount Horeb, 118, 127
Mount Moriah, 129
Mount St. Catherine, 4
Mount Sinai, 4, 10, 11, 12, 40, 45, 110, 112, 113, 114–19, 122, 123–24, 125, 126–29, 132, 133, 137, 146, 148, 153, 155, 163, 171, 181; climbing of, 127, 138–43
Mount Tabor, 129
Mukaddimah, The (Ibn Khaldun), 103
Murray, Sir Archibald, 16–17
Muzeina tribe, 64, 87, 88, 93, 97, 184
My Camel Ride from Suez to Mt. Sinai (Sutton), 15

Naama, 184
Nabateans, 7, 9, 39, 51, 86, 168, 169, 189
Nabk, 186
Nablus, 14
Nahal Yam, 200
Napoleon I, 12–13, 124–25, 146
Naram-Sin, 6
Nasser, Gamel Abdel, 23, 24, 25, 185, 239
nationalism: Arab, 18–19, 21, 44; and Bedouins, 103; Jewish, 14, 18–19, 82, 91
Nature Reserves Authority, 37, 100, 190
Naveh, Joseph, 167
nawamis, 5
Nazi Germany, 141
Neanderthal man, 5
Nebi Musa, 50, 123, 140
Nebi Saleh, 113, 140, 151
Negev, Avraham, 168–69
Negev desert, 1, 5, 22, 32, 35–37, 39, 40, 42, 49, 58, 73, 74, 83, 148, 175, 190, 191, 231–32
Nekhl, 12, 13, 16
Nelson, Raphy, 84, 85, 89
Neot Sinai, 76
Nessana, 39
Neviot, 88, 89–90, 91, 189
New Testament, 144, 145, 147. See also Bible
New Yorker, The, xi
Newlin, Michael, 193
Nile, 9, 16, 17, 235, 238, 240, 243, 249, 252
Nile Valley, 3, 7
Nimitz (ship), 172
Nineveh, 147
9th Brigade (of Israel Army), 87, 185, 190
9th Brigade Road, 87, 90, 188, 189
Nizana, 35, 37, 39
Nobel Peace Prize, 27
nomadism, 37, 103–104, 117–18
North Sinai Military Government, 60
Northern Route theory (of the Exodus), 40, 115–16, 171, 198
Nubians, 122
Numbers, Book of, 45, 111
Nura (daughter of Barakat), 158, 160, 161–63, 169, 170–72

Nuweiba, 83, 87, 88–89, 91, 130, 151

Occupied Enemies' Territory Administration, 20
Odeh Abu Abdullah, Breik, 64, 184
oil, 4, 25, 26, 28, 40, 44, 123, 176, 178–79, 181, 182, 202, 227, 244, 245, 247, 249, 253
Old Testament, editing of, 116–17. *See also* Bible
Ophir, 25, 39, 183
Ophira, 25, 183
Order of St. Catherine, 125
Osiris (deity), 166
Osman, Osman Ahmed, 244–45
ossuary, of St. Catherine's Monastery, 132, 149, 151
Ostracine, 9, 10, 11
Ottoman Empire, 12–14, 19, 37, 60

Paleanthropus Palestinensis, 5
Palestine, 3, 5, 9, 14, 29, 37, 42, 91; British disposition of, 17–20; partition plan for, 21–22; refugee camps in, 79
Palestine Liberation Organization (P.L.O.), 58, 62, 68, 191
Palestine Mandate, 20, 22, 38, 61
Palestinians, 22, 23, 27, 28, 35, 59, 77, 79, 182, 233, 249, 252
Palmer, Edward Henry, 15, 39, 54, 102, 113, 123, 136, 146, 153, 179
Paran, 153
Parker, Lt. Col. Alfred, 16, 20
partition plan, 21–22
Passover, 109, 171, 229, 232, 252
Paul, Father, 144, 146, 148, 149
Peace treaty (March 26, 1979), xii, 27–29, 36, 60, 61, 76–78, 127, 176, 178, 184, 206, 219, 230, 231–32, 234, 240, 248, 249, 252, 253–54
Pelusium, 9, 10, 11, 204
Persia, 8, 59
Persian (language), 144
Persian Gulf, 6, 235, 245
Petah Tikva, 121
Peter, St., 147
Petra, 9
Petrie, Sir William Matthew Flinders, 15, 45, 166

Pharaohs, 7–9, 85, 118, 142, 252
Philistines, 116
Phillips, James L., 5
Phoenician alphabet, 8, 166, 168
Phoenicians, 39
pilgrims, pilgrimage, 3, 10, 11, 35, 124, 125, 127, 136, 137, 140, 142, 143, 149, 151, 153, 168, 181
Pilgrims' Way, 138
Plain of Raha, 114, 126
poetry, Bedouin, 71, 96, 97, 101, 106–107, 138–39, 181, 185, 192
Poland, Poles, 29, 121, 196, 206, 207, 208, 242
Pompey the Great, 9
Port Fuad, 3, 246
Port Said, 3, 23, 24, 244, 245–46, 247
Port Tawfik, 247
Portugal, 12, 181
prehistory, of Sinai, 5–6
Press Center (Cairo), 240–41, 243
Procopius, 136
Proto-Canaanitic symbols, 8, 167
Proto-Sinaitic script, 8, 166–68, 169
Province of Sinai (Egyptian), 176, 244
Psalms, 146
Ptolemies, 8–9, 166
Ptolemy XIII, 9

Quarterhorse: *see* J-1
Qumran, 82

Rafa, 9, 11, 14, 17, 19, 22, 27, 74, 76, 77, 78–79
Rahmer, Christiane, 130–33, 136, 138, 141, 151
Rahmer, Elisabeth, 130–33, 136, 138, 141, 151
Ramadan, 137
Ramadan (driver), 243, 249
Ramses II, 8
Randall, Rev. D. A., 15, 136
Raphia, 9
Ras Muhammad, 61, 184
Ras Nasrani, 185–86
Rashrash (Saluki bitch), 100
Ravheden, Captain, 207–208
Red Sea, 3, 6, 13, 20, 39, 86, 115, 116, 122, 181, 183, 242, 248
"Reed Sea," 115

refugee camps, 35, 79
Rendall, M. J., 15
Rephaim, 6
Rephidim, 47, 116, 152–53
Rhinocolorum, 9–10, 59
Rhinokoloura, 59
Roberts, Owen, 212, 227–28, 229, 231
Robinson, Edward, 116
Rockwall (Watch Station 2), 224, 226–27
Rodeo: see E-1
Rodgers, Raphael Setchiel, 232–33
Roman Catholic Church, 131, 218
Roman Empire, 9, 11, 19, 39, 51, 59, 82, 122–23, 125, 138, 189
Rumania, 132, 163
Russia, 29, 124, 145–46. See also Soviet Union

Saad El Din, Dr. Morsi, 237, 239, 243, 252
Sabah, Prince, 246
Sabkhet El Bardawil, 198
sabras, 32, 68, 76, 77, 163
Sadat, Anwar El, xii, 238, 242, 243; peace initiative of, 27–28, 47, 61, 68, 75, 76, 77, 78, 91, 94, 127, 197, 206, 239, 240, 245, 249, 252, 254; and reclamation of Sinai, 244; and Sinai air bases, 231–32; and Yom Kippur War, 25
Sahara, 74, 208
St. Catherine's Monastery, 4, 31, 110, 111, 112, 113, 119, 126–27, 129–30, 153, 181, 189; chapel of the Burning Bush, 10, 122, 123, 127, 132, 147–49; church of, 137, 146–47; history of, 10, 122–25; interior of, 131–38, 143–44; library of, 144–46; ossuary of, 132, 149, 151
Saladin, 11, 12, 86
Saladin's Citadel (Cairo), 243
salamats, 41, 42, 44, 56, 99, 100, 155
Saluki, 43, 49, 88, 99, 100–101, 102, 106, 107, 108, 219
samak Musa, 200
Samaria, 82
Sanafir, 185
Sanjak of Jerusalem, 13, 14

Saracens, 200
Saudi Arabia, 1, 44, 86, 100, 103, 139, 160, 178, 185, 245, 246
Sawalha tribe, 113
sawan wa elmaz, 112
sayl, 96
Sde Boker, 58, 88
Sebai, Yousef El, 157, 249
Sela, Moshe, 112, 119–20, 121
Selim I, Sultan, 12
Semitic invasions, of Sinai, 6–7
Seneferu, 7
separation-of-forces agreements, 26, 68, 176, 201, 204, 205–206, 216–17. See also early-warning stations; Sinai Field Mission; surveillance stations; United Nations
Serabit El Khadim, 4, 7–8, 116, 151, 153, 155–58, 160–64, 166–72, 175, 242
settlements, Israeli (in Sinai), 25, 27, 28, 29, 47, 74–78, 183–84, 229, 253
Seven Pillars of Wisdom, The (Lawrence), 53
shahariya, 143
Shamash (deity), 6
Sharem Hotel, 184
Sharira Pass, 189
Sharm El Sheikh, 3, 4, 14, 23, 25, 61, 87, 169, 173, 183–86, 188, 253
Sharon, Gen. Ariel, 36, 47, 190
Sharon, Dr. Moshe, 37
sheikhs, Bedouin, 32, 42, 50, 61, 62–67, 69, 70–74, 99, 113, 118, 156, 183, 184, 190, 235
Shepard, Jim, 212–15, 222, 226, 228, 229
Sherafa, 49, 56
Shivta, 39
Shosha (Singer), 128
Shubra, 244
Shur, 7
Siha, 186
Siilasvuo, Lt. Gen. Ensio, 195, 246
Silwan, 81, 82
simsimiya, 66
Sin (deity), 6, 155
Sinai Campaign (1956), 22–23, 87, 181, 185

Sinai Field Mission, 26, 31, 34, 193, 197, 232, 233, 235; Base Camp, 209, 210, 211, 212–19, 222, 226, 227–31; operations of, 216–17, 220–27, 230. *See also* early-warning stations
Sinai in Spring (Rendall), 15
Sinai I, 26
Sinai peninsula: ancient history of, 5–10, 39, 59, 166–69; and biblical history, 1, 4, 6–7, 8, 9, 10, 14, 39, 40, 44, 45–47, 82, 85, 111, 114–18, 127–29, 138, 139, 141–42, 145, 146–48, 152–53, 189, 198; British interests and, 13–21, 37, 59, 73–74, 75, 89, 112, 173, 179, 200; and Christianity, 9–10, 30, 86, 111, 119, 122–25, 127, 130–33, 136–37, 139–40, 141–42, 143, 144–47, 153, 181, 186; Egyptian control of, 7–8, 12, 21–23, 29, 69, 74, 185; Egyptian-held territory (1978), 26, 31, 34, 176, 178, 193, 201, 229, 231, 237, 240, 244, 248; Egyptian and Israeli surveillance stations in, 26, 209, 211, 214, 217, 222, 230; geography of, 1, 3–4; historical paradox of, 4–5, 27; Israeli conquest of, 24–26, 36, 176, 183; Israeli-held territory (1978), 26, 27, 29, 31, 32, 36, 178, 179–88, 191–92, 201–202, 217–18, 231, 233; Israeli military presence in, 31, 36, 43–44, 56–57, 58, 59, 61, 62, 67–70, 72–74, 78–79, 88, 142, 162–63, 178, 182–83, 185, 191–92, 200–202, 204, 211, 217–18, 227, 230, 231; Israeli settlements in, 25, 27, 28, 29, 47, 74–78, 183–84, 229, 253; Israeli withdrawal from, xii, 22, 28–29, 36, 61, 76–78, 91, 94, 127, 169, 178, 184, 206, 219, 249, 253; keystone of Levantine arch, 252–53; mountains of, 4, 7, 10, 40, 88, 96, 112–13, 118, 119, 122–23, 126–29, 137, 138–42, 152, 155, 156, 162–64, 166–72, 179, 186, 192, 193; 1956 Campaign in, 22, 23, 87, 181,

185; northeastern tour of, 32, 34–80; oil in, 4, 25, 26, 28, 40, 123, 176, 178–79, 181, 182, 202, 227; origin of name of, 6; return to Egypt of (1979–82), 61, 78, 88, 127, 178, 184, 191, 206, 219, 231–32, 249, 252, 253; separation-of-forces agreement in, 26, 176, 195, 201, 204, 205–206, 216–17; Six Day War in, 22, 24, 34, 36, 40, 176, 181, 183, 185, 190, 207, 222; south-central tour of, 34, 81–192; and spread of Islam, 10–12, 124; Turkish rule of, 12–14, 15, 19–20, 59; U.N. buffer zone in, 26, 31, 34, 70, 81, 173–76, 178–79, 193, 195–98, 201, 202–12, 218, 219, 227, 229, 241, 244; U.S. early-warning stations in, 26, 31, 193, 209, 214, 216–17, 220–22, 224–27, 229, 230, 248; War of Attrition in, xi, 22, 24–25, 30, 200, 205; War of Independence in, 22, 39–40; and World War I, 16–18; and World War II, 21; Yom Kippur War in, 22, 25–26, 195, 196–97, 204, 207, 208, 225, 227, 231, 243; and Zionism, 14
"Sinai Sheikh," 70
Sinai Support Mission, 31, 216. *See* Sinai Field Mission
Sinai II, 26, 68, 176, 201, 204, 212–13, 216, 231
Sinaitic Inscriptions, 9, 166–69
Singer, Isaac Bashevis, 128
Six Day War (1967), 5, 22, 24, 34, 36, 40, 82, 91, 176, 181, 183, 185, 190, 222, 237
slaves: Bedouin, 36; Egyptian, 140; Hebrew, 118; Semitic, 7–8, 167, 170
Slavonic (language), 144
smuggling, 21, 63, 69–70, 87, 200, 207, 246
Sodom, 82
Solomon, 25, 39, 83, 86, 183
Southern Route theory (of the Exodus), 115–17
Soviet Union, 23, 25–26, 77, 146, 196, 218
Spann, Alex, 214–15

State Department, U.S., 31, 76, 216, 217
Stephanos (monk), 143, 149, 151
Stern Gang, 91
Strait of Tiran, 183, 185
Sudanese Camel Corps, 20
Suez, 24, 42, 54, 133, 195, 244, 245, 246–49
Suez Canal, 1, 3, 13, 16, 19, 20, 21, 23, 24, 25, 26, 30, 34, 68, 176, 201, 208, 215, 237, 241, 242, 243, 244–48
Suez Canal Authority, 245, 248
Suleiman (Tarabin passenger), 83, 86, 87, 88–89
sulha, 94, 103
surveillance stations, Egyptian and Israeli, 26, 209, 211, 214, 217, 222, 224, 230
Sutton, Arthur W., 15
Suwarka Bedouins, 200
Swedbatt, 197, 202–208, 210; mission of, 205–206
Sweden, Swedes, 89, 94, 197–98, 202–203, 205–206, 208, 209, 218
Swet, Ruth, 91, 94, 190
Swet, Zvi, 90–91, 93–94, 96, 189–90
Syria, 11, 13, 18, 21, 22, 23, 25, 30, 59, 69, 132, 203
Syriac (language), 144

tanks, 17, 19, 41, 78, 204, 207, 221, 232, 246, 247
Tarabin tribe, 42, 49, 61, 64, 66, 83, 84, 86–87, 88, 90, 93, 100
Tel Aviv, 14, 69, 75, 76, 81, 91, 112, 119, 121, 183, 189, 191, 218, 229, 230, 231, 233, 234
Tel Aviv University, 31, 39, 81, 117
Temple of Hathor, 4, 7, 164, 166
Ten Commandments, 142
terrorists, 22, 76, 82, 91, 157–58, 226, 233
Texas, Texans, 176, 202, 212, 213, 214, 216, 217, 218, 219, 220, 224, 225, 226, 229, 231
Thamudites, 6–7
Thebes, 166
Theodora, 138, 147
Third Army, Egyptian, 208
Thomas Lynch (ship), 248
Thoth (deity), 7

Timna mines, 83
Tiran, 185
Tischendorf, Konstantin von, 145–46, 147
Tiyaha tribes, 49, 86–87, 174
Tomb of Nebi Saleh, 113
Torah, 118, 128
tourism, 83, 88, 110–11, 112, 113, 125, 130, 136, 158, 175–76, 184, 191, 242, 244, 246, 253
Towara tribes, 113, 156, 179
trade routes, 1, 7, 8, 9, 12, 13, 23, 39, 69, 168, 181, 183
Transfiguration of Jesus, 147
Turkey, 21, 59, 69, 70, 190, 240; controls Sinai, 12–13, 20, 89; 1906 boundary with Britain, 14, 19, 29, 37; and World War I in Sinai, 15–17, 18–20
turquoise, 6, 7, 116, 151, 159, 161, 166–67, 170
Twelfth Dynasty (Egypt), 166
Twelve Tribes, 46, 47
Tyre, 39

Umm Bugma, 170
Umm Katef, 40–41
Umm Khisheib, 211
United Nations, 22, 47, 181, 185, 217; buffer zone in Sinai, 26, 31, 34, 70, 81, 173–76, 178–79, 193, 195–98, 201, 202–12, 218, 219, 221–22, 227, 229, 241, 244; General Assembly, 21; in Lebanon, 195, 196, 197–98, 203, 206, 208; Secretariat, 31; Security Council, 206
United Nations Disengagement Observer Force (UNDOF), 195
United Nations Educational, Scientific and Cultural Organization (UNESCO), 146
United Nations Emergency Force (UNEF), 23–24, 26, 195, 206
United Nations Interim Force in Lebanon (UNIFIL), 195, 197
United Nations Truce Supervision Organization (UNTSO), 195
United States, 23, 72, 77, 89, 144, 172, 185, 196; position on Sinai settlements, 29, 76; and reopening of Suez Canal, 26, 244;

United States *(cont.)*
  replacement of Israeli bases in
  Sinai, 231–32; role in Arab-Israeli
  peace agreements, 25, 26, 27–28,
  178, 206, 216–17, 219–20, 230,
  231–32, 253, 254; Sinai Field
  Mission of, 26, 31, 34, 193, 197,
  209, 210, 211–15, 216–31, 232,
  233, 235; and Yom Kippur War,
  25–26, 224–25
U.S. Embassy (Cairo), 241
Ur, 6

Vance, Cyrus, 29
Vatican Library, 144
Venezuelans, at St. Catherine's
  Monastery, 130–31, 132, 133,
  144, 148, 151
Via Maris, 3, 12, 59, 74, 78, 79,
  116, 197
Vietnam, 215, 220

Wadi Abbiyad, 39–40
Wadi Beirak, 153–54, 164, 172,
  173
Wadi El Arish, 59–60
Wadi El Sheikh, 6, 151, 152, 153,
  157
Wadi Firan, 10, 115, 122, 151, 153,
  154, 173, 179
Wadi Ghazala, 110
Wadi Kadeirat, 50
Wadi Saal, 110–11, 143, 189
Wadi Samaghi, 189
Wadi Taba, 84
Wadi Watir, 90, 96, 99, 100, 110,
  111
Wallachia, 119
war debris, 36, 208, 210, 224–25,
  227, 245, 247
War of Attrition (1969–70), xi, 22,
  24, 30, 200, 205, 245

War of Independence (1948–49), 22,
  39–40
Washington, D.C., 28, 214, 217
Watiya Pass, 112, 151
Weizman, Ezer, 47, 197
Weizmann, Chaim, 18
Well of Midian, 148
West Bank, 34, 35, 82
Wilderness of Zin, 46
withdrawal, Israeli (from Sinai), xii,
  22, 28–29, 36, 61, 76–78, 88, 91,
  94, 127, 169, 178, 184, 219–20,
  231–32, 249, 253; final phase, 78;
  Phase One, 61
women, Bedouin, 42, 62–63, 64–65,
  100, 105, 158–62
Woolley, Sir Charles Leonard, 15
World War I, 16–18, 37, 44
World War II, 21, 24, 29, 90, 163,
  247

Yahweh, 6
Yair Crossroads, 90, 91, 189
Yam Suf, 115
Yamit, 74–78, 122, 169, 253
Yesterday and To-day in Sinai (Jarvis),
  56
Yoffe, Gen. Abraham, 87, 185,
  190–91
Yom Kippur War (1973), xi, 22, 25,
  36, 120, 195, 196–97, 204, 208,
  225, 227, 231, 243, 246
Yossi, Colonel, 205
Youth Corps, 74

zarzamora, 148
zealots, Judean, 82
Zionism, 14, 18, 79
Zipporah, 118
Zohar, Basic Readings from the Kabbala,
  232